Te Papa

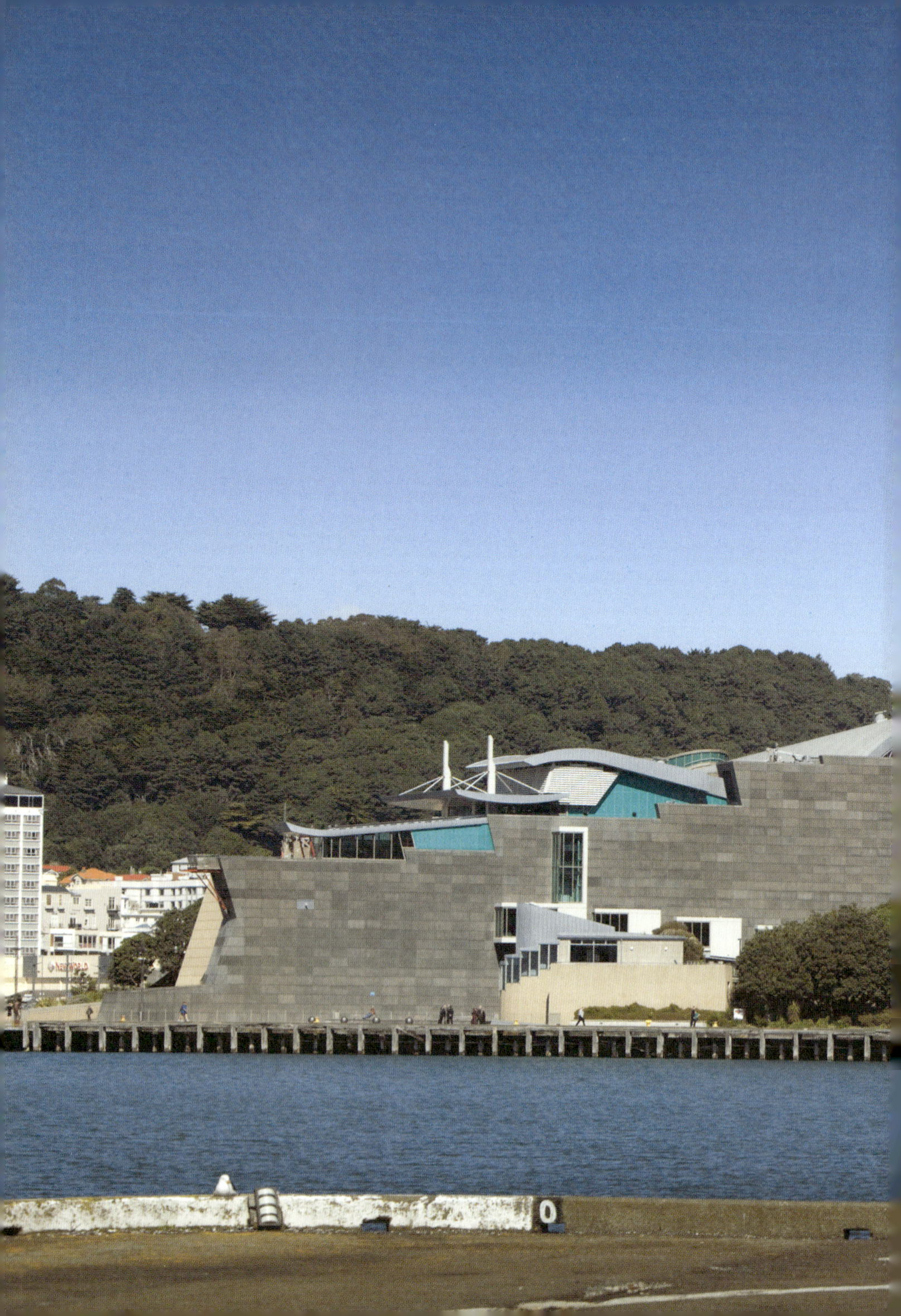

CONAL McCARTHY

Te Papa

Reinventing New Zealand's national museum 1998–2018

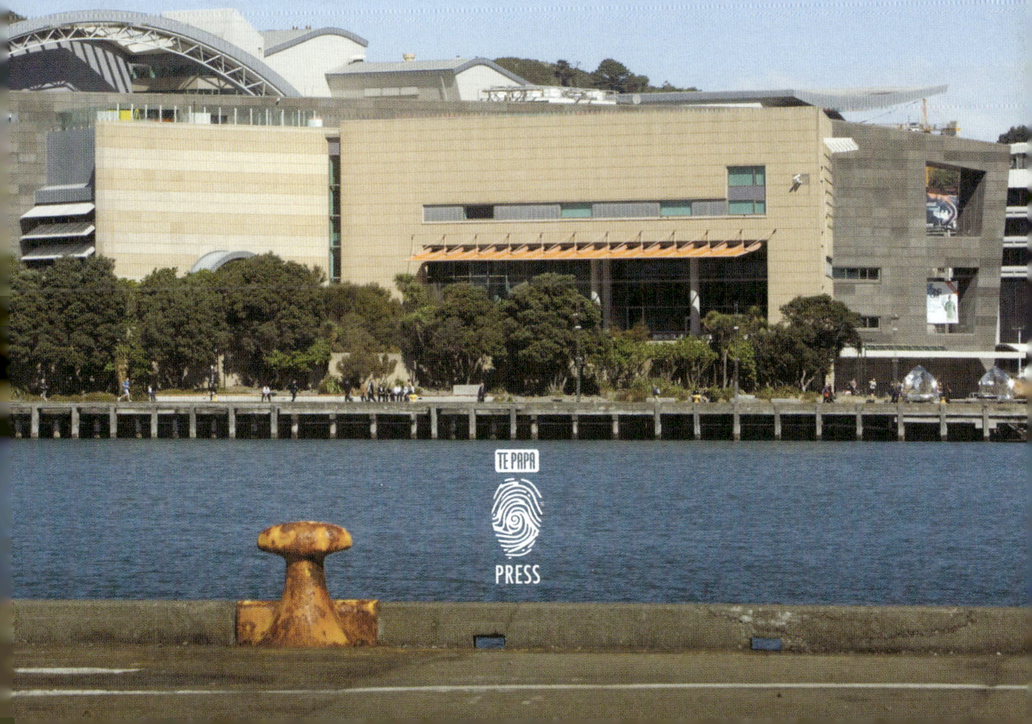

TE PAPA PRESS

contents

HE MIHI — A TRIBUTE TO THE LATE CLIFF WHITING

E te rangatira, te pītau whakarei o te Te Papa Tongarewa, haere, haere, haere atu rā. Te murau o te tini, te wenerau o te mano, te kaipūpuri i te whao, te tohunga toi Māori, te tōtara haemata o te wao nui a Tāne kei te mōteatea tonu te iwi Māori i tō rironga atu. Ko koe te pou matua o Te Papa Tongarewa i ngana, i ārahi haere ngā mahi kia tū tōtika te whare. Haunga noa ko to marae o Rongomaraeroa me te tipua kei runga a Māui Tikitiki-a-Taranga. Kua ripia kua haehaea mai te tau o te ate, ā, kei te hotuhotu tonu te whatumanawa mōu e te rangatira. Kua tangi mai tō iwi o Te Whānau a Apanui me Ngāi Māori mā, anō hoki ko Aotearoa whānui tonu. Waihongia ō mahi whakahirahira me ō taonga tiketike hei hiki te wairua o te tini me te mano e whai ake nei. Moe marire mai e te tohunga.

foreword

A national museum, like Te Papa, is a rare and strange thing. It is not simply a big museum created by the state to give citizens a nice day out. Oh, to live in such a world! A national museum is actually a rather more serious proposition. It speaks of, and speaks to, the nation. It represents us and it serves us.

And overtly or implicitly it helps shape how we think about ourselves and who we aspire to be. It then tells this to the world. And it does all this using real objects. We are all used to museums, but when you think about it, they are pretty strange.

You might think that these days all of this can be squeezed into a mobile phone app, but it cannot. The museum is a special public space. It removes us from the everyday, from pressures of work, the city, the news and people trying to sell us things. Museum visiting is not simply about looking and reading, it is about having a space to think, socialise and negotiate. It puts us into contact with new ideas that are not part of our daily life or upbringing.

Now when you think about it, we have created quite a list of expectations of this public institution. We might find fun and pleasure in the national museum but as an institution it is very different from the theatre, cinema or video game. Indeed, no other visitor attraction or entertainment carries its level of responsibility and risk.

Looking at national museums around the world we can see how all this can lead to unfortunate results. In many countries, national museums are subject to direct political interference. In Britain and New Zealand, we expect our museums to have an 'arm's length' distance from the partisan politics of government and the vested interests of the commercial sector. By these means, and aided by professional staff who seek balance, objectivity and neutrality, national museums are often among our most trusted institutions. This status has, however, made them useful to unscrupulous governments as sites of political propaganda. This happened in the Soviet Union and Eastern Europe before 1990, and can still be found in many parts of the world. Of course, the public is not stupid. Those living under Soviet influence soon learned to distrust the museum.

Elsewhere, national museums often display the evidence to support a national view of the history of a former conflict where the parties involved see things differently. Here you can find images and possessions of national martyrs. Other national museums have become home to political nationalism. They expect citizens to learn the defining symbols of the nation and to defend it against neighbours who are cast as threats to national security. These museums exist in very pleasant countries you might well visit.

Ever since Napoleon established the Louvre as a symbol of French greatness, national museums and galleries have been seen as essential institutions. They are among the first institutions a nation will build on achieving independence, regardless of its political persuasion or wealth. Fortunately, the vast majority of these museums are more likely to take inspiration from Te Papa and seek to realise a creative and autonomous population rather than disciples of narrow nationalism.

It is in this light that we should look at and reflect upon Te Papa. I cannot think of another national museum, built in the last forty years, that has been more globally influential in changing how these institutions represent the nation and, more generally, the indigenous peoples of the world. Indeed, it is hard to think of another national museum that has so fundamentally rewritten the ethics of being a museum. Te Papa is known and admired everywhere. It forced the big treasure houses of the northern hemisphere, like the British Museum in London and the Metropolitan Museum in New York, to think differently: to recognise their responsibilities and obligations. The product of a country of four million people, rather remotely placed on the globe, Te Papa is yet another example of New Zealand punching well above its weight!

In this book, New Zealand's leading museologist, Conal McCarthy, takes us back to the moment when New Zealand's biggest ever museum investment opened to the public 20 years ago. Fortunately for us, this is not simply a piece of historical research: Conal was there. Indeed, as I think about it now, Conal is as much a product of the revolution that affected the Museum of New Zealand as was Te Papa itself. His books *Exhibiting Māori* (Berg, 2007) and *Museums and Māori* (Left Coast Press, 2011) interrogate this revolution in museum practice, as well as its prehistory and its consequences.

The opening of Te Papa in 1998 was the culmination of a revolutionary journey that had begun in the early 1980s. That journey was not simply undertaken by the National Museum but by the nation at its heart as it redrew the Māori-Pākehā relationship, inventing a deep and sincere biculturalism that, as Conal explained in his earlier books, also possessed a helpful dose of local pragmatism. Even before the foundations of the new building had been laid, Te Papa was entering into debates in those parts of the world that have no indigenous minority as well as those that do. If, even now, Te Papa stands for a level of bicultural achievement rarely seen elsewhere, it is because the development of the museum and that of the country went hand in hand. Museums cannot bring about such changes on their own. They require government commitment. Nevertheless, the expertise and experience to be found in the museum and in its relationships are critical to the development of government policy.

Te Papa is very much what I would call a 'contemporary museum': it is focused on the needs of today and it does not shy away from the difficult issues. Indeed, it seems keen to face up to them. Without contaminating the beauty of the objects it displays, it nevertheless engages us with the lives of real people who speak directly to us from individual video displays. For me and many other visitors, this is a particularly effective form of interpretation, and it has been much copied.

Of course, no institution is perfect. As Conal explains, while visitor numbers were extraordinary and visitor feedback strong, the new displays were not without controversy. New museums are always of their time but the very best ones — like Te Papa — push the boundaries of what seems possible or desirable at that time. They challenge visitors to look and think differently. This means they have to change. They have to push us out of our normality.

The question is, what should they be like? What should they attempt to do? Te Papa is an answer to these questions, but given a different time and place that answer might have been very different. Had the money been found in the 1970s, Te Papa might well have ended up a national gallery, as this was much debated at that time. That vision underwent metamorphosis to eventually emerge from its chrysalis as *Parade*, the sensationally controversial opening exhibition of art and design. I would have loved to have seen that.

If Te Papa was to be built now, would the government be able to resist following the lead of the Guggenheim Bilbao? That museum opened just four months before Te Papa and established a trend that saw museum projects as being essentially about establishing a world-class piece of architecture. Over the last 20 years, shiny metal and glass contemporary art galleries have popped up everywhere.

It seems to me that only in that particular moment in time and only in New Zealand could Te Papa have been born. As this museum now moves forward, we can only hope that it never simply becomes a shiny bauble, that it retains its philosophical depth and by doing so drags the rest of the world towards a more egalitarian and cohesive future. We need this now more than ever.

Simon Knell
Professor of Museum Studies
University of Leicester
July 2017

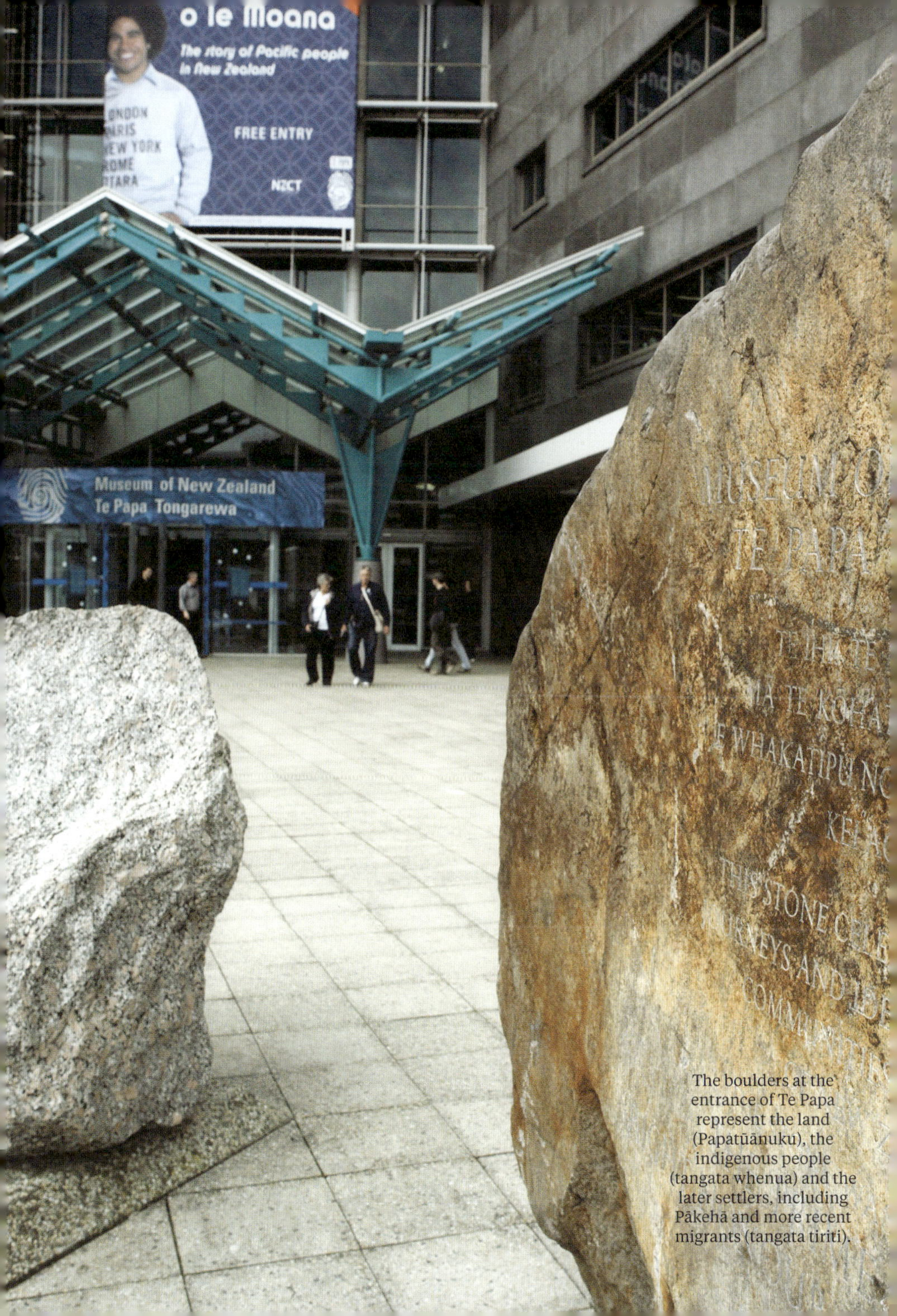

The boulders at the entrance of Te Papa represent the land (Papatūānuku), the indigenous people (tangata whenua) and the later settlers, including Pākehā and more recent migrants (tangata tiriti).

introduction

day one

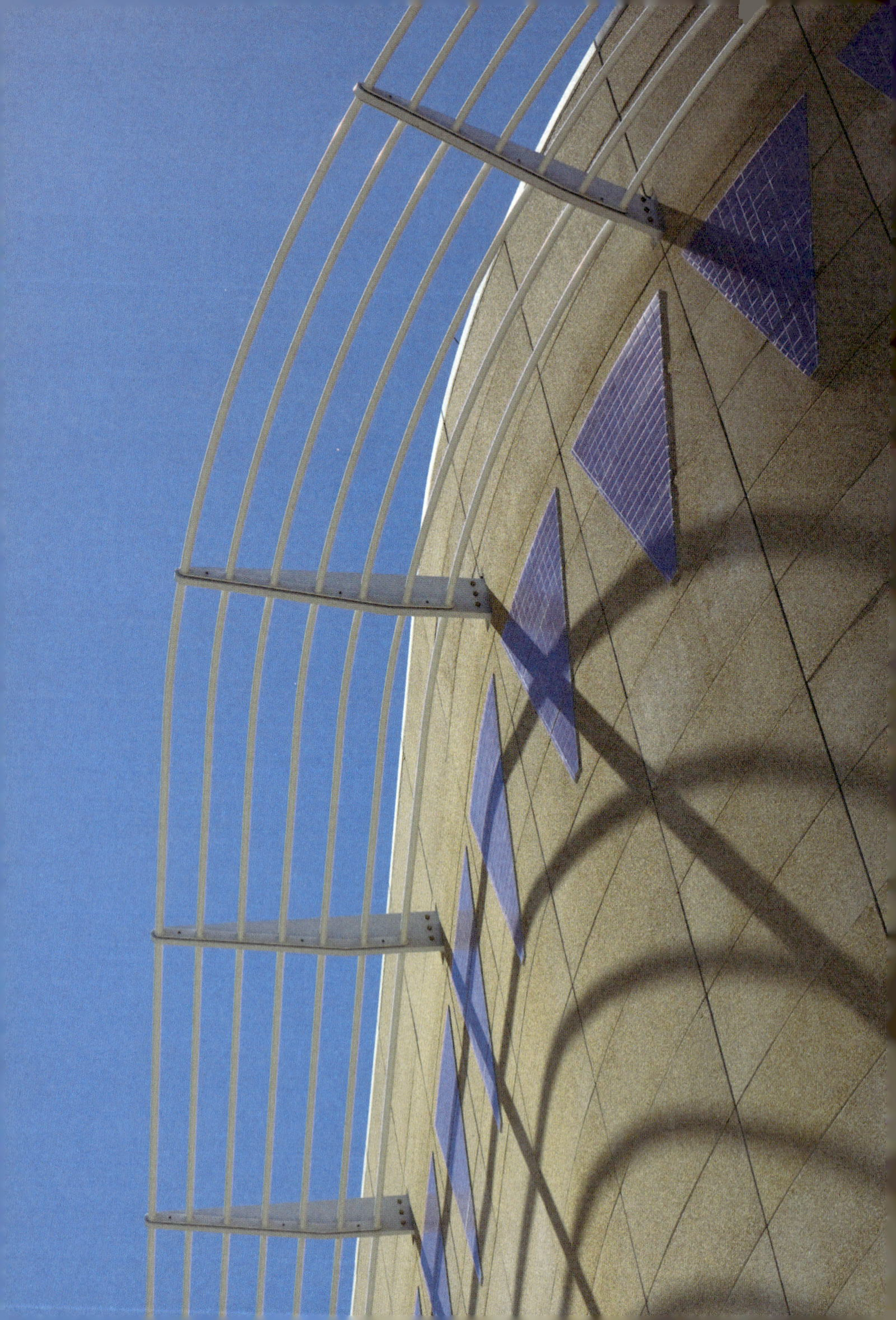

The Museum of New Zealand Te Papa Tongarewa (Te Papa) opened on 14 February 1998. The day was marked by food, music and celebration. Hay bales laid out on the forecourt of the museum lent the occasion a rural, and particularly Kiwi, flavour. New Zealand bands entertained the huge crowds. The sun shone, and the wind blew.

Just before midday, after a Māori ceremony, prayers, songs and speeches, Prime Minister Jenny Shipley said a few words:

> As New Zealanders, we think of ourselves as young, as raw and fresh, but one day, in looking in the mirror, we find, to our surprise, we have grown up . . . This building behind us is such a mirror. It is a place where we can look at ourselves, at our past and at our present, at our natural heritage, at the unique mosaic of cultures that is New Zealand.[1]

At 12 o'clock, two children, a Pākehā girl and a Māori boy, holding hands with famous yachtsman Sir Peter Blake, declared the Museum of New Zealand open.

For the public, this was the end of a long wait to see what was inside the new building on Wellington's waterfront. For several years they had seen (and heard) the construction, and witnessed collections being shifted from the old National Museum in Buckle Street into their new home. From early in the morning the crowds lined up, and after the short opening ceremony they poured in. They kept coming, all that day up to midnight, and again the next day, and the next. The numbers were unprecedented.

For the staff, this was 'day one', the culmination of several years of hard work, dreaming, planning, developing and realising. There were feelings of exhaustion, relief, joy, and sadness for those who did not live to see the project completed. I was one of those staff, and I remember looking down from above as the crowd swept in the front door for the first time, to the sounds of Gareth Farr's stirring music, specially commissioned for the occasion and performed by the New Zealand Symphony Orchestra. Then I ran up to level four to the Māori Discovery Centre *Te Huka a Tai*, which I had worked on, and was there when the first visitors came through the door, a local Māori family. 'Kia ora,' I said, 'welcome to Te Papa!'

And the verdict? One of the performers, Don McGlashan, spoke to the audience at the end of his set with The Mutton Birds: 'You *have* to go and look inside this place,' he declared, pointing to the building behind him. 'It is *fantastic*.' The whole front page of the next day's *Dominion* newspaper was emblazoned with the Te Papa brand, the now familiar stylised thumbprint, drawn on a cartoon hand raised in a thumbs-up sign of affirmation.

The public agreed, judging by the extraordinary response, which far exceeded the most optimistic visitor projections. The new museum attracted a large and genuinely diverse audience that included an unprecedented proportion of Māori visitors. Numbers averaged 2000 people on weekdays, rising to 6000 on weekends. Te Papa exceeded its annual target of 700,000 in three months. One million visitors came to the museum in five months and the first year, to February 1999, saw over two million.[2] Over the next few years, as the figures mounted, Te Papa became the most visited museum in Australasia and the Pacific.[3]

Te Papa was not just a popular success. It certainly attracted people who did not usually attend museums or galleries, but it was equally recognised and lauded for innovative museological features that were at the forefront of international developments. Though New Zealand boasts many fine museums, Te Papa is the only one widely known outside the country. It is often cited in studies of the visitor experience, postcolonial history, and engagement with indigenous people.[4]

Simon Knell, Professor of Museum Studies at the University of Leicester, argues that Te Papa has been the most influential national museum of the last forty years.[5] Barbara Kirshenblatt-Gimblett of New York University, who visited Te Papa in its first year, called it a 'new generation museum', which reflected the shift from the old 'memory palaces' to a contemporary form that worked against its immediate historical legacy.[6] Elaine Heumann Gurian, an American consultant who visited the institution over a four-year period leading up to its opening in 1998, saw the creation of a bicultural museum as a huge achievement:

> to me the most profound and interesting part of the process has been to watch the internalisation, institution-wide, of the bicultural process. It is one thing to mouth the aspiration of being inclusive, and another to try it . . . For all of us who have tried it, it is darned difficult. Difficult because integration is not only about content but also about world view, about values, about issues of time, of collaboration, disputational style, and the issues of supervision. In short, real biculturalism demands an understanding and acceptance by leadership of entirely different work and thinking patterns, and creating pathways, for it to work effectively in running an organisation.[7]

The things about the new museum that attracted mass audiences — the noisy interactives and busy public spaces laid out like malls, the affectionate exploration of New Zealand identity, and the friendly visitor services from hosts welcoming people at the door to readable labels — all signalled a shift away from the traditional style of the former National Art Gallery and National Museum with their somewhat stuffy image and small, elite audience.[8] Ken Gorbey, one of the key people responsible for Te Papa, who went on to oversee opening exhibits at the Jewish Museum Berlin, reflected that it was one of the world's great 'identity museums'.[9] He felt that its success was due in part to being firmly situated within the leisure industry, with its emphasis on customer service, strong brand presence and lively marketing that appealed both to overseas tourists and to local audiences who were previously non-visitors.[10]

These features all reflected the 'new museology', which favoured the museum as forum rather than temple, and stressed public scholarship and audience-focused exhibitions in place of the inward-looking preoccupation with collections and connoisseurship found in older museums. Similar features were seen at this time in other 'new' museums in Australia (National Museum of Australia, Canberra), Canada (Canadian Museum of Civilisation, Ottawa), and the US (National Museum of the American Indian, Washington), a trend that has generated much debate in the academic literature of museum studies.[11] Like those museums, Te Papa was shaped by a government-led agenda to celebrate national identity, reflected in its founding legislation (see Chapter 1), but was, equally, the product of an intellectual resistance by staff to this official discourse that stressed diversity, debate and cosmopolitanism (see Chapter 3).

Into this heady mix of nation building, project management and museological experimentation was added the distinctive local ingredient of 'biculturalism', the idea of two (bi) cultures in one country, based on the Treaty of Waitangi signed between Māori tribes and the Crown in 1840.[12] In contrast to ethnography museums in the UK, Europe and North America, which at this time still tended to depict native and tribal people as 'over there' and 'back then' (that is to say, distanced in time and space from the present), Te Papa sought to work *with* indigenous people and include them in the here and now. This strong sense of a living Māori culture was achieved by setting up a functioning marae (ceremonial space), employing Māori staff including a Māori co-director or Kaihautū, making exhibitions in partnership with iwi (tribes), integrating Māori perspectives into the collecting and display of taonga (treasures), and using bilingual labels and interpretation.

But if Te Papa was an immensely popular success, there were brickbats as well as plaudits. Art lovers wanted a more conventional gallery with pictures hung on white walls. Academics thought the museum was 'dumbing down' its scholarship to cater to the masses.[13] Te Papa was referred to variously as a 'giant amusement arcade', a 'glitzy expo' and the 'MTV of museums'.[14] The display of art in particular provoked much comment, even from the prime minister.[15] Anthropologist Michael Goldsmith observed that criticising Te Papa, at least among academics, was almost a national sport.[16]

Just months after its opening, a controversy erupted that suggested that Te Papa would always remain in the headlines. Christians furiously protested about an 'offensive' work by Tania Kovats in a travelling British art exhibition, *Pictura Britannica*, which depicted the Virgin Mary in a condom. The museum's forecourt was now witness to angry crowds with placards clamouring for the museum to respect their faith, when, they implied, the museum did exactly that for the sacred treasures of the Māori people. Then one day a container truck pulled up in the middle of the crowd of Christian protesters. The doors opened to reveal a living tableau of the Last Supper complete with a topless woman as Jesus Christ.[17]

Of course, this counter-protest about free speech, and the original protest, both demonstrated that Te Papa was, as it aimed to be, a public forum. From the very start the museum was at the centre of national debates about identity, race, the Treaty, the environment and other issues. It was and is the venue of choice for prestigious events, arts festivals, films and book launches, for welcoming overseas dignitaries, for ceremonies to mark the settlement of Treaty claims and discussions about current affairs, national politics and climate change. It was, and remains, 'our place', as the tagline states, in the middle of New Zealand's conversations about itself, whether good or bad, positive or negative.

So how did Te Papa come about? How was it that a small country in the South Pacific created such a bold statement of the latest museological trends, a museum that was a model for many others around the globe? What was Te Papa's impact nationally and internationally? How did it become the most loved, most visited, most debated, and therefore most prominent, museum in Australasia? What happened after it opened, and where is Te Papa going now?

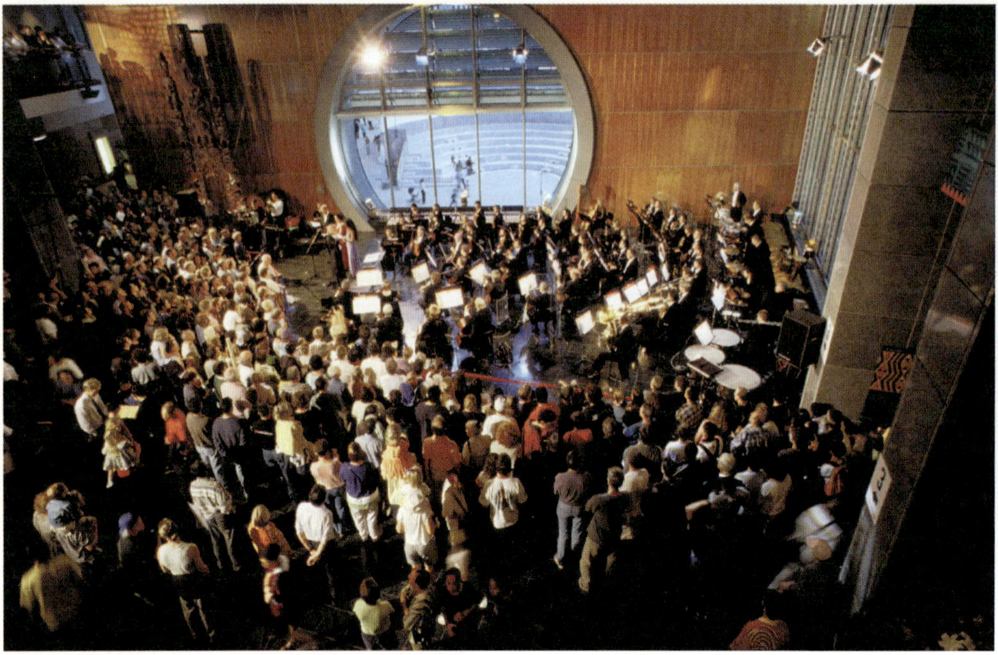

1.

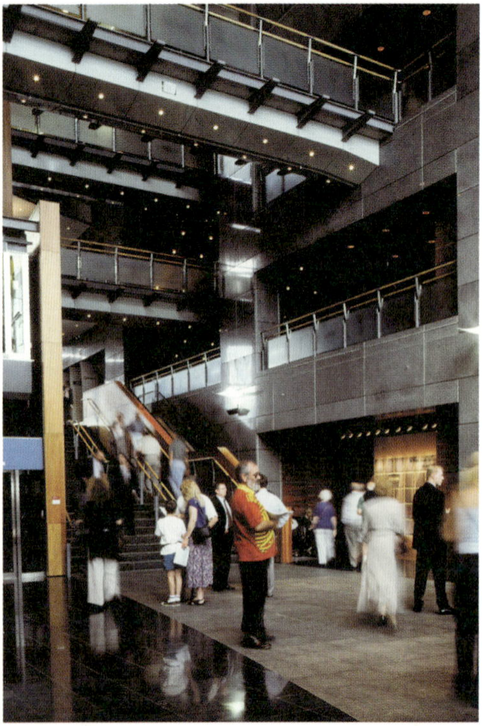

2.

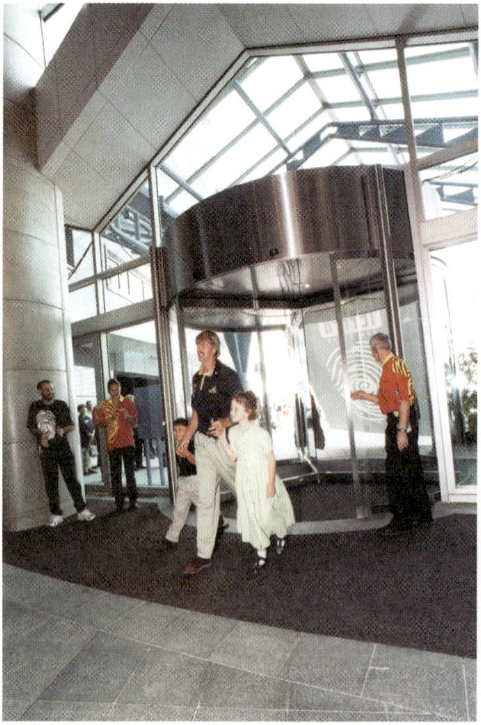

3.

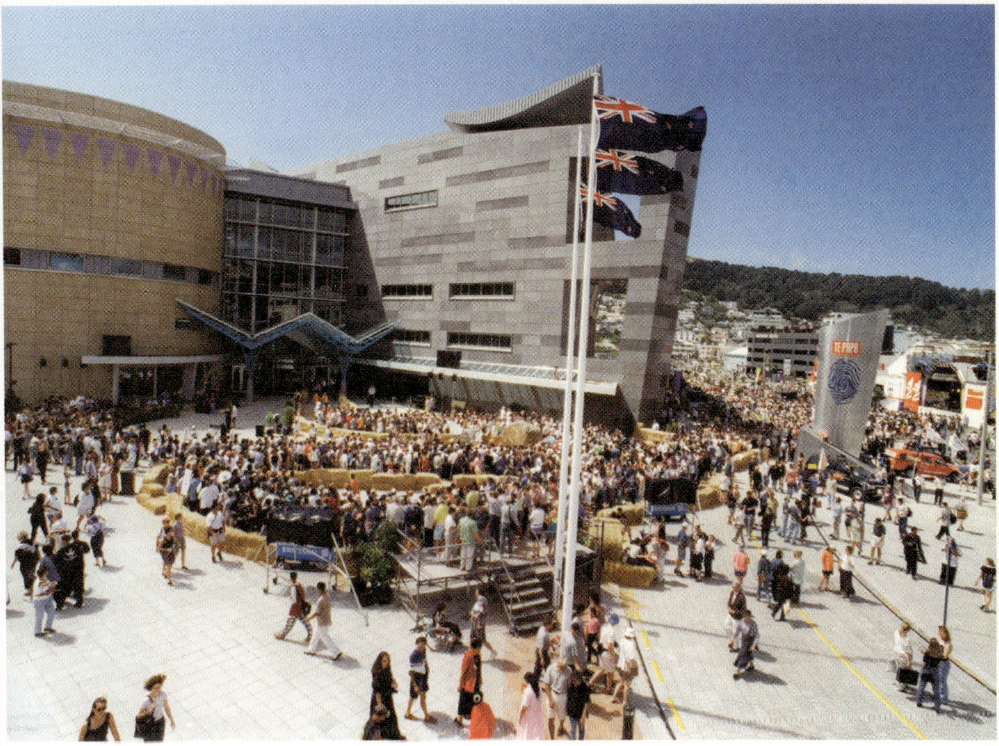

4.

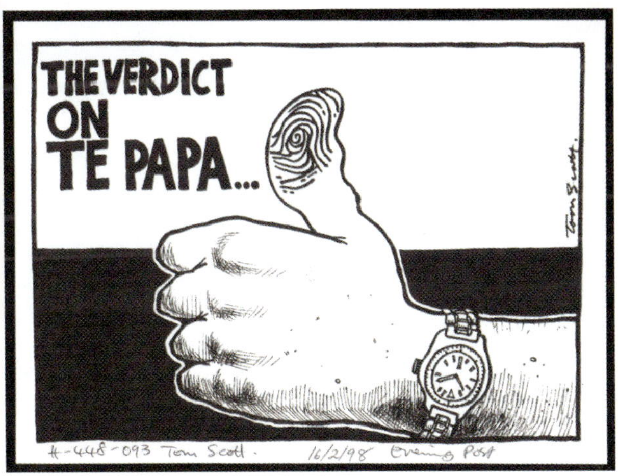

5.

1.

The New Zealand Symphony Orchestra performs in the Te Papa foyer on opening day, 14 February 1998.

2.

The crowds pour into Te Papa in 1998 (on the left, senior manager Stuart Park takes his turn working as a host).

3.

Peter Blake declares the museum open and enters the foyer, accompanied by two children.

4.

The crowds line the forecourt to see Te Papa on opening day.

5.

Tom Scott's *Evening Post* cartoon of 16 February 1998.

Having recalled day one in 1998, let us return to the beginning and retrace the steps to Te Papa's opening, and then on up to the present, as it celebrates its twentieth anniversary. In Chapter 1, I sketch the historical, social and museological background for Te Papa's reinvention of the national museum within the broader context of Aotearoa New Zealand, as well as the museum project, and the architecture. In Chapter 2, I give a guided tour of Te Papa as it was when it opened in 1998, walking around the building's interior and looking at the exhibitions. In Chapter 3, I review the development of these exhibitions, and what the staff set out to do, noting the innovative aspects of their professional practice, before considering the popular and critical reception of the displays, including research on visitor responses. Chapter 4 analyses one of the most important aspects of Te Papa's legacy, its experiments in biculturalism and its emerging Māori museum practice, both of which have attracted international attention. In Chapter 5, I reveal the people behind the scenes who made, and make, Te Papa what it was and is, with profiles of the staff who work there today, in a range of roles across the organisation, showing what they do in order to keep a large national museum going and why they do it. Lastly, in Chapter 6, I take a look at what Te Papa has achieved and what might be learned from its first 20 years.

At this point I want to tell you the reader a bit about myself and my approach to writing this book. After a background in teaching, I worked at the National Art Gallery and National Museum from 1988–92, and then again at Te Papa from 1996–2000, in a variety of roles including education, exhibition interpretation and public programmes. Since leaving Te Papa I have become an academic teaching museum studies at university, but I have kept in close touch with developments at the museum, not least through my research and writing and that of my students, which deal extensively with Te Papa, and on which I draw for this study.

My perspective is personal, and is necessarily limited and selective — I could not possibly hope to cover every aspect of the national museum's work in a short book like this. Consequently I deal with it only in general terms. Readers are referred to the notes, the appendices and other works for more detail on Te Papa's staff, programmes, collections and exhibitions from 1998 to

2018. Moreover, this study does not attempt a chronological account of every event, exhibit and person in Te Papa's history over the last 20 years. Annual reports and other documents, and Te Papa's website, are a better guide for that operational detail.

This is not an official authorised account, and I have had no restrictions on what I have written. At the same time this book is not an academic work, but is aimed at a general reader, while being informed by wider scholarship on Te Papa, and museums in general, to which I refer in the endnotes. I see it as an example of museum history, a sub-field of museum studies that interrogates the history of museums not as a celebratory march of progress but as the critical analysis of the ways in which social institutions are constructed in particular times and places and shaped by contemporary ideas, values and practices. The analysis tries to consider both theory and practice, the view from the inside and the outside, the local setting and the international context.

So, in that spirit, let us leave the crowds swirling around Te Papa in February 1998, and ask: How did this extraordinary museum come to be?

01.

getting to day one

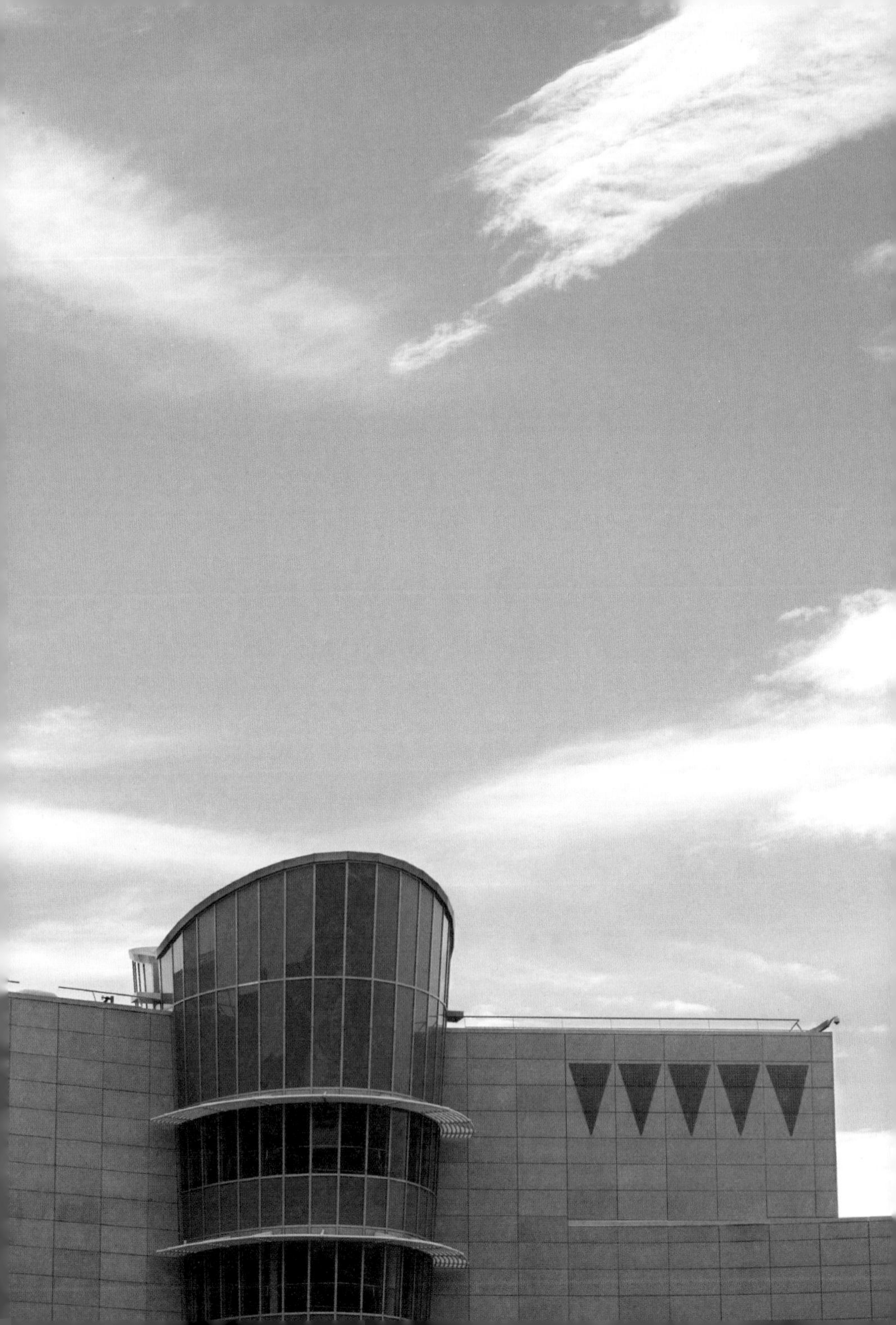

The 'new' museum that opened in 1998 was in fact not new at all, but a reinvention of its various predecessors: the Colonial Museum founded in 1865, which became the Dominion Museum in 1907, the National Museum in 1972 and, in 1992, with a new Act of Parliament, the Museum of New Zealand Te Papa Tongarewa, commonly known by its short name Te Papa.[1]

This was the third building in which the institution was housed: the first was a wooden structure in Museum Street behind Parliament Buildings, much criticised for being a mouldy, cramped fire risk, and the second a grand neoclassical building in Buckle Street, designed by Gummer and Ford, which opened in 1936. The new National Art Gallery and its sister institution the Academy of Fine Arts were housed on the first floor of the same building above the Dominion Museum.[2] In the British world from the mid to late nineteenth century, 'museums' were generally seen as institutions housing natural history, anthropology and related collections, and sometimes fine arts, set up in the wake of the popular international exhibitions of the period, which attracted enormous crowds.[3] Art galleries had a distinctive and slightly different history. In British colonies they developed later than museums, often growing out of private art societies that held annual exhibitions.[4]

Along with the Colonial Museum in Wellington founded in 1865, a museum in Auckland (actually a rather modest shed) began operating in the 1850s, the Canterbury Museum was established in Christchurch in a fine Gothic Revival building in 1870, and the Otago Museum opened its doors in Dunedin in 1868 as part of the University of Otago.[5] These first museums in the young settler colony were, not surprisingly, designed along British lines and reproduced on a modest scale the emerging professional form of public museums in the mid to late Victorian period. They were initially concerned with collecting and displaying specimens of flora and fauna and were closely connected with wealthy gentlemen naturalists and collectors who were members of philosophical societies, as opposed to the working-class users of mechanical institutes and libraries.

In New Zealand, as elsewhere in the Empire, museums concentrated on geology, amassing large collections of minerals, rocks and fossils, along with specimens of native plants and animals. Māori 'curiosities' were often seen in the same light, and displayed together with birds, fish and insects.[6] This campaign to collect nature and put it under glass, and on the end of a pin, was integral to the process of exploration, colonisation and economic development.[7]

How did Māori respond to the western museum culture introduced by Europeans during the nineteenth century? In many ways museums were part of the technology of colonisation and were regarded with suspicion for their complicity in the appropriation of ancestral material culture, not to mention the human remains that were regarded as tapu (sacred, restricted) by Māori. However, in other ways museums were not unlike indigenous forms of preserving and presenting the past, and there is evidence of Māori visiting museums and participating in collecting, display and other heritage practices.[8] By the early twentieth century, prominent Māori leaders engaged with museums and participated in anthropological research.[9] Influential Māori politician Sir Āpirana Ngata had close contact with the Dominion Museum in the 1920s and 1930s, and particularly the shed in nearby Sydney Street that housed the Māori collection, where the carvers from the School of Maori Arts and Crafts worked to 'restore' the meeting house Te Hau ki Tūranga, subsequently installed as the centrepiece of the Maori Hall in the new museum building in 1936.[10]

The new building in Mount Cook, housing the National Art Gallery on the first floor and the Dominion Museum on the ground floor, with the National War Memorial and Carillon in front, was referred to as Wellington's Acropolis, a shrine to the war dead and a showcase of the nation's history, culture and

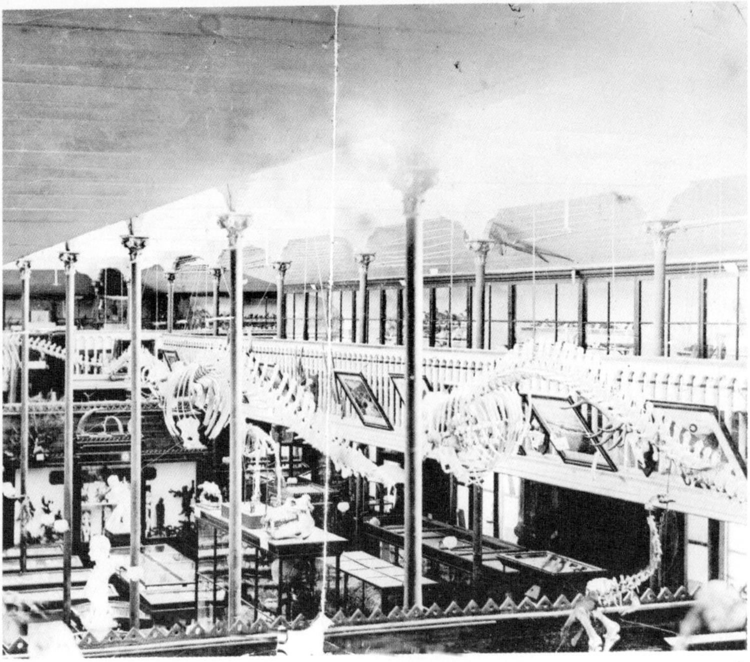

1.

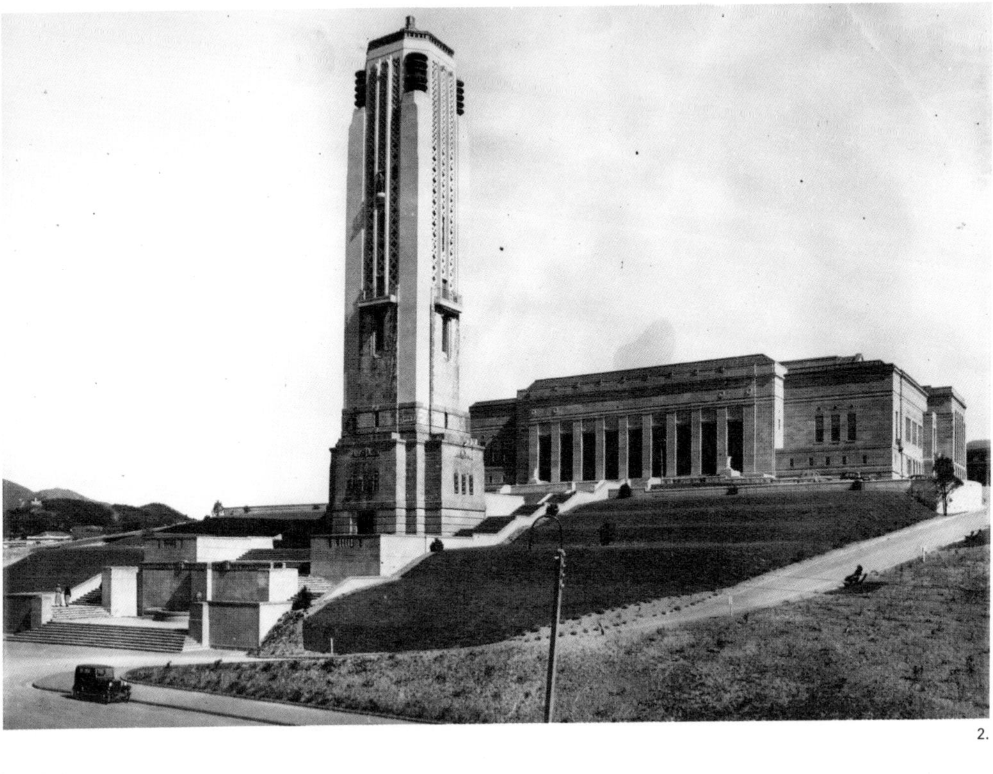

2.

1.

The interior of the Colonial Museum, Te Papa's predecessor, on Museum Street, Wellington, photographed in the late nineteenth century.

2.

The Dominion Museum, National Art Gallery and National War Memorial photographed not long after opening in Buckle Street, Wellington, in 1936.

art. It served its purpose well for a few years but, sequestered out of the city centre on a hilltop that was not connected to public transport, it quickly lost broad popular appeal and visitor numbers appear to have tailed off. There was a hiatus when the air force took over the building during World War II and it did not reopen until 1949. In the postwar decades other new attractions, such as television, competed for the attention of visitors in their leisure time.[11]

Turning inward from public and external demands, the institution focused on professional and scientific concerns: adding to its collections of fishes, plants, insects, birds and artefacts. Expeditions were mounted, new species were described, academic papers were written, and staff came and went.[12] The postwar period saw growth in the number and variety of New Zealand museums: there were expansions in buildings and staff numbers, developments in professionalisation, improved display techniques, and growing awareness of education for schools (if not interpretation for the general public). Though they followed museological trends in Britain and, increasingly, Australia and the US, New Zealand museums began to look at the country's own cultural heritage and national identity. In the 1960s and 1970s New Zealand history became a subject in schools and universities, and there was keen community interest in local museums, historic buildings and heritage sites.[13]

Then came a museological revolution. In the 1980s the famous *Te Maori* exhibition changed the direction of New Zealand museums and became a touchstone for the Māori Renaissance, a dramatic resurgence of Māori people, culture and identity that had been gathering pace for some time.[14] *Te Maori* opened at the Metropolitan Museum in New York in 1984 and toured the US before returning to tour New Zealand in 1986–87, during which time it was seen by almost a million people. It was widely praised and emulated for the way it acknowledged Māori understandings of their carving as taonga, living ancestral treasures with a spiritual dimension, and also for the way it incorporated tikanga Māori (cultural practices) into opening and closing ceremonies. The exhibition has been credited with initiating sweeping changes in museums including an increase in Māori staff, the use of Māori language in labels, and stronger relationships with local iwi.[15]

When *Te Maori: Te hokinga mai* opened at the National Museum in 1986,

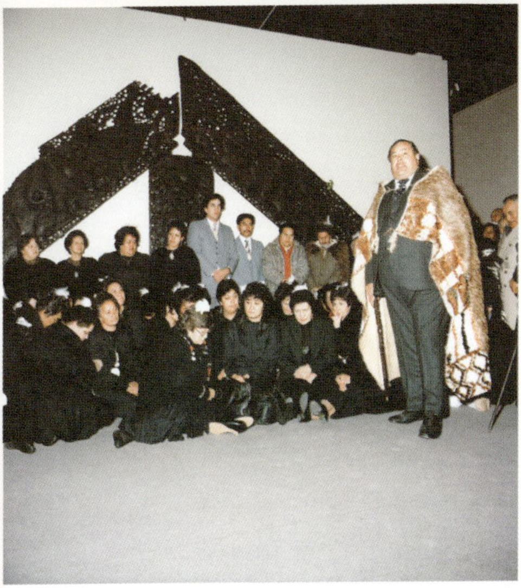

1.

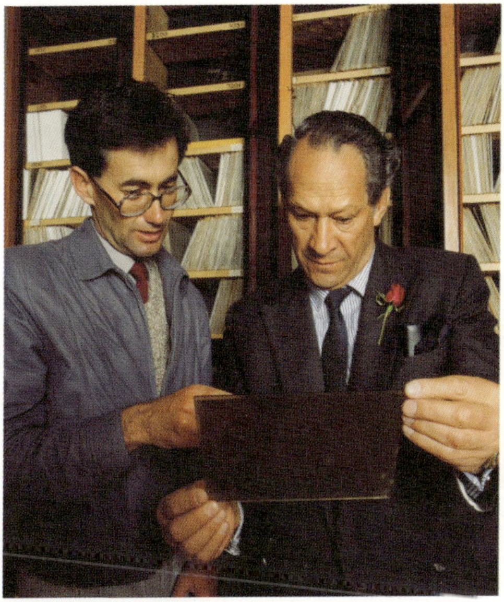

2.

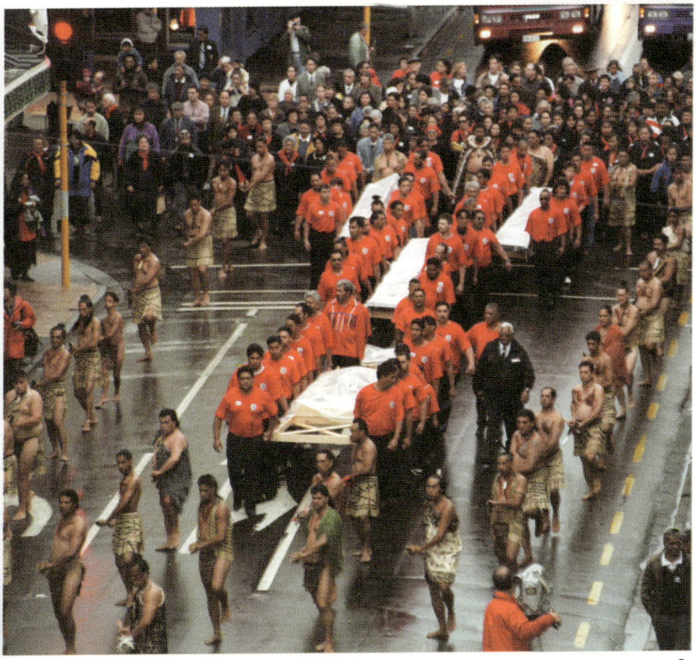

3.

1.

A scene at the opening ceremony for the exhibition *Te Maori: Te hokinga mai* at the National Museum, 1986.

2.

Dr (now Sir) Peter Tapsell, Minister of Arts, with history curator Michael Fitzgerald at the National Museum, Buckle Street, in the late 1980s.

3.

Iwi moving taonga to the new building on the waterfront, 22 March 1997.

there was widespread debate about the future role and mission of museums. Art critic Hamish Keith urged the museum sector to face the challenges posed by the exhibition. 'None of these could be resisted,' he said. '*Te Maori* had in any case made them inevitable.'[16] By this time the National Museum had outgrown its building in Buckle Street, and its Māori, Pacific and history displays were showing signs of being out of step with a changing society. Plans for a new national museum overlapped with, and to some extent grew out of, the *Te Maori* exhibition. Certainly the museum came under pressure for change from Māori leaders in a period of intense debate about the contemporary relevance of the Treaty of Waitangi, New Zealand's founding document.[17]

Historian James Belich has argued that this period of New Zealand history was marked by domestic 'decolonisation'.[18] Beginning in the 1960s and 1970s, when formal ties to Britain were loosened, externally New Zealand learned to make its own way in the world, while internally a sense of independent national identity sprang up. Confronted by Māori protest over land, language and political rights, Pākehā (European) New Zealanders were forced to re-examine their difficult relationship with their own colonial past. The stark reality of Māori impoverishment dispelled the old myth that God's Own Country had 'the best race relations in the world'. Simultaneously, cultural nationalism found expression through the visual arts, architecture, music and literature. Local debates were spurred on by international social movements: conservation of the natural environment, women's liberation and the legalisation of homosexuality.[19]

Much of this political and cultural foment came together in the early and mid 1980s during the term of the Fourth Labour Government (1983–90), when Prime Minister David Lange oversaw a progressive social policy agenda that, ironically, was matched by neoliberal economic policy that resulted in restructuring, deregulation and unemployment. Some in the Museum of New Zealand project office thought that landmark cultural investments such as theirs got the go-ahead precisely because they represented an antidote to, perhaps even a distraction from, this gloomy backdrop.[20] Meanwhile, the mood and tenor of government policy on Māori issues switched from paternalistic integration to a degree of self-determination. For example, the 1984 Hui

Taumata (Māori Economic Summit), chaired by Professor Ngatata Love of Victoria University, heralded a decade of social and economic development further stimulated through the later settlement of Treaty claims.[21]

One of the themes that came out of the hui was the notion of 'biculturalism', or two peoples in one country, based on the Māori-Crown partnership enshrined in the Treaty of Waitangi. The evolving interpretation of 'partnership' based on article two of the Treaty was to prove effective in addressing Māori grievances through the Waitangi Tribunal. Crucially, from 1985 the Tribunal considered retrospective claims concerning breaches of the Treaty, opening a flood of major claims that, when they began to be settled from the mid 1990s, effected significant changes in the fortunes of iwi. The Treaty, given effect by the Tribunal's reports and a series of important court cases, became highly influential in the public sector, where institutions were expected to demonstrate their responsiveness to Māori through bicultural processes, bilingual names, hiring Māori staff, etc.[22]

The assertive Māori engagement with idealistic Labour politicians in the early and mid 1980s was led by a generation of university-educated Māori leaders: Pat Hohepa, Ranginui Walker, Donna Awatere, Ripeka Evans, Tipene O'Regan, Bob Mahuta and many others. Several of these leaders — Hirini Moko Mead, Kara Puketapu, Piri Sciascia and Tāmati Reedy — were to play important roles in the *Te Maori* exhibition.[23] However, there were also strong individuals working within the parliamentary system. One of these was Dr (later Sir) Peter Tapsell, of Te Arawa, MP for the Eastern Māori electorate, Minister of Arts, and later speaker of the House of Representatives, who played a key role in Te Papa's history, as we will see below.

Te Papa came out of a dynamic period of New Zealand's history. This explains much in terms of how the museum project developed from the late 1980s, and through the 1990s. The major social changes described above reshaped the relationship between majority settler (Pākehā) culture, indigenous Māori, and the other social groups making up this increasingly diverse country, namely Pacific Islanders who had arrived in greater numbers from the 1960s, and Asian migrants from the 1990s. Demographic trends indicated that Māori could no longer be ignored on the national or local stage.[24]

Greater political representation boosted Māori assertiveness — after the 1994 election, the new MMP Parliament boasted 15 Māori MPs spread across the political spectrum.[25] Despite its antipathy to many Māori political demands, the National government that came to power in 1990 oversaw the settlement of the Tainui Treaty claim in 1995 and the Kāi Tahu claim in 1998 (and saw the national museum project through to completion). But if this was the political and social background, what was the museological context of Te Papa?

THE NEW MUSEOLOGY AND NEW NATIONAL MUSEUMS

The 1990s and 2000s saw an unprecedented museum boom in New Zealand, with several new or redeveloped museums and art galleries becoming the focal point of regional and national identity and culture.[26] Te Papa led this trend, and after it opened a wave of change swept through local museums. A number of these institutions, like Te Papa, were combined, all-purpose cultural facilities that integrated gallery, museum, library or archive functions into one 'converged' operation.[27] They had a different focus and feel to the older style of museum — a broad interest in cultural and natural heritage of many different kinds, attractions that included physical interactives or computers, and a strong appeal to visitors and especially tourists through aggressive marketing, and enhanced public services.

New Zealand may have been ahead of the curve, but around the world new museums looked different in the late twentieth century. Going to a museum felt less like going to church — quiet, reverent, contemplative — and more like hanging out at a cafe. Many of their features were aimed at greater audience engagement, inspired by 'the new museology'.[28] In this movement, the museum was seen as a forum for debate not a temple on a hill. Rather than looking inwards, professionals reached outwards to the community through active public programmes.

Initially the *new* museology was directed at the *old* museology, and sought to move away from a conservative focus on *what* the museum did to *why*, resulting in a more critical analysis of the institution and its social purpose. Inspired by a wider postmodern intellectual climate that questioned western master narratives and revealed the constructedness and partiality of cultural representation, museum professionals and scholars abandoned the idea of the authoritative museum display of the 'truth', and experimented with multiple voices and divergent perspectives.[29] The museum's focus shifted to the audience. To paraphrase American commentator Stephen Weil, museums changed from 'being *about* something to being *for* somebody'.[30]

The new museology was translated into professional practice on a number of levels: collections, exhibitions, management and public programmes.[31] By collapsing distinct collection boundaries, mixing up objects from different disciplines, and including elements of popular culture in 'high culture' spaces, museums left behind the grand European model, those vast storehouses of encyclopedic collections made famous by the British Museum, the Louvre, and a handful of other treasure palaces; instead they embraced 'edutainment', new technology and shopping. The separation of art and culture/history, and the authority of science and anthropology, were subject to trenchant critique for their links to social exclusion, environmental issues, racism, imperialism and colonisation. Many things later associated with Te Papa — the blurring of high and low, the colourful, dramatic design and layout, and the emphasis on interactivity and the visitor experience — can be seen in other new national museums in Australia, Canada and the US at this time.[32]

The first of these was the Canadian Museum of Civilization, which opened in Ottawa in 1988 and claimed to be the first museum of the television age. It was a 'reboot' of an older institution, the separation from the past signalled dramatically by a bold architectural design by native Canadian architect Joseph Cardinal. There are many similarities between this museum and Te Papa, notably the collaborative approach to the indigenous exhibits.[33] Other new museums that followed Te Papa, such as the Melbourne Museum (2000) and the National Museum of Australia in Canberra (2001), were likewise characterised by controversial buildings and displays that grappled with difficult national histories.[34]

Another museum with which Te Papa was often compared was the National Museum of the American Indian in Washington — a striking contrast to the sober and somewhat conventional institutions on the Mall such as the National Gallery of Art or the National Museum of Natural History — which attempted to represent what director Rick West called the changing view of Native American culture in contrast to the Indian 'frozen' in the ethnographic past.[35]

These and other museums, usually located in former settler colonies of the 'new' world, explored different ways to display national histories that took account of indigenous presence: using self-reflexive and dialogic techniques to include native voices alongside curators, collecting and exhibiting modern or transitional objects to counter the historic portrayal of tribal culture, and consulting those represented so that they would have a say in how their culture was shown.[36]

Despite innovative experiments with design, collections and display, and positive responses from a new and larger public, new national museums often received negative reviews for the way they negotiated questions of indigenous, settler and national identity.[37] Jette Sandahl, who ran the Museum of World Cultures in Gothenburg, Sweden, and later the Danish National Museum in Copenhagen, worked at Te Papa in the 2000s, and regarded it as a model for the decolonisation of European ethnographic museums. While new museums like Te Papa were 'not infallible' or above reproach, she points out that the hysterical criticism of them overlooked their fundamental challenge to traditional museology:

> At times a radical rift is felt between European museum traditions and the new, Indigenous-driven museums in other parts of the world, like the NMAI, Te Papa or the National Museum of Australia, carrying a — in professional circles often only whispered, hinted at and intimated — delegitimization of the epistemologies of Indigenous curating. The idea of Indigenous self-representation, and that of other oppressed groups, is not easily integrated into or absorbed within the framework of White Western interpretative monopoly and its foundation in the binary hierarchies of European scientific rationalism.[38]

Comparing Te Papa with its predecessors, and analysing it in the context of other new national museums of the time, it can be understood as a radical example of the new museology, and a strikingly original reinvention of the national museum as it was then understood. However, Te Papa's connections to the wider international context should not take anything away from the originality of its concept and the thoroughgoing way in which it was brought to fruition, working in isolation and against great odds.

How did this happen? It is a remarkable story, which involves a small group of politicians, developers and professionals who worked for over ten years to see the project completed. In the next section I trace the evolution of the ideas, the architecture and the exhibitions up to 1998.

STEPS TO DAY ONE: THE MUSEUM OF NEW ZEALAND PROJECT

Te Papa was the product of *Te Maori*. It emerged from the social and political context of the 1980s, with its peculiar mix of indigenous politics, liberal reform and cultural nationalism. When *Te Maori* was held at the National Museum, a major gathering of Māori elders called for greater input into the care of their taonga.[39] In 1985 a report titled *Nga Taonga o Te Motu* laid out a vision for a radically different kind of national museum, which could bring together all the separate collections to tell the story of New Zealand.[40] In 1988 a Project Development Team was set up, led by Ken Gorbey. Gorbey had come from running the Waikato Museum in Hamilton, where several important exhibitions of contemporary Māori art and colonial history had been staged. A small team under Gorbey produced a concept in 1989 recognising the Treaty and acknowledging the two main cultures of the nation: Māori and Pākehā.[41]

This concept, and the fact that the museum project got the go-ahead in the first place, was due in large measure to the astute Māori politician Dr Peter Tapsell. Then Minister of Arts, it was Tapsell who got Cabinet approval, persuading his Labour Party colleagues that it was worth spending over

$300 million on a major building construction project in straitened financial times. As Gorbey recalls, Tapsell had the advisory committee's report but he needed something 'more fundamental' to get the project across the line, a 'set of principles that reflected what he saw emerging in our cultural landscape at the time'.[42]

One day Gorbey was called into Tapsell's office in Parliament. There, the minister laid out the three main ideas that became the foundational principles of the institution. Gorbey recalls Tapsell telling him that they did not want something like 'the old museum up on the hill', which he saw was of 'very limited relevance to modern New Zealand'. He wanted the project team to capture the 'essence of a new cultural place'. 'What emerged, to be consistently restated in each and every presentation and in every press interview,' Gorbey wrote later, 'were three stakes in the ground':

The museum will:

- be for all New Zealanders: an inclusive place that welcomes people of all ethnicities, and educational and socioeconomic groups; that works to bring in an audience that is expressive of the full New Zealand demographic
- tell all our stories: be about all of the peoples who live in the country, their lives, beliefs and values; be a narrative, rather than collection-based, museum
- be bicultural: the museum will share governance between the tangata whenua (Māori) and the peoples of New Zealand.[43]

These concepts — social inclusion, narrative storytelling and collaboration with indigenous people — were well ahead of other national museums at the time. What is even more remarkable was that bold ideas became reality, thanks to the support of politicians, senior management and trustees (including former Labour Prime Minister Bill Rowling as chair of the board). It should be pointed out that this was also the case with the centre-right National government that came into power in 1990, with prime ministers Jim Bolger and later Jenny Shipley both keen supporters of the new museum.[44] Cheryll Sotheran, formerly director of the Dunedin Public Art Gallery, became CEO

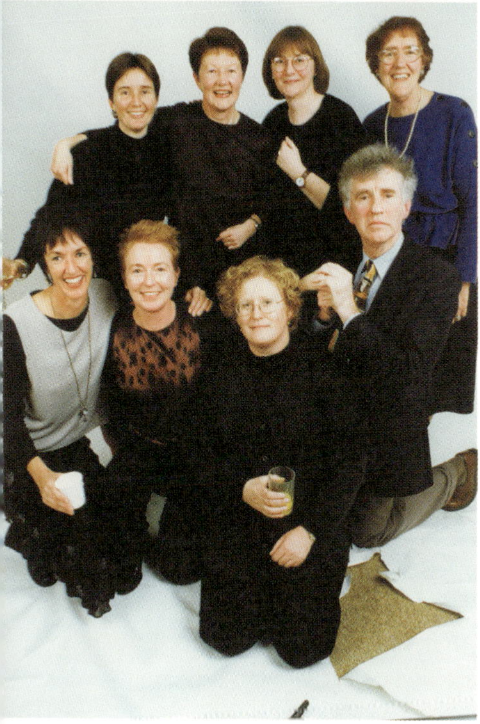

1.

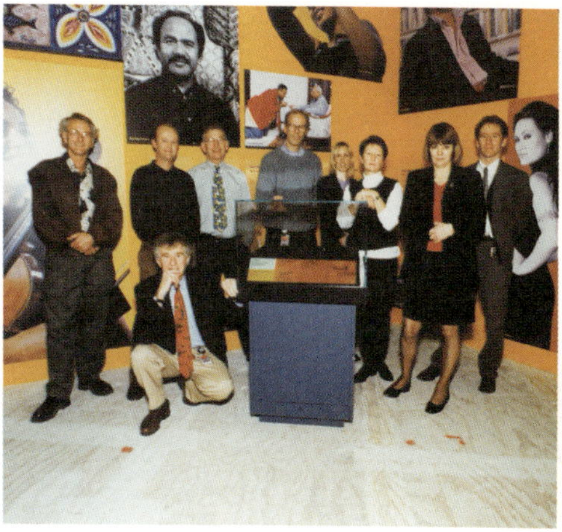

2.

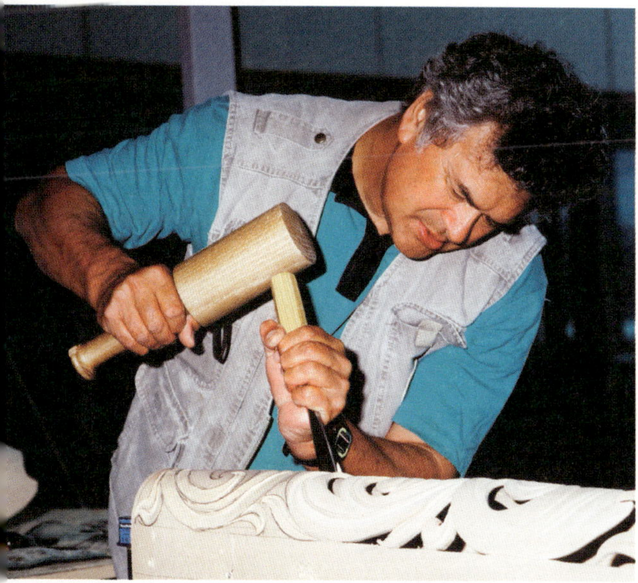

3.

1.

Staff from the Museum of New Zealand project office in 1996. Front row, from left: Karen Mason, Michelle Taylor, Bronwyn Simes, Ken Gorbey. Back row: Sue Harrop, Raewyn Smith, Diana Minchall, Pearl Cunningham.

2.

Staff with the first display installed in the new building, the *Mana Pasifika* exhibition, June 1997. From left: Alan Grey, Neil Kemp, Ken Gorbey (kneeling), Mack Morum, Robin Parkinson, Raewyn Liddle, Raewyn Smith, Cheryll Sotheran and Sean Sweeney.

3.

Cliff Whiting, Concept Leader Māori and later Kaihautū, who led the carving of the contemporary marae Te Hono ki Hawaiki.

in 1992 and worked with steely determination to see that its mission would be realised on time and under budget.[45] With a strong mix of management skills, museum experience and passionate commitment to the vision, Sotheran led Te Papa through numerous challenges during the project phase leading up to opening in 1998.[46]

Te Papa's proactive style of museum economics, an essential ingredient in the mix, was something that often attracted adverse comment and has been little analysed.[47] One of the corporate principles, along with more lofty ideals, was that Te Papa would be 'commercially positive'. Many decisions about day one were driven by this imperative: value management of exhibitions, the hosts' bright costumes, the shop and donation box prominently positioned at the entrance along with names of sponsors and donors, the staff training in customer service, and the funds development, events, marketing and communications programmes drawing on leisure industry models. All this was part of a conscious 'repositioning' of the museum by senior management.[48] In hindsight, much of Te Papa's success with the public must be attributed to this element, despite the complaints of those who think the state should fully fund cultural institutions. Indeed, the museum was remarkably successful in raising half of its income, from various sources, on top of the government funding, as shown in Appendix A, 'Selected highlights 1998–2017'.

The other essential ingredient was the reassertion of mana Māori. From the late 1980s planning was well advanced for extensive Māori input into the museum project according to bicultural principles, including significant Māori staffing to take responsibility for taonga.[49] Māui Pōmare, a member of the National Museum council and the board of the Museum of New Zealand, assembled a group of elders to advise the project team in 1988. This became Ngā Kaiwawao (meaning those who interrogate or dissect) — influential Māori leaders, artists and academics who played a key role in forging relationships with iwi that underpinned the development of the new museum. Ken Gorbey recalls their crucial input:

> Officially Ngā Kaiwawao was the new project board's Māori advisory committee, but under the driving chairmanship of Apirana Mahuika

> . . . it became a visionary force that helped redefine what a museum in New Zealand might be. Balancing vision with pragmatic good sense they formulated new ideas on the nature and nurture of collections; created the ceremonials for our unique cultural mix; struggled with ideas of how all cultural and origin groups might be drawn into Te Papa and stand as equals; fed into and reviewed architectural concepts; and brought deep cultural understandings to formulating approaches to visitor experience development.[50]

The chair of Ngā Kaiwawao, Dr Api Mahuika of Ngāti Porou, took the proposals out to iwi in a series of meetings around the country. He wrote at the time that: 'Te Papa Tongarewa is seen by Māori as the first physical demonstration of a bicultural approach to *taonga* and, therefore, a first step towards the recognition of Māori cultural values.'[51] In a world first, indigenous people were active partners in the development of a new museum. Certainly, no one at any level of the project team — whether architects, managers, concept developers, writers or interpreters — had any illusions about the central place of Māori themes within the building and exhibitions and the role played by their Māori colleagues and the iwi that they represented.[52]

The Museum of New Zealand Te Papa Tongarewa was formalised by legislation in 1992, guided through the parliamentary process by then Executive Director Michael Volkerling. A gifted arts administrator who had run the Arts Council (now Creative New Zealand), Volkerling oversaw the early planning for the institution.[53] The purpose of the new museum was set out in the Act as follows:

> Te Papa is a forum for the nation to present, explore, and preserve the heritage of its cultures and knowledge of the natural environment in order to:
>
> - better understand and treasure the past
> - enrich the present and
> - meet the challenges of the future.[54]

The new name of the museum was an interesting example of how a national museum took on a Māori identity without alienating a mass audience. The short form 'Te Papa' was easy to pronounce and quickly caught on.[55] The full name, Museum of New Zealand Te Papa Tongarewa, suggests an equal pairing of Treaty partners. The Māori name can be translated as 'the receptacle of treasured possessions'. 'Papa' alludes to mother earth in the Māori creation story (Papatūānuku), but also means land, foundation, platform and a papahou, or treasure box, containing a rare variety of pounamu or tongarewa.[56] As Ken Gorbey remembers it, the name came out of a waiata (song) sung by Sir Timoti Karetu in response to discussion within Ngā Kaiwawao.[57]

The 1992 Act integrated the collections of the former gallery and museum. This was a controversial step then, and 25 years later it still rankles for some, though it was this integrated approach, along with the audience and bicultural focus, which distinguished Te Papa internationally. Today it is hard to believe how hostile the reaction was to something now taken for granted. At the old National Museum building in Buckle Street some visitors, alarmed by signs of a dramatic change in direction, saw the museum project as Māori-centric, and the de-installation of old favourites like the Egyptian mummy, the Elgar furniture in the Colonial Gallery and the stuffed lion 'King Dick' were greeted with anger. 'It's a shame that this is called a National Museum,' one disgruntled person wrote in the visitors' book. 'It should be called a Maori museum.'[58]

Despite the reactionary and, at times, openly racist opposition, the project team forged ahead.[59] Once the concept was established, concept leaders started work on exhibitions in four broad zones. They were a diverse and multi-talented group: marine biologist Dr Geoff Hicks for natural environment; historian Dr Jock Phillips for history; poet, art critic and curator Ian Wedde for art; and artist Cliff Whiting for Māori. Whiting, a well-known artist and educator, had been a member of Ngā Kaiwawao, and later became Kaihautū or Māori co-director alongside Sotheran. He was a remarkable man, fluent in Māori and a staunch advocate of Māori rights, but flexible, creative and open to new possibilities. As Kaihautū (navigator), his was the gentle but firm guidance that kept the waka going through the storms of the next few years. Phillips writes in his memoirs that this group was stimulating and rewarding, but working with Whiting in particular was a 'privilege'. 'He had a real feel for what would work on an exhibition floor,' Phillips recalls. 'Cliff never spoke loud, was never assertive, but always made his point with a twinkle in the eye.'[60]

The concept leaders worked to the framework below, established in 1988. This conceived of Māori as tangata whenua and Pākehā as tangata tiriti. European settlers were therefore seen together with *all* later arrivals (i.e. Pākehā and recent migrants from Asia alike), who related to the country through the Treaty. This formulation, according to art historian and former National Art Gallery director Jenny Harper, then working in the project office, was suggested by Eddie Durie, chief judge of the Māori Land Court.[61] The exhibition conceptual framework was as follows:

- Papatūānuku: the earth on which we all live
- Tangata Whenua: those who belong to the land by right of first discovery
- Tangata Tiriti: those who belong to the land by right of the Treaty of Waitangi
- Integrated Exhibitions: zones of cultural overlap[62]

But what about the building itself? In the next chapter, we will tour the interior and exhibitions to see how the concepts materialised (or not) on the floor. For now, a brief account of the exterior design must suffice. The architecture of museums is a notoriously fickle topic, subject to personal taste and stylistic fashion.[63] The famous global museums commonly seen in coffee-table books, such as Frank Gehry's Guggenheim in Bilbao or I.M. Pei's Louvre in Paris, are the creations of 'star-architects'. More concerned with the container than the contents, they are often formally beautiful, like sculptures, but not necessarily effective designs from an operational point of view.[64]

Te Papa's architects were Ivan Mercep and Pete Bossley of Jasmax. The Auckland firm had experience with building museums and marae, and, in the case of the Waikato Museum in Hamilton, which opened in 1987, designs that attempted to bring the two together. They won an international competition against much-favoured and famous competitors, Frank Gehry included. Factors in their favour were that they answered a very specific brief and had a much better practical sense of how the build was going to be completed, and moreover how the interior would operate as a museum.

1.
View of Te Papa from the harbour.

2.
The entrance to Te Papa from Cable Street.

3.
View of the building looking up to the marae from *Bush City*.

4.
The waharoa or gateway to the marae.

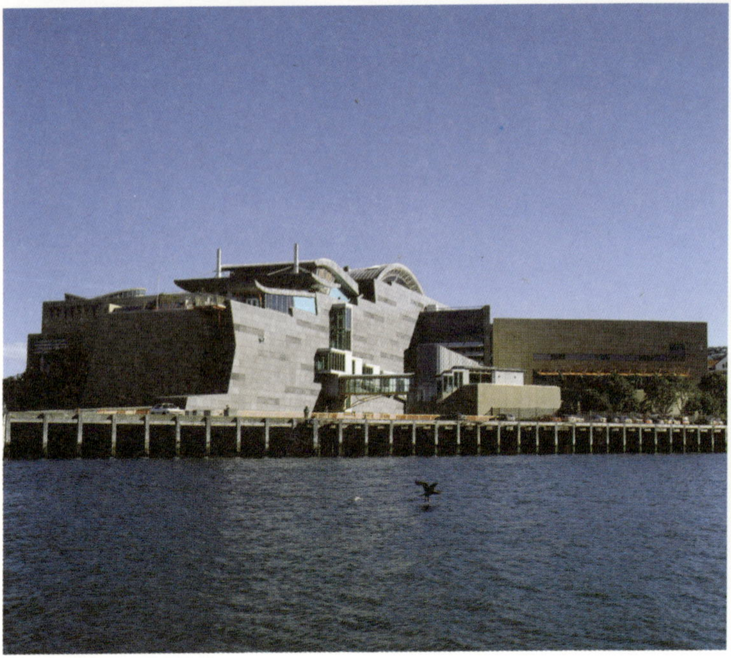

1.

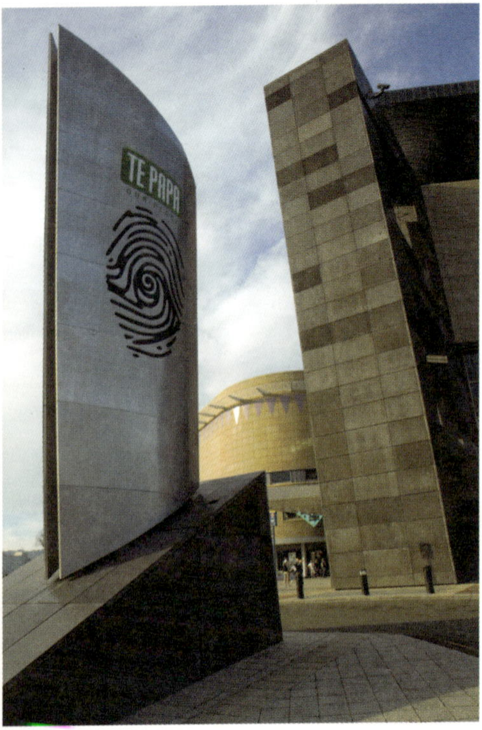

2.

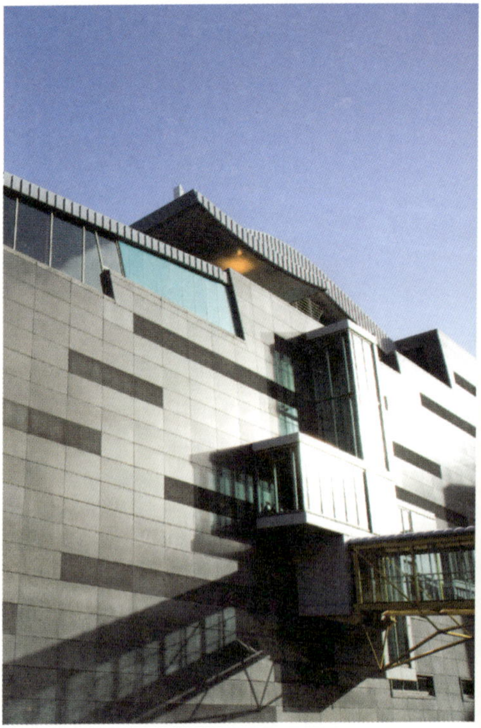

3.

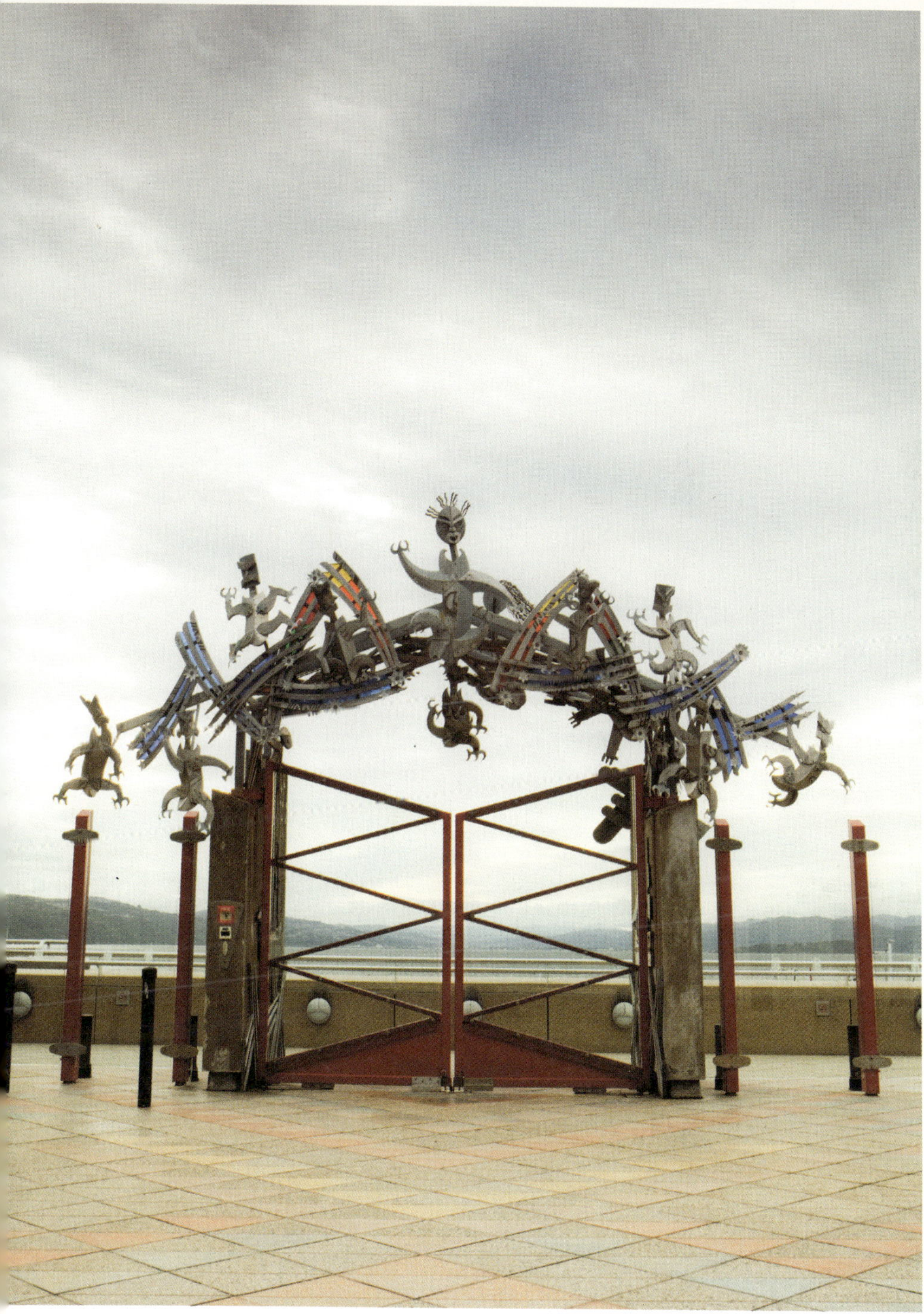

4.

The architecture of Te Papa can be read in terms of the conceptual framework described above: the land, and the people/culture arising from it, reflecting the nation's origins in the negotiation of Māori and Pākehā coming together around the Treaty. The square facade facing the city, with its rectilinear design (the coloured windows on the facade an artwork by Milan Mrkusich), represents the country's European settlers and the grid-like pattern of the city they established. On the other side of the building, facing the sea where according to local tradition the explorer Kupe arrived 1000 years ago, curvilinear shapes suggest the Polynesian heritage, particularly the marae that juts out into the harbour like a hilltop pā. Running right through the building from north to south is a large wall, representing the earthquake fault line, splitting in two the 'European' and Polynesian heritage — two peoples living on a few trembling islands. Inside the building, the people and their cultures are seen to grow up out of the environment, with nature exhibitions lower down and culture and history above them.[65]

Despite this conceptual integrity and the skill with which the architects responded to the brief, providing a building that, for example, shielded exhibits from the harsh New Zealand daylight and housed collections on upper floors to protect them from tsunamis, the design of Te Papa is regarded by critics as somewhat literal and unimaginative.[66] More consequential than the design, perhaps, is the choice of location. On its spectacular site at the edge of Wellington's inner harbour, the building faces downtown Wellington, in stark contrast to its predecessor in the leafy seclusion of Mount Cook, signalling that it is part of the leisure and tourism sectors, not standing aloof from them.

As a building, Te Papa is perhaps most distinguished by its sheer engineering ingenuity. Many critics thought the government was mad to put a museum next to the harbour in the earthquake-prone capital of the shaky isles. But thanks to the base isolaters, a New Zealand-designed technology that 'isolates' the movement of the earth from the foundations, it is one of the safest places in the city. All this work on what was at the time one of the largest buildings in the country, along with the landscaping and gardens around it, took several years from the early 1990s.

Meanwhile, as the building took shape, staff in the project office in nearby

Wakefield Street were hard at work on what to put inside it. An Interpretive Plan in 1991 and an Exhibitions Conceptual Plan in 1994 provided a framework for more than twenty exhibitions on thematic and narrative lines that mixed objects from different collections. In this document, the stress was on 'ideas of journeys, place, identity, and how each of these has changed over time'. A 'lateral and inclusive approach to storytelling' was called for. Interpretation and writing were seen as 'imaginative bridges' to the audience, which was centre stage.[67] The central idea underlying and focusing all this work was 'exact imaginings', the notion of storytelling that was creative and imaginative but precise, that straddled different disciplines like science and art, and different world views, European and Māori.[68]

Clearly this number and variety of exhibitions could not be delivered by the typically informal and serendipitous process of curators deciding their content and approach, pitched invariably to their peers rather than a broad general public. Within each exhibit, therefore, emphasis was placed on developing clear objectives that were underpinned by audience evaluation. Strict documentation ensured designers stayed true to the brief and did not follow the latest fashions to impress other designers. Multi-disciplinary teams included concept developers who were subject experts (but not 'curators'), interpreters who worked out how to get the ideas across, and professional writers who wrote labels.

A distinctive feature of the process was the stress on accessible audience engagement, led by Neil Anderson who, in place of didactic 'education', championed engaging personal stories, and lively and even irreverent text. Each stage of development was signed off by an Exhibition Approvals Team. The pressure was huge, the hours were long, and debates, conflicts and tears were inevitable. One particularly fraught exhibit tackled the hot topic of the Treaty of Waitangi (see next chapter) as can be seen in the fly-on-the-wall documentary *Getting to Our Place*.[69]

We will see in the next chapter how these exhibitions materialised in 1998. A year before opening, the collections had been moved to the new waterfront building, the staff were on-site, exhibitions were being installed, programmes were being fine-tuned, and the brand 'Te Papa: Our place' (shortened from the full title) had been launched. The widespread adoption of the catchy name 'Te Papa' reinforced the popular brand of the national museum as strongly bicultural.[70] Another key piece of the jigsaw puzzle, also captured in *Getting to Our Place*, was the creation of the logo, the koru/thumbprint/topographic map image developed by Saatchi and Saatchi, which has become so well known.[71]

So, by early 1998, Te Papa was ready. Opening day drew near. Expectations rose. The staff were apprehensive but confident that they had developed an experience that would capture the nation's imagination. But what would the public, and their peers, think? They were about to find out.

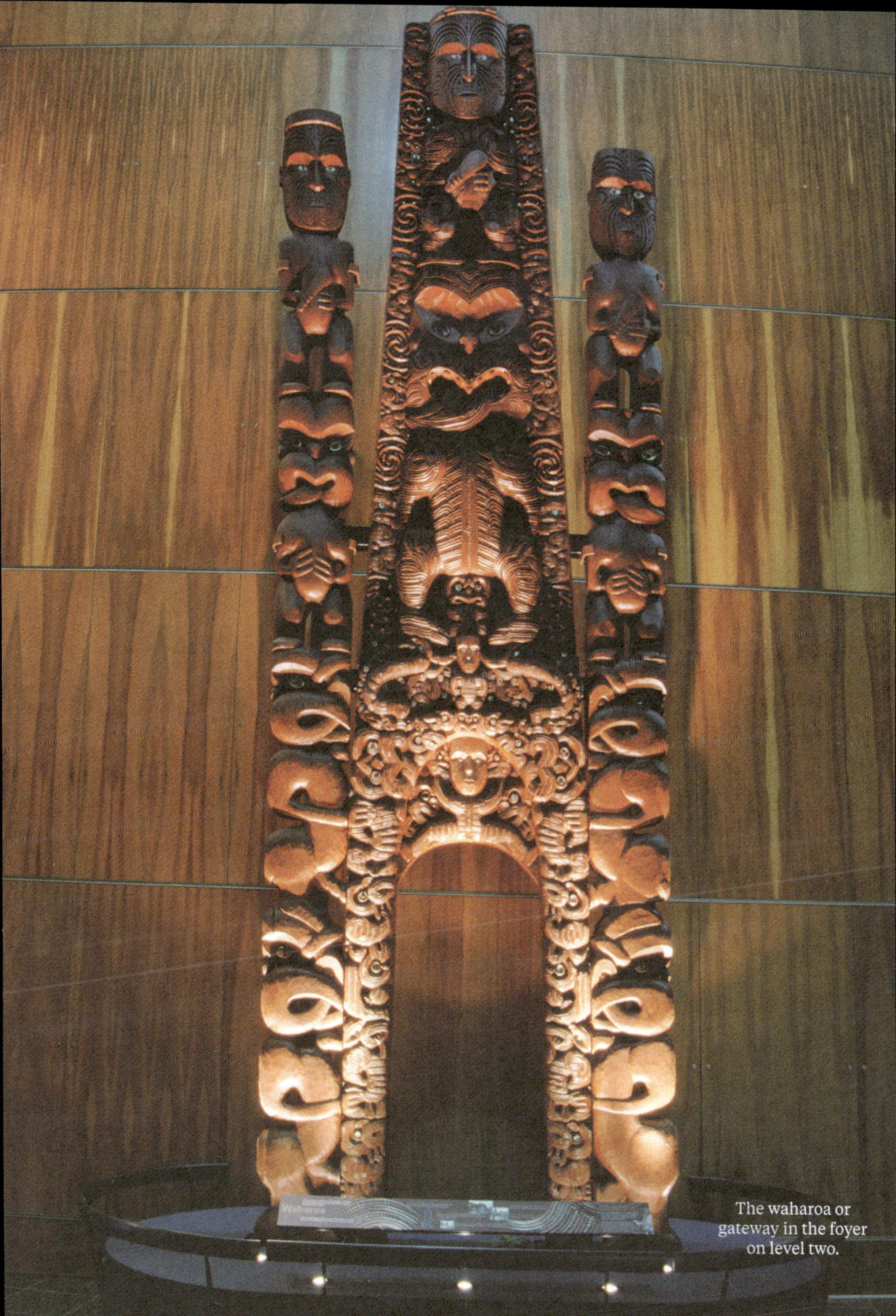

The waharoa or gateway in the foyer on level two.

02.
a guided tour of the museum

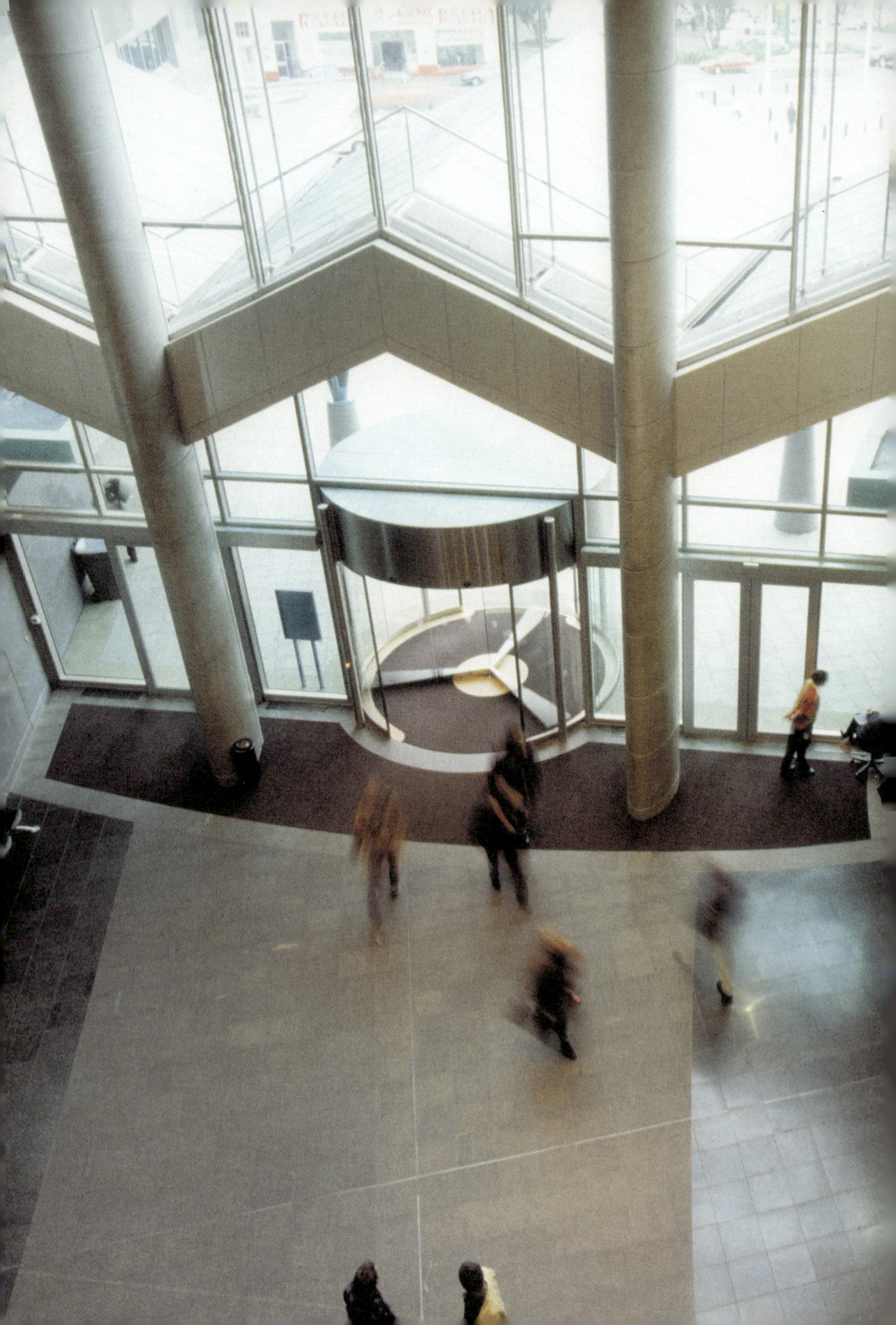

Kia ora and welcome to Te Papa. I will be your guide on this tour of New Zealand's new national museum.[1] Today I will show you some of the treasures housed here, part of a collection that numbers more than two and a half million taonga (treasures), historical artefacts, specimens, artworks and other kinds of objects. The new museum contains 8000 square metres of display space comprising over twenty exhibitions. There is a restaurant, two cafes, four classrooms, an amphitheatre, an auditorium, a functioning marae, four Discovery Centres, plus a computer database, 26 AVs (audio-visuals), and over a hundred mechanical interactives.

Here we are standing outside the building. Now over here in front of the main entrance you can see three boulders, different types of rock that represent the concept behind the museum: the land (Papatūānuku), the indigenous people (tangata whenua), and the later settlers, including Pākehā and more recent migrants (tangata tiriti). The wall jutting out into the street, as you can see, runs right through the building — representing the earthquake fault line running through Wellington — so we will see that inside the building as we walk around. The end of the wall symbolises the stern post or taurapa of a waka taua (fighting canoe), which reminds us that the Māori name of the museum — Te Papa Tongarewa — refers to a waka huia, or feather box, or if you like a vessel containing precious things.

INTRODUCING TE PAPA: LEVELS ONE AND TWO

On entering the building, we find ourselves in an atrium with a wide staircase leading to the foyer and exhibitions. It is an impressive space, rising up 30 metres above us to the roof. Although the architecture is modern, this grand entrance refers back to the history of museums, which were often designed as cathedrals of science and culture.[2] But in other ways this may not look like a museum, but rather a mall — there's the cloakroom and car parks, here's a large shop right by the entrance, and there's a cafe over there. You may wonder why there are no exhibits here on level one? Of course if there is an earthquake, and (God forbid) a tsunami, then it is not a good idea to have objects down here, so they are housed on the upper floors.

Mind you, there is one large artefact high up on the wall. Look — can you see what it is? That's right, it's an anchor. This is one of the oldest objects left behind by European explorers to Aotearoa in the eighteenth century. Without knowing it, one dark night during his circumnavigation of these islands in 1769, Captain Cook passed a French ship, the *St Jean Baptiste*, under the command of Jean François Marie de Surville. The French ship got into some difficulty in a storm while anchored in Doubtless Bay (in New Zealand's far north) and had to throw this anchor overboard — it lay on the ocean floor for over two hundred years until it was eventually recovered in the 1970s.

Displayed here, it reminds us of the ships in nearby Wellington Harbour, and for Pākehā New Zealanders it brings to mind our ancestors who sailed here from Europe in the nineteenth century. The anchor also speaks to the meeting of two cultures, Polynesian and European, as well as the arrival of iron technology — a momentous event in the history of local Māori, who eagerly acquired new technology through trade and exchange with the wider world.

Let's walk up the steps to level two and have a look at the way the museum is organised. This is the Wellington Foyer, where visitors are welcomed to the Museum of New Zealand. It's appropriate that on our left stands a waharoa, an example of the carved gateway that forms the entrance of Māori settlements — you might have seen a famous one similar to this in Rotorua at Te Puia: The New Zealand Māori Arts and Crafts Institute? This one was carved by a well-known Māori carver, Neke Kapua, and his two sons in 1906 for an international exhibition in Christchurch.[3] Actually the waharoa also talks about the mission of Te Papa, which is to act as a waharoa/gateway to New Zealand's cultural and natural heritage.

If you turn around and look where we are on level two, you can see the way in which the interior of the museum is structured. So there is the earthquake wall running right through the building, and we can look out that big round window to the city. Some people even interpret the window as the eye of the fish. The North Island of New Zealand of course is the fish caught by Māori demi-god Māui — Te Ika a Māui.

Now I referred before to the rocks outside symbolising Te Papa's concept of the land and the two peoples who live on that land, the indigenous Māori and all those who came later. Well, you can see if you look up through the floors of the building that the land is represented in the exhibitions here on level two; on level three is an exhibition exploring how the land was shaped by people; and on level four, growing out of that interaction, the people and culture — the Māori, Pacific, art and history exhibitions — are displayed. The building thus symbolically combines our natural and cultural heritage, which reflects the fact that this is an encyclopedic or general museum with integrated collections that bring together objects from different disciplines to tell stories about New Zealand and the world.[4]

Folks, if you look right up through this big open space in the middle to the roof of the building you can see at one end a giant glass facsimile of the Treaty of Waitangi, Aotearoa's founding document, which was signed in 1840 by Māori chiefs and representatives of the British Crown. Of course the actual Treaty is held in Archives New Zealand on the other side of town, but here this exhibit expresses the idea of bicultural partnership that is one of the foundations of our nationhood.[5] We'll talk more about that when we get up to level four.

As you walk around the building you can orientate yourself by coming back to this central space running up through the core of the building from level one to level four. We call it the 'core', but its other name is 'te ihonui', referring to the Māori creation, and the concept of the 'nothingness' out of which life emerged. To be honest, though, this space did not work out exactly as the architects planned — it was envisaged originally as a symbolic space where everything would come together, and there were all sorts of ideas for it (including hydroponic trees growing up it!), but it remained empty space . . .[6]

In a moment we will explore the two exhibitions directly in front of us, which are devoted to the natural environment; namely, *Mountains to Sea* and *Awesome Forces*.[7] But before we do, I thought I should point out *Time Warp* in the centre of this floor, with the bright lights and rides. A first for museums in New Zealand, this is a 'themed attraction' that uses the latest technology to tell stories of our past, present and future. Now I have to admit this has been quite a controversial feature of Te Papa as many of our older visitors don't like this kind of commercial attraction, which is more associated with theme parks — one writer calls this theatrical style of display 'Distory' (Disney history)![8] However, young people seem to like it, and it raises money for the museum, which is important to keep the place running. Speaking of which, over there on the right you can see Soundings Theatre, a 300-seat theatre where lectures and films are staged, and over here Icon restaurant.[9]

MOUNTAINS TO SEA

This exhibition, as the name suggests, is a walk through our landscape, from alpine terrain down to the coastal environment.

As we walk along you see on your left different habitats presented in these large window cases: alpine and tussock grasslands, bush, freshwater, coasts, open ocean and offshore islands. Originally we called the exhibit 'biotic realms' because we wanted to get across the idea of these different areas where biodiversity can be found — the amazing variety of plants, insects, birds, fish, etc. in New Zealand — but we decided that name was a bit obscure. The concept developer, Geoff Hicks, wanted to get away from the old style of natural history exhibition, which was I guess a bit like a school lesson. Instead he aimed to immerse visitors in an environment that gives them a strong sense of what it is like to walk through these settings. Still, the cases actually look a bit like dioramas, don't they?

There's lots you can do here, not just standing and looking. Over there you can actually climb up into the canopy of a giant kauri tree to look out over a rimu and rātā forest and see a sweep of sea birds. In the corner, you will see the entrance to *NatureSpace*, a children's Discovery Centre, which has all sorts of specimens, games, books and objects you can touch: check out the models of the dodo, the sun fish and the spider crab. Kids love it. There are four of these in the museum: the others are on level four: one each for Māori, Pacific, history and art. If you go right to the end of this exhibition you can look through into what we call the 'x-ray room' or Display Storage, where part of our extensive collection of marine mammal skeletons is stored. Te Papa has one of the largest collections of these in the world.[10]

Look up! What do you see? It's a gigantic skeleton of a so-called 'pygmy' blue whale . . . it looks a bit large to be called a pygmy, right? A pygmy blue whale (*Balaenoptera musculus brevicauda*) is a little smaller than a southern blue whale, by a few metres. This whale was only a teenager when it was hit by a container ship in 1994 just north of New Zealand, probably on its way to feeding grounds near Antarctica. It was towed to Motutapu Island, flensed (removing the blubber), then taken to Napier, where the bones were dropped in a cage in the sea so the sea lice and the salt water could clean them. Sorry . . . a lot of visitors find this process a bit yucky! From there, museum staff brought it here. The lower jaw was attached later because it was leaking oil.

This little whopper is about the length of a cricket pitch and as heavy as a truck. Fully grown, male pygmy blue whales are 24 metres long. This one's only 20 metres, but still would have weighed 50–60 tonnes. It's a baleen whale, which, unlike toothed whales, feeds by sucking in tiny fish called krill. It would eat nearly two tonnes of krill per day. In times past, when Māori found these

1.

Te Ara a Hine, or the pathway of women, leading up to the marae on level four.

2.

Bush City, the outdoors natural environment display next to the harbour.

3.

The exhibition *Mountains to Sea* on level two, including the pygmy blue whale.

4.

The earthquake house in the exhibition *Awesome Forces*, on level two.

5.

Visitors in *Mountains to Sea*, which has proven to be one of the most popular exhibitions at Te Papa.

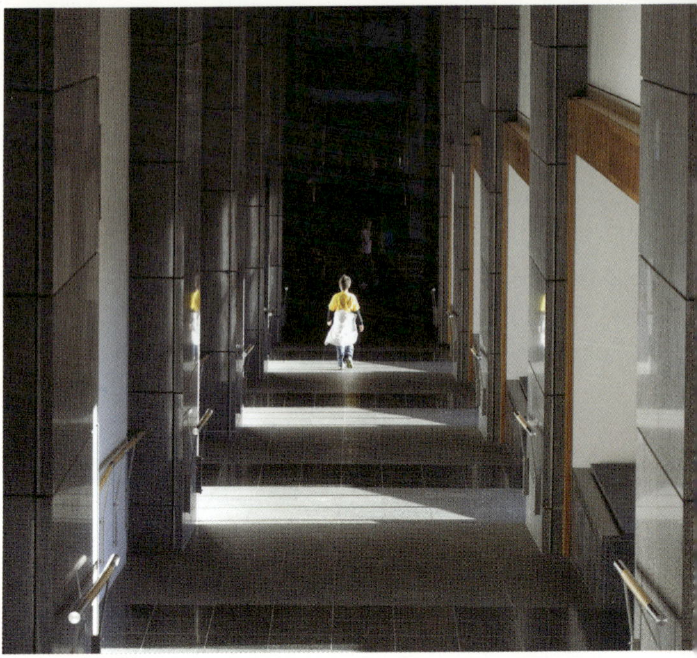

1.

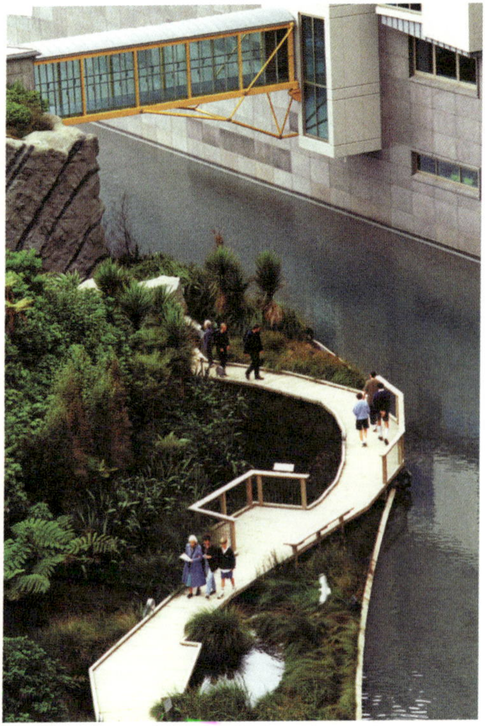

2.

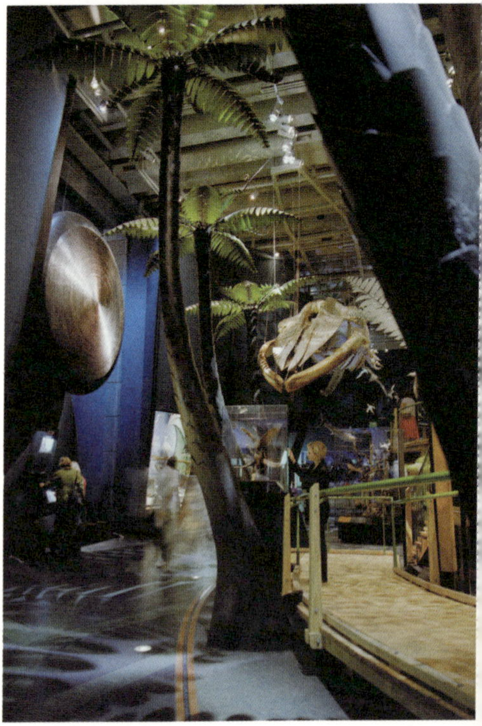

3.

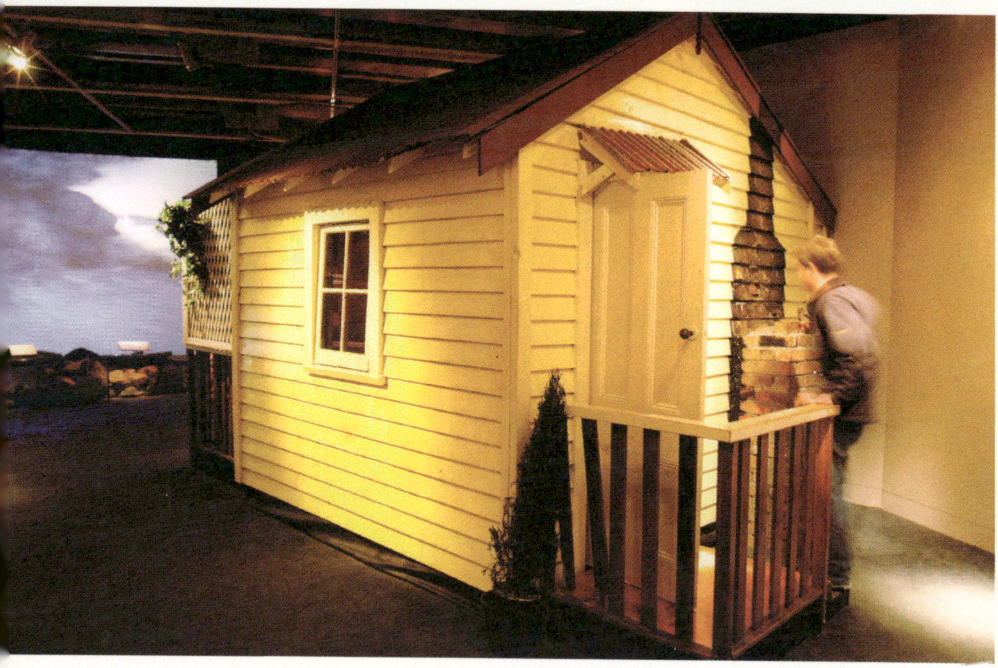

4.

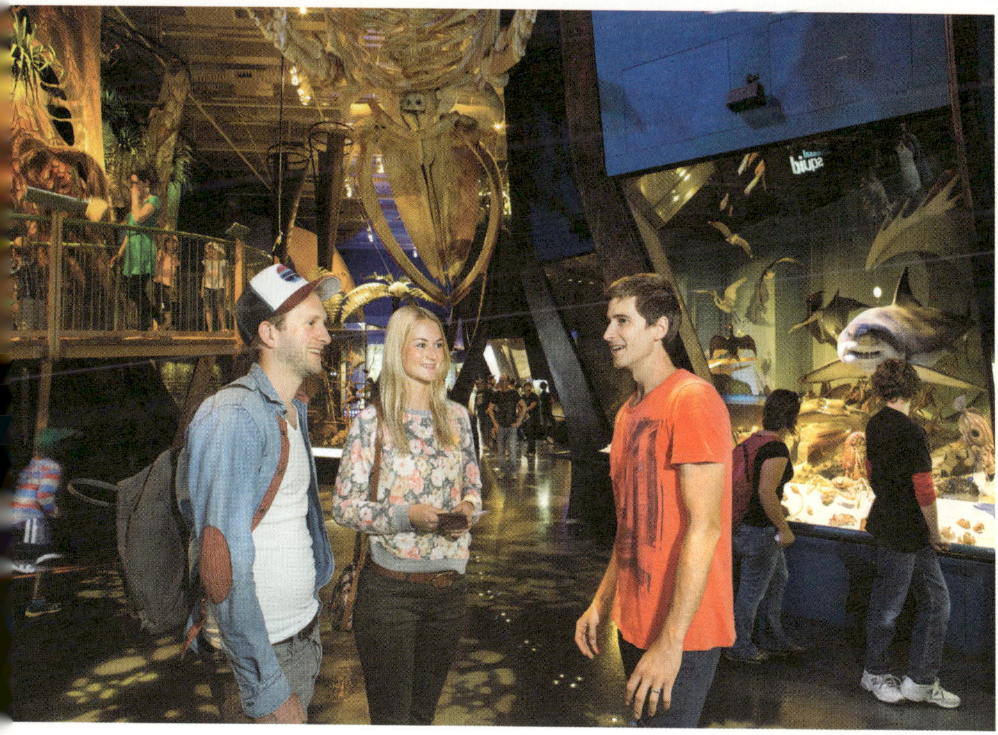

5.

whales stranded on beaches, they harvested the bone for clubs and other weapons — hoeroa or whalebone rib clubs were prized ceremonial indicators of rank. Whales or tohorā can also be seen in Māori art, for example the pātaka (storehouse) upstairs, as a symbol of plenty. Obviously whaling does not happen anymore — so how do we get the skeletons, you ask? Every year around eighty strandings occur on beaches around our coasts — most of the 2000 specimens in the collection come from this source.

Now let's walk through this entrance into another exhibition — can you feel how it seems hot and noisy, like we're walking into the centre of the earth?

This is the exhibition devoted to the creation and transformation of the land on which we live. Again we had another name for it when we were developing it, 'Ancient Lands', but we wanted something more dynamic that conveyed a sense of the power of geological and tectonic forces, so we called it *Awesome Forces*. You can read up about geology, volcanoes, earthquakes, etc. in the book that was produced with the exhibition. But the scientist who worked on this display, Hamish Campbell, didn't want it to be like a book on a wall. He was looking for an experience that was more, well, 'awesome'!

There is a lot to see and do as you walk around and explore this exhibit: there's a model of the giant New Zealand eagle, pouākai, and the moa, tallest bird in the world, locked in mortal combat (you can see real specimens as well); a 145-million-year-old fossilised ammonite (prehistoric sea shell), the largest ever found in the southern hemisphere, which was pieced together over two years by scientists; and one of our most popular exhibits, the earthquake house that gives you a chance to feel what it was like to experience the 1987 Edgecumbe shake. Finally, there is the amazing Chinese seismoscope, or 'di dong yi', a replica of the original designed nearly 2000 years ago during the Han dynasty by famous astrologer Zhang Heng.

As you walk out, check out the small theatrette where the Māori story of creation is told through an AV. As you go out you can also see an amazing carving by Māori artist Greg Whakataka Brightwell depicting Rūaumoko, the atua or denizen of earthquakes. This is an important message that we wanted to get across to visitors, that western science is not the *only* way of understanding the natural world. Māori have an intimate relationship with mother earth (Papatūānuku) and a quite distinctive way of thinking about humans and the environment that does not separate out culture and nature.

Now let's go up to level four along this passage. On the way, we can see out the windows on our left a harbourside park that is another 'living' exhibition: *Bush City*.

This is a 3500-square-metre outdoor 'museum' that links thematically with the indoor natural environment exhibitions. It recreates sections of natural landform overlaid by an extensive planting of 1400 native trees and shrubs. The central theme deals with the way the land has been transformed by catastrophic phenomena such as plate tectonics and volcanic eruptions and by the 'clothing' of the land over millions of years. *Bush City*, which gives you a sense of what the Wellington shoreline was like 200 years ago, was planted well in advance of the opening of Te Papa. Our curator of botany Patrick Brownsey wanted to give visitors the 'flavour and feel' of the New Zealand bush, including a range of different plant communities: mānuka-kānuka scrub, coastal plants, coastal rainforest, wetland plants and plants in volcanic areas. Go out and have a look later.

As you walk up this path, which is the internal entrance to the marae on level four, you will notice that it is decorated with artworks. This is called Te Ara a Hine, or the path of women, because of their role in the karanga, the call of welcome on to Te Marae above. The figures on the walls on either side of the passage are contemporary artworks made from electrical wire by Jacqueline Fraser, and show different female Māori atua (goddesses, or guardians).

Phew. We've made it to the top. Now we're on the end of the building, the tauihu (prow) of the waka that juts out into the harbour. Good views, eh?

While you catch your breath, you can turn around to face back at the building. We have reached the entrance to Te Marae. On the outside stands the waharoa or gateway, carved in a modern style with figures representing all sorts of people, including European sailors. When groups come here for a pōwhiri, or welcome, they either come up the internal entrance, as we did today, or from the outside up another external path called Te Ara a Tāne (the pathway of men). Visitors pass through the waharoa, and across the open marae ātea. That large coloured-glass window there is actually a door depicting Ranginui the sky father. During the welcome ceremony it rises up to allow manuhiri (guests) to enter, thus re-enacting the separation of Rangi and Papa, sky and earth, in the Māori creation. Let's go inside and have a look . . .

TE MARAE

Have a seat while we talk about the marae. What is a marae? It's a traditional Māori ancestral base where tribal or iwi business is undertaken, issues are debated and visitors are formally welcomed. Te Papa's marae, Rongomaraeroa, is a functional, living marae underpinned by Māori protocol and customs but radically innovative in its design and form, and, unusually, it belongs to all the cultures of New Zealand. *All* visitors to Te Papa are given the chance to become 'family' or tangata whenua (people of the land). If you go into the whare (house), you can participate in an activity through which you identify with certain geographical features and ancestors as Māori do, but using your own maunga (mountain), awa (river), waka (canoe), and so on. Look at the non-Māori figures in the carvings: European and Asian figures, and new ideas and technology, represent the whakapapa of Pākehā that comes down through James Cook and Abel Tasman, parallelling the Polynesian whakapapa that comes down through Kupe, the waka traditions and iwi history.

The marae itself consists of a courtyard (marae ātea), which extends indoors, and a wharenui (meeting house). The courtyard is covered in colourful, patterned tiles representing Papatūānuku — designed by artist Kura Te Waru Rewiri. Magnificent, multi-coloured glass panels representing Ranginui — an artwork by artist Bob Jahnke — open into a large hall, an indoor extension of the marae ātea. The carpet continues the pattern of the tiles outside.

Typically in a meeting house you would have carved poupou, or posts, latticework tukutuku panels along the walls, and painted rafters. What have we got here? On the walls, painted panels and weaving in a contemporary style have been created by artists Sandy Adsett, Steve Gibbs and students from Toi Hou Kura (the Māori art school at Gisborne Polytech).

The wharenui, called Te Hono ki Hawaiki (the link to Hawaiki, the mythical homeland), features spectacular wall and roof carvings completed by students, Māori and Pākehā, from polytechs around the country under the direction of our Kaihautū (Māori co-director) and master carver Cliff Whiting. Customwood has been used because it is an adaptable modern material: it can be bent in hot water to create different shapes, it is quick to carve with modern saws and other machinery, it is easily decorated with the full range of bright modern paint available to the contemporary artist, and it does not use up limited resources of native timber.

All iwi, or tribes, are represented in the carvings, which tell the stories of how they are all related to the common ancestor Māui, who fished the North Island (Te Ika a Māui) out of the sea from his waka, the South Island (Te Waka a Māui). Of course Māui is an ancestor of many other Polynesian people as well. You can see Māui standing on top of the house, holding over his head the rope with which he fished up Te Ika a Māui, which can be seen at the end of the maihi (bargeboards) with the fish hook made from his grandfather's jawbone. Alongside Māui are his four brothers, Māui pae, Māui roto, Māui taha, and Māui waho. Beneath him is the sun, Tama nui te Rā, which he snared to slow its progress through the sky and lengthen the day (so people would have time to work and do all the things they needed to do). There are lots of other stories depicted in the carvings as well.

So how does this marae work? Basically we hand it over to iwi to run. The tangata whenua for the first two years are the local people, Te Āti Awa, who are represented by the door to the left of the Ranginui window and the amo, the post on the front left of the whare, where Te Āti Awa elders stand while they are 'sitting on the paepae'; that is to say, while they are officiating at welcome ceremonies. The other amo represents the Ngāti Toa people, another local tribal group. Every two years or so, one tribe is iwi in residence while their

1.

The exhibition *Signs of a Nation: Ngā Tohu Kotahitanga* about the Treaty of Waitangi in the centre of level four.

2.

A view of Te Marae, showing the contemporary meeting house Te Hono ki Hawaiki, level four.

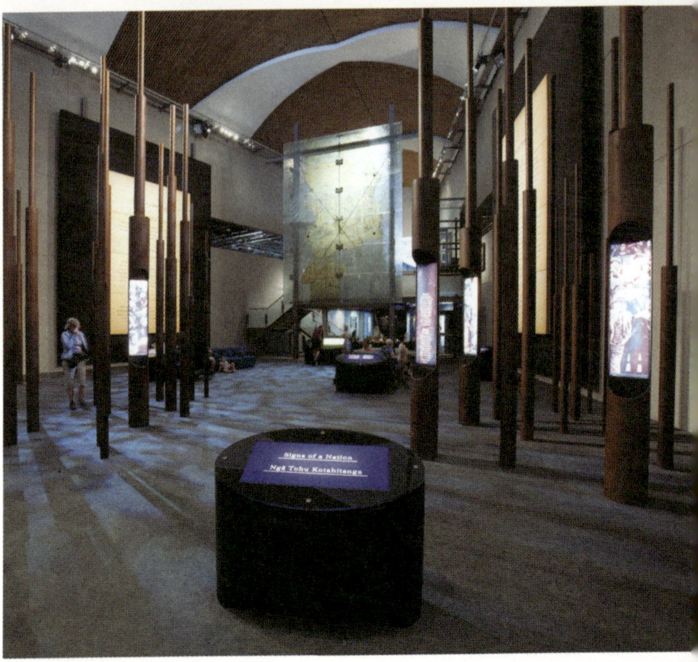

1.

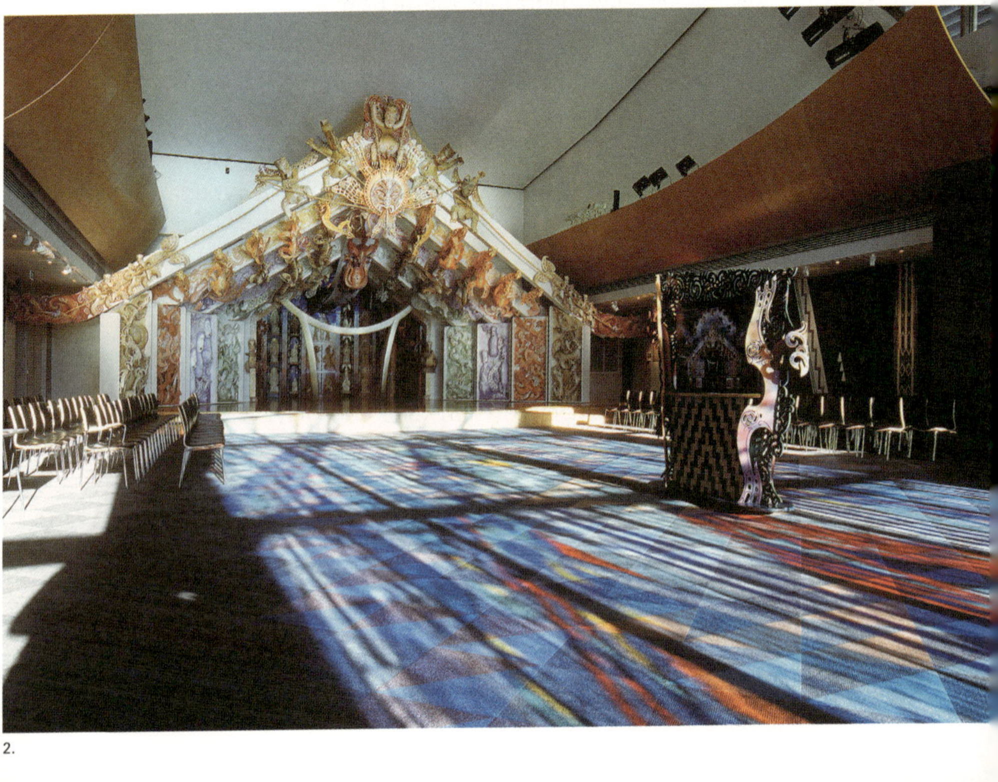

2.

exhibition, which they co-curate with museum staff, is on display. During this time they are the kaumātua (elders, people with status) for Te Papa, their kawa (protocol) is followed on the marae, and the staff learn their waiata (songs).[11]

Okay, we need to keep going — there's lots more to see.

Oh . . . as we leave the marae, don't forget to look at this large boulder. This is the mauri stone, a huge piece of pounamu, or greenstone. It was given to the museum at the time of the exhibition *Taonga Māori* (1989–91) by the Kāi Tahu people of the West Coast of the South Island (Te Waipounamu). It represents the mauri or life essence of all things animate and inanimate. Feel free to rub the boulder as we pass through to the Māori exhibition zone.

MANA WHENUA

You can see now as we come out of this passage that we are entering a large open space. It's quite dark, like a forest, with dappled light coming through the trees. We can hear birdsong. Now you can make out objects — carved figures standing sentinel. There are no glass cases, so you could almost touch them if you wanted to (don't tell anyone I said that!).

Anyway, here we are in the exhibition *Mana Whenua: Mai i a Rangi ki a Papa: The people, the spirit that binds*. This title refers to whenua (the land) and the people who claim mana over it — their authority arising from ancestral connections that come down from Rangi and Papa, the ancestral parents, sky father and earth mother. It tells the story of the establishment of Māori as tangata whenua, and presents a strong Māori perspective by using oral tradition, whakapapa (genealogy), mythology, language and tribal traditions.

Let's stop here, in the middle of the floor. From this point we get a sense of the overall contents of *Mana Whenua*. As you can see the space is dominated by the big house there in the centre, the whare whakairo (carved house) Te Hau ki Tūranga, which belongs to the Rongowhakaata people. On its right, there is the Ngāti Pikiao pātaka Te Tākinga. Further to the right against the wall is a section devoted to pounamu (nephrite/greenstone), and next to it a large wall display of weaving including kākahu or cloaks. On the opposite wall is the waka hourua, or ocean-going canoe, *Te Aurere Iti*, built by navigator Heke Busby as a replica of one he sailed back to Rarotonga in 1992. This one was crewed by staff out on the harbour the day the museum opened!

In a large island case across from that is a small exhibit devoted to the Moriori people of the Chatham Islands (that's been a hot topic of debate). Here on our right is a small raupō whare called Mākōtukutuku, which is a reconstruction of a fifteenth-century site discovered several years ago by our archaeologist Janet Davidson. It was built in partnership with Ngāti Hinewaka of the southern Wairarapa region.

As you can see, the exhibition features ancient taonga integrated with contemporary pieces that are really different in style and media: for example, that painting by Robyn Kahukiwa about Hineteiwaiwa (the goddess of weaving). Sadly, we didn't get quite the money we wanted from Lottery grants — there *was* going to be much more contemporary art and culture in this space. You might get the impression this display is mostly old stuff, quite similar to the Maori Hall in the former National Museum in Buckle Street, but that's a bit misleading. The Māori staff who worked on this exhibition were adamant that, in contrast to the 'ethnographic' nature of old museum displays, this exhibition should be organised in *partnership* with iwi whose taonga these are — an innovation for museums. At Te Papa we believe that we don't *own* the taonga, we look after them as guardians for the people whose cultural property they are. This is the principle of mana taonga, which means that the mana or power lies with the people who own them.[12]

The main feature of the exhibition of course is the meeting house. Some larger museums you may have visited in New Zealand have a carved whare. But this one is special. Te Hau ki Tūranga is the oldest carved meeting house in existence. Built of tōtara in the early 1840s by master carver Raharuhi Rukupō, it is one of the first houses built using steel tools. It is not just a place to meet and sleep in, but it is also a tupuna whare — an ancestor house. Many meeting houses represent the body of an ancestor of the tribe, usually but not always male — the kōruru (figurehead) is his head, the maihi and the raparapa (bargeboards) his arms and fingers, and the amo (side posts) his legs. Go and have a look inside (don't forget to take your shoes off). Remember that when you enter, you are inside the ancestor's body — the heke (rafters) are his ribs, the pou tokomanawa (centre post) his heart, and the tāhuhu (ridgepole) his backbone.

There's quite a story behind this house, which in a way reflects the history of museology in this country and how it has changed. It has been in the museum since 1868. At that time it was seen as a sort of specimen, or even a curio, from a European perspective. In 1936 it was rebuilt within the National Museum in Buckle Street, as part of the Maori Hall, and was seen as an artefact that reflected a 'traditional' way of life. In the last few years, through an evolving partnership established with the Rongowhakaata people, the house was taken out of the old museum and completely restored using customary methods and materials by workers from this iwi, and re-erected as a freestanding structure for the first time since it came to the museum. And that's not all. What you may not realise is that this house was actually confiscated by the government during the conflicts of the 1860s. There is a strong chance that one day it may be returned to the Rongowhakaata people.[13]

PACIFIC, ART AND HISTORY EXHIBITIONS LEVEL FOUR

Let's continue on our tour, following this pounamu path in the floor, with the pāua shell trim, which will take us across level four through the exhibitions devoted to the Pacific, history and art.

Along this route, which staff call The Promenade, are large feature objects from the museum collections. The first, which we can see here right outside *Mana Whenua*, is *Teremoe*, a famous waka taua (war canoe) from the Whanganui River that was used in the battles of the 1860s, and which was given to the museum by the Hīpango family in the 1930s — see their photograph on the label.

The hull of the canoe is made from the trunk of a single tōtara tree. The tree was felled and hollowed out with fire and adzes, a process that was governed by strict observances of tapu because of the association with death. The taurapa (sternpost) and tauihu (prow) were carved separately and lashed on, often being taken off and stored when the canoe was not in the water. *Teremoe* is 30 metres long, and would possibly have held 40 or 50 warriors. It must have been a fearsome sight on the water. The symbolism of the carving is rich and complex — some say that the figures on the tauihu refer to atua such as Tū, 'god' of war, and Tangaroa, 'god' of the sea. In the carvings along the side, called rauawa or strakes, which were done by a museum carver in the 1900s, there are graphic images of procreation. Actually, like many large carvings in the museum, this canoe was assembled from various elements; in this case the taurapa came originally from Matatā (in the Bay of Plenty) and the tauihu from Horowhenua (on the west coast of the lower North Island).

We have arrived in the middle of level four, and can now see all of the various exhibition zones. In the centre, between the Māori and history exhibitions, is *Signs of a Nation: Ngā Tohu Kotahitanga*, which talks about the Treaty of Waitangi in relation to modern New Zealand nationhood. This is a good place to sit and read the texts of the preamble and three articles of the Treaty, English on one side, Māori on the other.

See how the glass facsimile of the Treaty sits in the centre of the museum, bringing together (or perhaps separating out?) Māori and Pākehā culture on either side. Now we talk here at Te Papa about tangata whenua (the people of the land) and tangata tiriti (people of the Treaty, that is to say Pākehā *and* everyone else who lives here by right of the Treaty). So you might say that this exhibit operates conceptually and architecturally as the hinge of the nation, cleaving the space into tangata whenua and tangata tiriti sections, uniting (or dividing) us, depending on your perspective. So on the tangata tiriti side, we have the history exhibition *Passports* and the art exhibition *Parade*, which we will see in a moment.

If we turn around and look directly opposite the Treaty exhibit, there is the void in the centre of the museum that we saw from below. Up above we can see another floor where there's an art exhibition under the roof. On the other side of the void, next to the waka, is another cafe. You'll notice a motorbike on a plinth at the edge of the cafe — yes, over there where the crowd of men are standing around with their mouths open gazing at it lovingly (if no one's looking, I have seen blokes reach out and touch it!). This is another of those feature objects I was telling you about along The Promenade. They are meant to be 'icons' of Pākehā New Zealand identity — often with a transport theme — so here is John Britten's superbike, down there you can see Jeff Thomson's corrugated-iron Holden car/sculpture, and a Tiger Moth plane. Finally, in the distance there by the staircase, you might just be able to make out a skeleton — this is the famous racehorse Phar Lap. Down the stairs on level three you will find Captain Cook's cannon, thrown overboard on the Great Barrier Reef off Australia during one of his voyages to the Pacific.

Let's go and have a look at the Britten bike. So this may not be what you expect to see in a traditional museum, but we have all sorts of things in our collections here and this really is quite something in terms of design and technology. It has a top speed of about 300 kilometres per hour, and broke four world speed records in 1993. The bike has a revolutionary body design, with light, strong carbon fibre and a new type of 60-degree V-1000 twin engine. The most notable thing about this bike, however, is that the prototype was designed and built by someone who, although he was a motorcycle enthusiast, was not a professional designer — John Britten. Sadly, in 1995 he passed away at the age of only 45. I guess people love it because it symbolises the so-called Do It Yourself Kiwi ingenuity that we love to claim. Not sure about that myself — I'm useless at fixing things — but there you go.

Okay, let's go and see Phar Lap. Now this is another one of those New Zealand myths, something we love to give Australians a hard time about for 'stealing' and claiming as their own. I beg your pardon, no offence Bluey. The famous racehorse, whose name is Thai for 'Lightning in the sky', was born near Tīmaru in 1926, but was sold to an Australian trainer and won many races over the ditch, including the Melbourne Cup in 1930. Then he died mysteriously the night before a big race in California in 1932. Phar Lap's heart was donated to what is now the National Museum of Australia in Canberra, his hide was sent to the Museum of Victoria in Melbourne, and the skeleton was returned to New Zealand, where it was mounted using funds donated by the public.

Now let's walk down to the art and history zone in the centre of level four, and have a closer look at these other two remarkable objects.

On our right, outside the exhibition *Parade*, we have a car, but not like any you've seen before — it is in fact a work of art. Jeff Thomson, the 'iron man' of New Zealand art, is well known for his sculptures made from that classic Kiwi building material, corrugated iron, with which he has clad the classic Aussie car (note the tribute in the aerial — bent into the shape of Australia). In 1991 he painstakingly converted his own 1974 Holden Kingswood station wagon into this artwork, curving the old roofing iron from the Criterion Hotel in Napier, which had burned down. He used to drive it around, but now it's part of the art collection here at Te Papa.

Why would he do this, you ask? I guess it's the idea of raising questions about the nature of art — is art only 'beautiful' objects made from fine art materials, or is it part of popular culture, a 'ready made' artwork that has been 'found' by the artist and placed in a museum context, to be seen for its aesthetic rather than its utilitarian qualities? These are some of the issues raised by this exhibition. *Parade* has been very controversial with art critics, though it's proved to be very successful with the kind of mass audience we get here. Let's go in and take a look.

PARADE

Stepping into *Parade*, it is immediately apparent that a whole variety of art, craft, design, technology, ceramics, photography and advertising is mixed up together.[14] There is certainly plenty of painting and sculpture here, from historical works like the so-called 'Ranfurly Goldies' — Charles Goldie portraits of *The Widow* (Harata Rewiri Tarapata) and *Darby and Joan* (Ina Te Papatahi)

(1901) — to modern and contemporary art such as Rita Angus's *Rutu* (1951), Gretchen Albrecht's *Indian Summer* (1974) and Rick Killeen's *Age of Fishes* (1980).

There are also several prominent sculptures, among them Chris Booth's *Silent People* (1991) made from Northland river stones, and Christine Hellyar's *Clutch, Brood and Echo* (1990), an evocative work that recalls collections, museum displays and nests. There is even a project space, currently a commissioned installation by Māori artist Maureen Lander called *String Games* (1997), and in an adjoining space a group of artists, including Lisa Reihana, Greg Semu and Destiny Deacon, who confront new technology in a very interesting show called *Facing IT*.

But clearly we can see here a lot of other objects from a wider range of what we might call visual culture. Not your typical art exhibition, eh? We have already seen Jeff Thomson's car. Also on display are the zany costumes from Split Enz, designed by Noel Crombie for this ground-breaking post-punk band, and a dinghy designed when he was just 14 by Bruce Farr, who went on to design the yacht *KZ7* that won the America's Cup.

Perhaps the most surprising thing we can find, over here in this corner, is a group of three 'products' of the 1950s placed side by side: a Kelvinator slim-line refrigerator, airline crockery from TEAL (the forerunner to Air New Zealand), and Colin McCahon's famous *Northland Panels* (1958). I am not sure about you, but if you like your art neat, then I guess this will be a bit like mixed drinks?[15]

Walking through the show, you will notice that another strong thread is the intermingling of the European and Polynesian traditions throughout New Zealand's cultural history: for example the Māori artist Tene Waitere using western realism in his carving, right through to a painting by Pākehā artist Gordon Walters using the koru motif. Some complain that Pākehā artists should not 'steal' Māori art. The emphasis here, though, is on cross-fertilisation and exchange, not cultural 'appropriation'. In the 'Whakaoratia' segment over there, for example, curator Megan Tamati-Quennell has displayed ink drawings, a marble patu, a muka tea cosy and kiwi feather muffs, which showed Māori artists responding enthusiastically to new materials.

And another thing you may have noticed on our tour is that there is a lot of contemporary Māori art displayed in different exhibitions around the museum. Downstairs in the natural environment zone on level two, you may have seen Brett Graham's abstract sculpture *Tangaroa* hanging in *Mountains to Sea*, while in *Mana Whenua* there was a large painting by Peter Robinson. So, you can see we've tried to mix things up a bit. In this 'art' exhibition there are objects from the history and Māori collections, and over in the history and Pacific exhibitions there are paintings and sculptures, etc. But you know what? We didn't really go as far as we wanted with this. Despite our best intentions to make interdisciplinary exhibitions with integrated collections, you can still see there are walls between the exhibitions — right? — and you kind of know you are in the 'art' area or whatever, cos people pretty much stuck to their separate areas.

Anyway I digress. As well as this exhibition *Parade*, there is a lot more art to see here at Te Papa: in fact we estimate there will always be between 3000 and 4000 square metres of art on display, about four times that of the old National Gallery. Up the stairs, in The Boulevard on level five, the temporary exhibition *The Dream Collectors*, developed with Auckland Art Gallery, is on display. Right in the middle of that you can see an amazing sculpture: Shona Rapira Davies' moving terracotta figures of Māori women, *Ngā Mōrehu* (1988). Then, across the bridge on level four, there is the touring gallery where at the moment you can see a show of Old Masters from overseas. Around the corner children can visit *Inspiration Station*, the Discovery Centre, which also has original prints by New Zealand artists such as Hodgkins, Angus and Kahukiwa. Next door to that, visitors can also see decorative arts, ceramics, jewellery, textiles and other objects, in *Eyelights*, as well as prints in the nearby Ilott Gallery.

And, on top of that, you can make an appointment to see the works on paper in the Ilott print room, where the large collection of prints and drawings is looked after by our collection manager Tony Mackle. It is also possible to do a back-of-house tour, where staff take you through the paintings, sculpture and other works kept in storage. So, enough art to keep everyone happy, or so you would think . . .

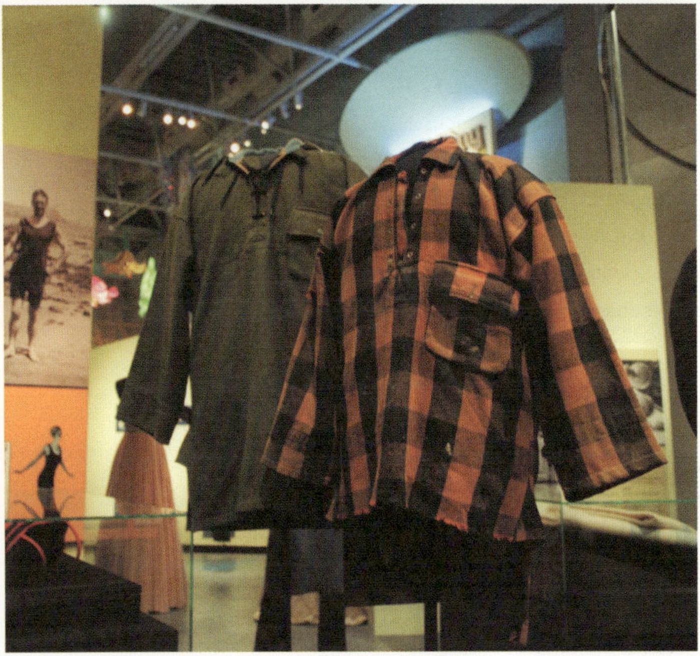

1.

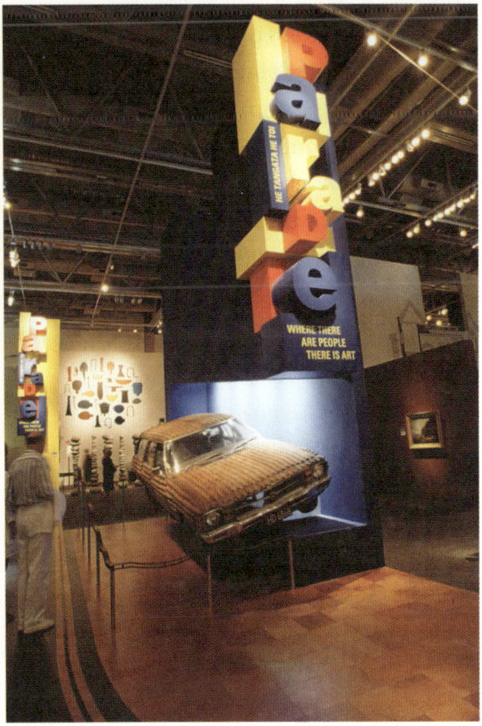

2.

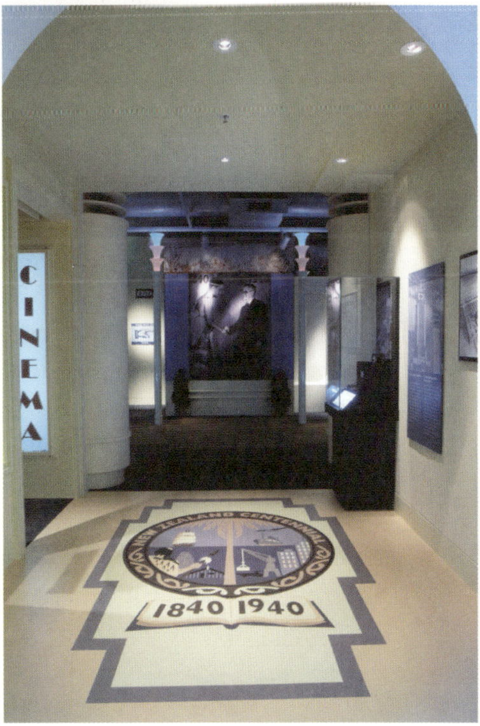

3.

1.

A display from the exhibition *On the Sheep's Back*, showing a Swanndri.

2.

The entrance to the art exhibition *Parade* on level four, showing Jeff Thomson's corrugated-iron Holden.

3.

The *Exhibiting Ourselves* 1940 court.

PASSPORTS

Now having had our taste of art, we're back outside the *Parade* exhibition and we can see three history exhibitions here in this corner of level four.

The first, *Passports*, tells the story of migration, how people came to New Zealand from the nineteenth century to today. Then the second, *On the Sheep's Back*, talks about daily life here in New Zealand from the nineteenth century to the late twentieth century, in this case through the lens of wool. The third, *Exhibiting Ourselves*, explores how New Zealanders have thought about their culture and identity, seen through national displays at four different international exhibitions: London in 1855, Christchurch in 1906, Wellington in 1940 and Seville in 1992.

And right above us you can see a plane hanging from the ceiling. This is a Tiger Moth, a biplane designed initially as a training aircraft by de Havilland in the UK and first flown in 1931. This plane, on loan from its owner in Hamilton, is in working order. Many Tiger Moths no longer needed by the air force found a new use as New Zealand's earliest topdressing aircraft. Many of our early topdressing pilots had flown with the RNZAF during the war, and for them getting behind the controls of a plane to topdress seemed a natural progression. But Tiger Moths were not ideal for the task. Many of the early farm airstrips were short and very rough, and the constant low flying in hilly country was very dangerous. Many Tiger Moths crashed during operations and a number of pilots were killed. By the late 1950s more suitable aircraft began to be used for topdressing, which was an important part of agricultural development in this country.

Moving right along. It should be obvious from the luggage piled up at the entrance that this first history exhibition, *Passports*, is about migration. When they first came up with the ideas for this exhibition, Jock Phillips and the other developers called it the 'peopling of New Zealand'.

Grab yourself a passport from the machine at the entrance here. You can see each tells the story of a different migrant and their journey to a new land — you can get it stamped as you move through the exhibition. These profiles, as well as other stories in the drawers, show colonial New Zealand was a more diverse place than you might think: we have Bartolo Russo, a cabin boy from Italy; assisted migrant Mary Player from Ireland; refugee Lislette Turnovsky from Czechoslovakia; and soldier Kimble Bent from the USA.

The first section of *Passports*, 'Leaving Home', explores the push and pull factors that produced mass migration at the time: like the push of war, and the pull of a new life somewhere else. You might like to try the interactive there to see if you would pass the entry tests for migrants today!

Next we move into the 'Crossings' section, which gives you a sense of what it was like to spend six months in a leaky boat on the 12,000-mile voyage to this British settler colony. The next section, 'New Country', then shows what happened to people once they got here and how they adapted to their life in a different environment. There are lots of great things to see that settlers brought with them: former Wellington mayor George Hunter's piano, landed on Petone beach in 1840 (yes, just like the movie), and relics from the Guard family, including the whaler Jacky Guard, whose family were kidnapped by Māori after a shipwreck. That's an amazing story!

Finally, at the end of the show is the community gallery, a changing exhibition that features a different migrant group every two years. First up, *The Making of a Chinese New Zealander* charts the ups and downs of the Chinese in New Zealand, from the gold miners of the 1860s to recent migrants, including the 'dark' history of things like opium addiction, European racism against Asian migrants, and an unjust poll tax levied on Chinese. You might think this is a bit sobering for a museum exhibit, which we expect to be nostalgic and often celebratory, but sometimes we have to examine history without the pain edited out. The next community to be featured will be the Italians, and then the Indians.

Now let's have a quick look at the wool exhibition, before we go to the last exhibition on the Pacific. Now, I have to let you in on a little secret. Come closer so I can lower my voice . . . There. Okay, what you don't know is that there was originally going to be another larger exhibition here, not about wool, but about love. Yes, that's right, love . . . and sex and all that stuff. Well, you can imagine that the board got a bit anxious, cos the museum was getting criticism at the time for being anti-Pākehā. So management decided Te Papa needed to have some more 'celebratory' exhibits. Next thing the topic for this exhibition was switched to wool (much less risky, right?) AND then the space and budget was cut in two and the rest given over to this object theatre called *Golden Days*. Now, I have to admit it's very popular with the punters, a nostalgic look back at the way we were, but I can tell you some of the staff were annoyed about that.

Anyway, *On the Sheep's Back* shows you a glimpse of life in New Zealand through wool: from sheep farming and shearing gangs, to knitting and craft, to high fashion and the Swanndri. Here furniture from the famous Elgar collection, usually thought of as being 'colonial', is displayed in its historical context as part of the pastoral industry. These pieces belonged to Ella Elgar, the wealthy grand-daughter of Charles Pharazyn (the first man to establish a sheep farm in the Wairarapa, who drove his flock around the south coast from Wellington Harbour). Ella lived in the 'Fernside' mansion near Martinborough, which she furnished in the 1920s with a diverse range of objects bought in Europe and Asia (which don't actually have a connection with colonial New Zealand at all). Here, for example, we have a cabinet on a stand, dated 1690, in the William and Mary style, and an eighteenth-century mahogany table along with two chairs in the Chippendale style. Did you know that Ella had 300 pairs of shoes? Obviously the lives of wealthy landowners were on another level from the workers who toiled in the paddocks and shearing sheds.

In contrast, next door we have a more utilitarian object that speaks to the working man rather than the southern gentry. This wool press was built in Australia in about 1860 of jarrah timber, and was shipped to New Zealand and used on the Terawhiti station at Makara, near Wellington. It is of the old type used in this country before Donald Donald's 'lift and swing' wool press became standard in the 1880s — here the wool is loaded in the top and the bale is pressed by rope winches. Nowadays presses are electric, but this old press was used until quite recently when it was outlawed by new safety regulations.

MANA PASIFIKA

Before we finish our tour, there is one more exhibition you should see — *Mana Pasifika: Celebrating Pacific Cultures* — which we can find down here behind the history exhibitions, connected to the Māori exhibitions at the back of level four. Like other exhibits, this one has a few surprises. It focuses on the seven main island groups of the South Pacific represented in New Zealand's population: Samoa, Tonga, the Cook Islands, Fiji, Niue, Tokelau and Kiribati. Oh, and there are objects from other parts of the Pacific too, and don't miss the Hawaiian chief's feather cloak, which was given to Captain Cook, just around the corner there.

But — and here's the thing — it *also* looks at the vibrant urban youth culture springing up in places like Porirua and South Auckland. The show is structured around a series of themes important in Pacific Island life: music and dance, food and feasting, costume and adornment, warfare, sport, religion.

There are a lot of beautiful old artefacts here from the Pacific — tivaevae, tapa, a tamtam (slit gong drum) from Vanuatu, a paroe (huge food bowl) from the Cook Islands — including rare and beautiful things collected on Cook's voyages. However, you will also find a surprising range of modern manufactured products that reflect the everyday experience of New Zealanders of Pacific descent: Jonah Lomu phone cards, Margharet Matenga's netball uniform, music by Annie Crummer, fiction by Albert Wendt, art by Michel Tuffery.

Don't miss the Discovery Centre *PlaNet Pasifika*, under the (fake) coconut tree and (real) Samoan fale, especially built for Te Papa, and you *must* try the computer interactive on cooking a feast in a Cook Island umu for a wedding!

So folks, that's the end of our tour. I hope you enjoyed it. You are welcome to wander around and explore by yourselves, and don't forget to buy a souvenir of your visit in the shop on the way out.

Kia ora!

03.

what the staff intended . . . and what the critics thought

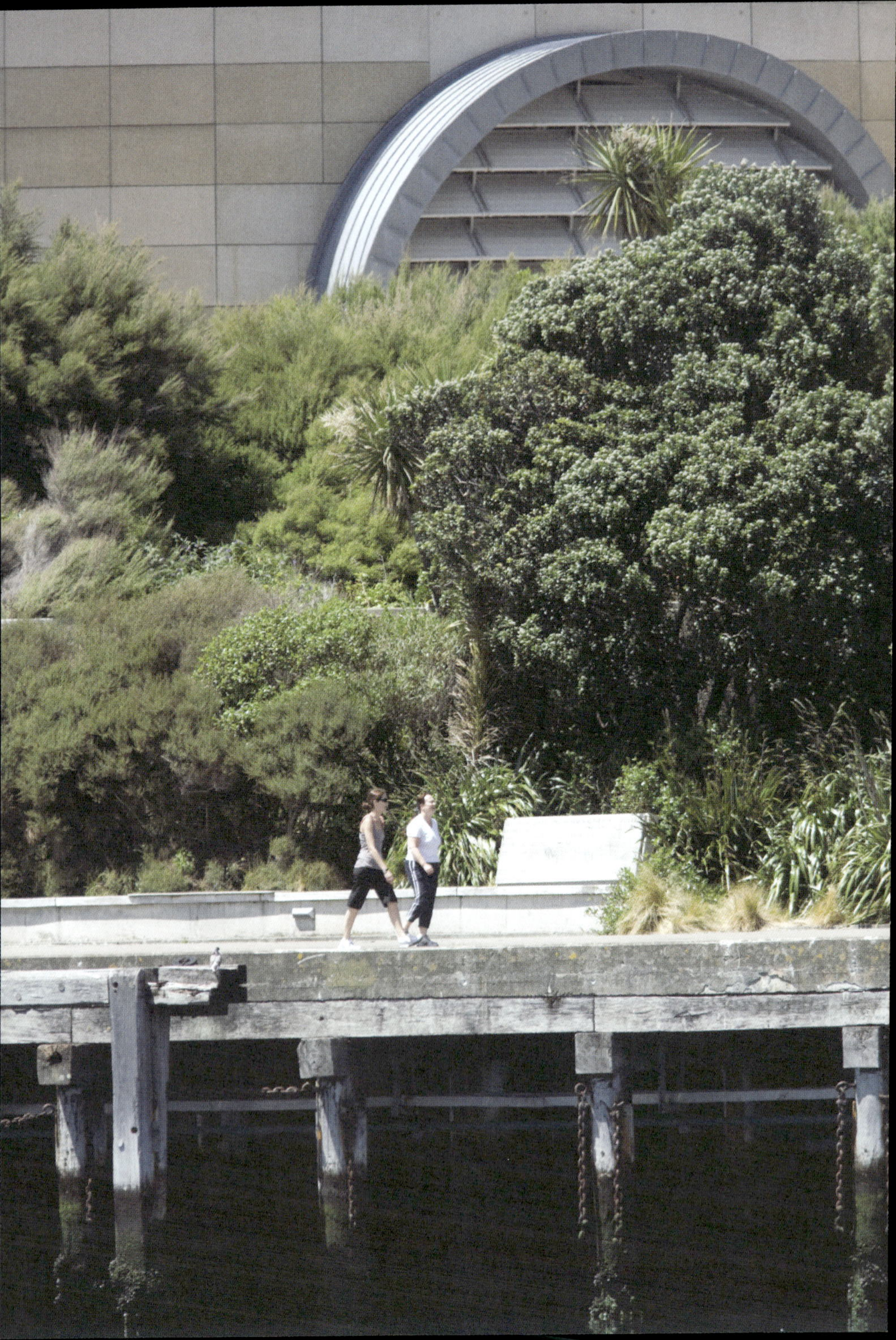

The guided tour of day-one exhibitions in the previous chapter conveys a sense of what was on the floor of New Zealand's new national museum in February 1998. But what it doesn't do, and this is invariably the problem with an individual critic's subjective reviews of exhibits, is give you an idea of how it got there. In other words we need to understand the *process*, and not just the final *product*, i.e. how the exhibitions were actually made. We also need to appreciate both the production *and* the reception of the displays; that is to say, what the developers' intentions were, and what meanings visitors made from them (which are not always the same thing).[1]

If we were to leave our tour group and step back of house to the offices where we could talk to the staff, then we could get a glimpse of what the exhibition developers were trying to do. A brief review of how the exhibitions were put together will identify what it was that was innovative at the time, and why the visitors came (in droves) and why they, mostly, liked what they found. This is the subject of this chapter: the developers' intentions, the visitors' reception, and the critics' reviews.[2]

Simply put, what made Te Papa's day-one exhibitions so successful was the strong emphasis on the visitor experience as an integral part of the development. For the first time in New Zealand on a comprehensive scale, exhibitions were strategically planned and produced in line with the tenets of the new museology, that is to say, they were audience-focused (see Chapter 1 for the work of the museum project office). A key part of this process was that everyone in the exhibition team was working to common goals and objectives, and that interpretation was an integral part of this — not just in the form of a role for an interpreter on the team, but also in the sense that interpretation was an overall function of the institution and in line with its public service mission.[3] As art curator Tim Walker remembers it, 'the audience-centric approach was a *tactical* HOW WE THINK response driven by the *strategic* WHY question — what does it mean to be "a museum for all New Zealanders" — and the philosophical tenets of the new museology.' This meant, he continues, 'an integrated approach to design, content, interpretation etc.'[4]

A clear example was the writing of labels and text, which was not done by curators but rather by professional writers from diverse backgrounds who had written for the screen, stage and page in a variety of settings.[5] Labels were written in an accessible and engaging style in everyday New Zealand English, often enlivened with cheeky humour, personal stories and individual experience of the subject matter being displayed. Even though summative evaluation showed that these labels were, for the most part, very effective, they were often derided by academic critics who thought experts should have written them (for other experts), and who delighted in pointing out errors of fact, complaining that they were 'dumbing down' the content.[6]

To one such complaint, Ken Gorbey replied: 'We at Te Papa make no apology for our basic label-writing approach. In this we seek to make every word written so as to make the Te Papa experience available to the broadest New Zealand audience. Our language is openly conversational and we frequently use the device of drawing parallels and comparisons to engender understanding and engagement.'[7] This commitment to communication was shared by most in the project office, not just interpreters but also designers, concept developers and senior management. When I interviewed the Kaihautū, Cliff Whiting, who had worked on early ideas for *Mana Whenua*, he stated in no uncertain terms that the exhibition worked with Māori audiences because 'they can bloody understand it, eh?'[8]

NATURAL ENVIRONMENT EXHIBITIONS

So, what were the messages that the developers were trying to get across, how did they do it, and did it work? Let us start again, as on our tour, with the natural environment exhibitions on level two.

Here the developers wanted to get away from the conventional museum displays of flora and fauna that presented specimens as a 'dead zoo' and instead show that the natural world was dynamic, diverse and interconnected with people. A key player in this quest was concept leader Geoff Hicks, a scientist with a passionate commitment to bringing science to life. 'No longer is it a case of plonking objects in display cases and expecting them to speak for themselves,' he told a reporter on a tour of *Mountains to Sea*. 'That's the Victorian approach to museums.' Now a 'multi-faceted' approach was possible. 'It's a mix of art, of history, of science and technology, of the Māori . . .'[9]

A striking example of this in the exhibition was the push-button audio labels in which children explained in their own words the features of plants and animals — a simple but effective technique. Another example could be found in *NatureSpace*, where Jane Martin, an experienced teacher and interpreter, had a real gift for working with children. In a flip book aimed at children, cartoons and text told the extraordinary tale of the discovery of the first dinosaur fossil in a quarry in England by naturalist Gideon Mantell, whose son Walter brought the specimen to New Zealand and deposited it in the Colonial Museum. When children turned over the last page, there was the iguanodon tooth, embedded in a tiny case under the book. Real object and graphic storytelling combined to produce a moment of pure magic.

Science communication was also the aim in *Awesome Forces*. Parts of the exhibition, for example the segment on plate tectonics, and the book that accompanied the show, had serious scientific material. But overall the aim was to explain complex concepts, such as the major earth processes that have created and shaped New Zealand, in an accessible way to a diverse audience.[10] Here the concept developer was Hamish Campbell, a geologist at Geological and Nuclear Sciences (GNS), who won a national award in science communication because of his work on *Awesome Forces* (which consistently came out in visitor surveys as the most popular permanent attraction). Campbell told a reporter that the real reward for his work was 'seeing the delight on people's faces' when they start comprehending aspects of geology.[11]

Also apparent in *Awesome Forces* is the bicultural element mentioned by Hicks. A key objective was to present Māori perspectives on, and relationships with, the natural world as an integral part of the exhibition. The interweaving of western science and mātauranga Māori was realised in part through inserting Māori characters and stories in the narrative where possible, for example in the volcanology section the episode about the Tarawera eruption and the 'buried village' of Te Wairoa, but also through artworks and the AV telling the Māori story of creation. This work was facilitated by a Māori science interpreter, Greg Motu, who worked on the exhibition.[12]

So, did it work? Did they get it? The evidence shows that the natural environment exhibitions were an outstanding success.[13] Summative evaluation of *Awesome Forces* suggested that it largely met its stated learning objectives, with most respondents identifying the central theme of earth processes, about half identifying ideas about how New Zealand has been shaped by those processes, and basic earthquake preparedness, but only a minority picking up the Māori connection with the land.[14] This study found *Awesome Forces* to be Te Papa's most popular exhibition, having been seen by 65 per cent of all visitors and being reported as a highlight by 22 per cent of visitors.[15] There were few reviews as such, but one long attentive article praised the level two exhibitions, along with other exhibits.[16]

The earthquake house was often cited as a highlight of a visit to the museum. On Trip Advisor you will find nearly 10,000 comments, mostly positive, with things like the x-ray room, and the colossal squid put on display in 2009, standing out for international visitors.[17] *NatureSpace* was a hot spot for children, and organised school groups.[18]

What arguably did *not* work, and what was a sore point with traditional museum-goers from the beginning, was the *Time Warp*, the high-energy attractor next door on level two. Although it was popular for a few years with young visitors, staff felt that it was very expensive to develop, quickly became dated, and was difficult to refresh or change. After another experiment with a digital space in later years, which also had mixed results, the area has now reverted to exhibition space, with *Gallipoli: The Scale of Our War* marking the centenary of the World War I campaign in 2015.

MĀORI EXHIBITIONS: 'MĀORI TALKING ABOUT MĀORI'

Upstairs in the marae and the Māori exhibition *Mana Whenua*, the drive for social inclusion, which was a feature of the exhibition development generally, was also apparent, but matched with a strong statement of Māori political assertiveness (reflecting the museum's historical context, described in the Introduction). What was remarkable about this space on level four was not just that it was a contemporary working marae within a national museum, but that it was also intended to embrace *all* visitors — on both counts this was a challenge to Māori traditionalists, just as the art exhibitions challenged the old art history.

'It's a Māori marae but it belongs to all the cultures of New Zealand — all our spiritual things are here,' Cliff Whiting told a Māori reporter. The whare was a 'working model of biculturalism' as carvers both Māori and Pākehā worked side by side 'creating images from their own histories'. 'The marae is a challenge to ourselves,' he added. 'We're moving ourselves along as a people and as a nation.'[19]

This became a controversial point for some Māori critics of Te Papa, as we will see, but it was more of a problem for non-Māori who invariably have an idea of indigenous culture as traditional and unchanging — a restrictive and arguably ethnocentric view that assumes western culture can adapt and innovate but native and tribal people must remain in the past, a people without history. Some visitors accepted this 'souped-up and modernised marae', but many felt it was tacky, gaudy or demeaning in contrast with the 'real' Māori art on display in *Mana Whenua*.[20] In contrast historian James Belich responded positively to what he called the 'postmodern' marae: 'It's recognising that Māori culture is not frozen circa 1769, but is still living and growing.'[21]

Overall, however, the visitor reaction to the marae was very positive, especially when there were events on in the space that they could see — staff waiata practice, pōwhiri for visitors, etc. — which goes to show that visitors like to see planned events but even more to observe a museum at work, and a culture going about its business, something that seems more 'real' than a spectacle that appears staged. Cliff Whiting's generous and inclusive vision for a marae to which everyone could belong was realised successfully and has been borne out by 20 years of busy activity.

As Arapata Hakiwai, the current Kaihautū, has observed, Rongomaraeroa has become the de facto national marae where events of national importance are staged — ceremonies associated with the settlement of Waitangi Tribunal claims, major conferences, hosting visiting dignitaries, and so on.[22] Internally, it seems that the marae really has become the beating heart of Te Papa's biculturalism, providing a focus for iwi in residence to present themselves to the world, but also for Māori staff to maintain their cultural practices, and non-Māori to develop their knowledge and understanding of tikanga Māori. The questions that have arisen over the years have been more to do with how the marae was run, and where it was situated — these are discussed in the next chapter.

Next door in *Mana Whenua*, the same mix of political sovereignty and cultural democracy was evident in the way in which staunch beliefs and claims to culture, identity and land were presented and interpreted — in terms that were accessible to a mass audience made up not just of Māori themselves but also Pākehā and overseas visitors.[23] *Mana Whenua* is 'a celebration and affirmation of kaupapa Māori', declared Arapata Hakiwai, then a concept developer. 'In many ways we broadened museum practice to not only become facilitators in the exhibition process,' Hakiwai said, 'but to increase iwi involvement and participation in the display, interpretation and ultimately the future of our people's taonga.'[24] The process of developing the exhibition worked 'from the outside in', through collaboration with iwi, in order to empower Māori in decisionmaking.[25]

This intention was well meaning, but one of the challenges the exhibition team faced was getting across to the public an understanding of this partnership with iwi. Surveys showed visitors often did not realise the exhibition had been developed by Māori staff, let alone that it was co-curated with iwi.[26] One tactic to make this apparent to the public was to write labels that used first person plural pronouns — 'we' rather than 'they' — which may have been an improvement on the old impersonal ethnographic 'othering' of indigenous people, but some curators later felt was too generalised and impersonal.[27] Another tactic was to use the present tense in labels — 'are' rather than 'were' — which helped convey the sense that Māori culture was alive and dynamic, one of the main concepts of the show.

One segment where the partnership process *was* clear was the display of the small house Mākōtukutuku. Here archaeologists Janet Davidson and Foss Leach worked alongside Hāmi Te Whaiti and a group of Ngāti Hinewaka people from the Wairarapa to reconstruct an ancient wharepuni, or sleeping house, the remains of which had been discovered in Palliser Bay. This community project involved making the tools, collecting local resources, building the house and constructing props such as nets and traps — all in the style of their ancestors 500 years before. The comments from the people in the accompanying video suggest that this process was more about fostering identity and iwi development than archaeology.[28] In fact these discussions led the team to discard what they called the 'archaeological/ethnographic approach' to exhibition making because it 'infuriates Māori people and does not convey any sense of our history and meanings we attach to taonga'.[29]

The completed installation design of *Mana Whenua* was not everything its developers had wanted (it lacked the contemporary focus they sought because a funding shortfall meant modern Māori life was not as well represented as they would have liked). Nevertheless, it can be seen in hindsight as a compromise between their political aspirations and the museum's overall goal of communicating to a mass audience. There was little of the postmodern experimentation, social critique and irony evident in the art and history exhibitions. The design and layout of *Mana Whenua* was therefore not fundamentally different to other Māori exhibitions from the late 1980s, which similarly set out to celebrate ancestral culture, but this was less a museological conservatism than the pragmatic outcome of a genuine empowering of iwi to tell their own story as they saw it.[30]

So, how did the Māori exhibitions fare with the public? There were some reservations about *Mana Whenua* both internally and externally. Some felt that it did not show the depth and range of the museum's collections, and that it was relatively static and conservative compared with other Te Papa exhibits, concentrating on a rural, historical view of Māori life.[31] Whatever the professional and critical quibbles, the public voted with their feet. Surveys showed that the exhibition was extremely popular with visitors, especially international visitors, and usually ranked in the top two to three exhibitions behind the natural environment.[32]

The summative evaluation of *Mana Whenua* showed that it was a big hit with Māori visitors in particular. The Te Papa Visitor Profile showed that 17 per cent of New Zealand visitors to *Mana Whenua* were Māori, and the summative evaluation revealed that 40 per cent of those interviewed in the exhibition for the study were Māori.[33] The comments of Māori visitors reveal a positive reaction to the way in which, as one visitor put it, 'taonga are treated as taonga', and as another said, 'Māori are talking to Māori here.'[34]

Most of the learning objectives were met successfully but, as stated above, it was not always clear the exhibition had been co-curated, and the idea of presenting Māori culture as contemporary was perhaps not as apparent with the audience as the exhibition team would have liked. This was partly due to the content, which was predominantly historical, and partly the lighting and design, and the dark, moody atmosphere that tended to reinforce the notion of 'traditional' Māori ways of life as pastoral, and spiritual, rather than urban or modern.[35]

On the other hand, art critics' reviews of the Māori exhibitions were, ironically, more positive than those of the art exhibitions as they found the installation design more 'traditional'. Art historians thought taonga were treated with the 'respect' lacking in the treatment of artworks.[36] Overseas critics usually liked *Mana Whenua* due to what they saw as its 'seriousness, calm and spirituality', which contrasted with other exhibitions on level four that they found too noisy, colourful and eclectic for their tastes.[37] The display of contemporary art and Māori life today, however, did not always meet with the approval of many Pākehā who preferred to see Māori art and culture along more 'traditional' lines.[38]

One controversy erupted in 2000 when Peter Munz, Emeritus Professor of History at Victoria University, criticised the Moriori segment of *Mana Whenua* because the labels did not mention the 1835 massacre of Moriori by Taranaki Māori, calling the display a 'historical distortion' and 'political propaganda'.[39] But according to Arapata Hakiwai, Moriori leader Maui Solomon told museum staff that they did not want to be represented yet again as 'victims'. For his part, Hakiwai did not see it as a deliberate 'omission'. If iwi were genuinely 'empowered to tell their story,' he said, 'and if they chose certain things that were important to them and not others . . . so be it.'[40]

MANA PASIFIKA: AFTER 'TRADITION'

Similar questions about how to exhibit culture and identity were being dealt with next door in the Pacific exhibition, where issues to do with the history and theory of museum representation were related but distinctive.[41] *Mana Pasifika* focused on tropical Polynesia and Fiji but also explored life in 'Niu Sila' for New Zealanders of Pacific descent.[42]

As in *Mana Whenua*, a key tool in developing *Mana Pasifika* was consultation and collaboration with communities, in this case through two advisory groups, one in Auckland and one in Wellington. The exhibition reflected the shift in focus in the museum over recent years, concept developer Janet Davidson explained, from an older ethnographic approach to material culture, to collecting and exhibiting Pacific Island communities in New Zealand through a broader range of objects and media.[43] This objective was conveyed successfully through the finished exhibition, which, as our tour in Chapter 2 showed, was full of everyday popular culture, sport, music and fashion as well as finely crafted old artefacts from Samoa, Tonga, the Cook Islands, etc. Right in the centre of the space, a reporter from the *Dominion* noted, was an area evocative of the lounge in a Pacific Island home in Ōtara or Porirua.[44]

But this emphasis on everyday material culture was not an easy idea to convey, and it was contested even among Pacific visitors. Curator Sean Mallon related an incident that occurred while he was giving a tour of the exhibition for a Pacific group. When they stopped in front of a display case showing an old paint tin that had been used as a drum, a young Pasifika visitor questioned why this mundane object was in the museum at all. Surely the museum should display authentic traditional objects, not ordinary stuff like this? Mallon explained that a respected Niuean elder and member of the advisory group, the Reverend Lagi Sepeli, had donated the drum. Later Mallon wrote about the problem with the notion of 'tradition', which tends to freeze cultures in the past and does not allow them to grow and develop. In fact this word, often imposed on non-western cultures by museum anthropologists, had been 'banned' from the exhibition by Albert Wendt, the prominent Samoan writer and intellectual who was on the advisory group.[45]

Nothing conveyed the dynamism and energy the curators were seeking better than the extraordinary contemporary sculpture by artist Michel Tuffery. *Pisupo lua afe* (Corned beef 2000) (1994), a cow made from recycled corned beef cans, was part of a group of similar sculptures, one of which was used as the centrepiece of a spectacular performance with fireworks and dancers. At the same time, it was a strong political statement on colonisation, diet and the environment.

SIGNS OF A NATION: DEBATING THE TREATY

As we learned in the last chapter, the exhibition *Signs of a Nation* was positioned in the centre of level four in 1998, and was conceptually and structurally the heart of the Museum of New Zealand.[46] Not surprisingly, given the political ferment of the 1980s and 1990s around Aotearoa's founding document, this exhibition was the most difficult to realise. It took at least three attempts over several years to get a concept that was accepted by the Exhibition Approvals Team, who were very conscious of the current debates and public disquiet about the Treaty.

The painful process of exhibition production was documented warts and all in Gaylene Preston's documentary *Getting to Our Place*.[47] Two concepts regarded as ponderous and unpalatable were turned down, until finally a new group of developers reworked the ideas and got the green light to proceed. The film shows the penultimate team, which included concept developers Paul Thompson and Jock Phillips, designer (and the building's architect) Pete Bossley, interpreter Haniko Te Kurapa, historian Kerry Taylor and project manager Annette Meates, pulling together a plan that would work for a diverse audience in a tricky space. Front-end evaluation demonstrated that there was very little knowledge of the Treaty of Waitangi and its text, especially among young people.[48] It was a tall order.

Then the breakthrough came. Thompson skilfully negotiated a concept that was not a history lesson that would turn off a reluctant audience, but rather a combination of memorial and forum that allowed people to make up their own minds about a controversial topic. The team decided to create an empty space where people could simply see the Treaty and decide for themselves what it meant to them.[49] Thompson remembers that 'because we wanted the Treaty to speak for itself and the words of the Treaty to have the mana and for people to think for themselves, we didn't make the downstairs [area] too didactic with too much information, it wasn't supposed to be a book on a wall.'[50] This explicit aim to create a 'sacred and dignified place' is of course closely related to nation (re)building.[51]

The resemblance to a constitutional shrine came following a visit to the Lincoln Memorial and other monuments in Washington DC, quiet and almost sacred spaces where visitors were able to read and think about the words of documents such as the Constitution. The talking poles — which pulled visitors into the space and the debates about the Treaty — were inspired by an Aboriginal exhibit at the Museum of Sydney.

This was a clever and elegant solution to a practical problem, but the critical reception and visitor research show that, whatever the developers' intentions were, people make up their own minds about the exhibit. One review, written by British historian Peter Hudson, found it 'powerfully moving and inspirational'.[52] During a school programme in the space one day I had a challenging encounter with a Māori visitor who was adamant that the display did *not* give 'the Māori view', only that of the Crown, and did not talk about the alienation of Māori land. In the academic literature there is a veritable library about this exhibition, much of it highly critical, but often paying little heed to either the process of exhibition making or the response from the mass audience. In the most balanced analysis, Australian academic Kylie Message wrote that the quiet cathedral-like space of the Treaty exhibition was at odds with the rest of Te Papa with its busy interactives, and likened it to the nation's classroom in its pedagogical display of the official government policy of biculturalism.[53]

It is not one of the most popular exhibits, but it has also aged quite well, despite the fact that the Treaty, and biculturalism, are perhaps no longer as central to nation building as they were in the 1990s. This raises the question of what kind of exhibit would go in the middle of level four that would reflect how the nation sees itself in the twenty-first century? For an answer to that, we will have to wait for the next generation of exhibitions.

HISTORY EXHIBITIONS: OUR NATION'S STORY?

The day-one history exhibitions at Te Papa also attracted this kind of hyper-critical analysis of nationalism, race relations and settler identity, but were, equally, embraced by the visiting public. They were developed by a team led by Jock Phillips who, as a respected historian, was very aware of academic debates about national identity and other issues. The team included concept developers/curators Bronwyn Labrum, Lyndon Fraser, Paul Thompson and Michael Fitzgerald, and interpreters Jane Martin and Jean-Marie O'Donnell.

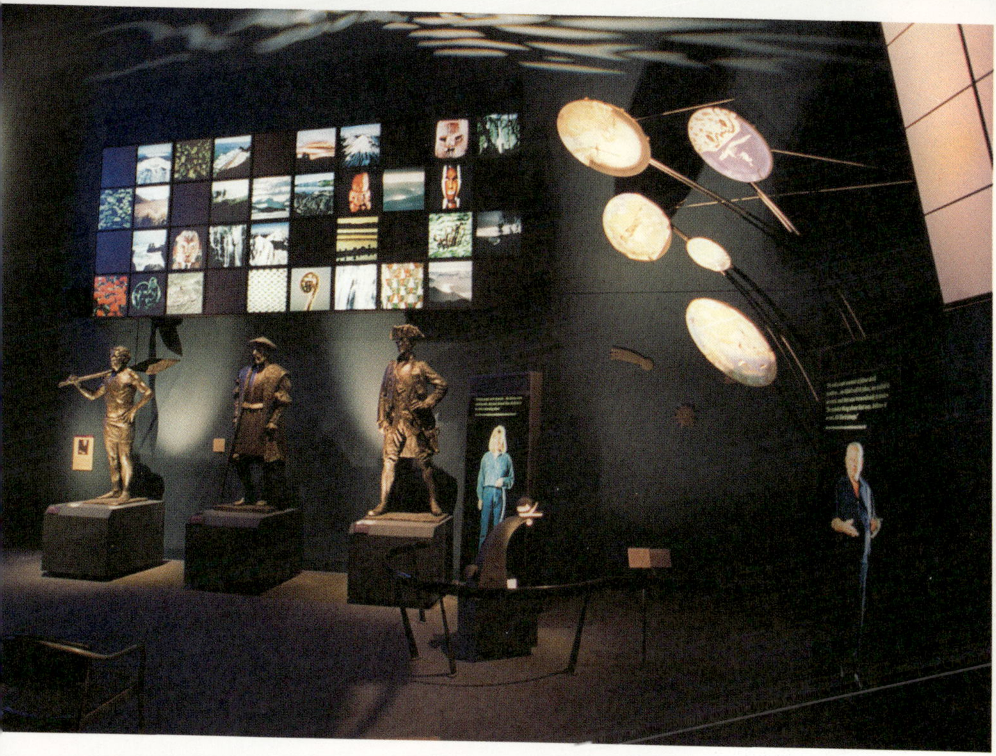

1.

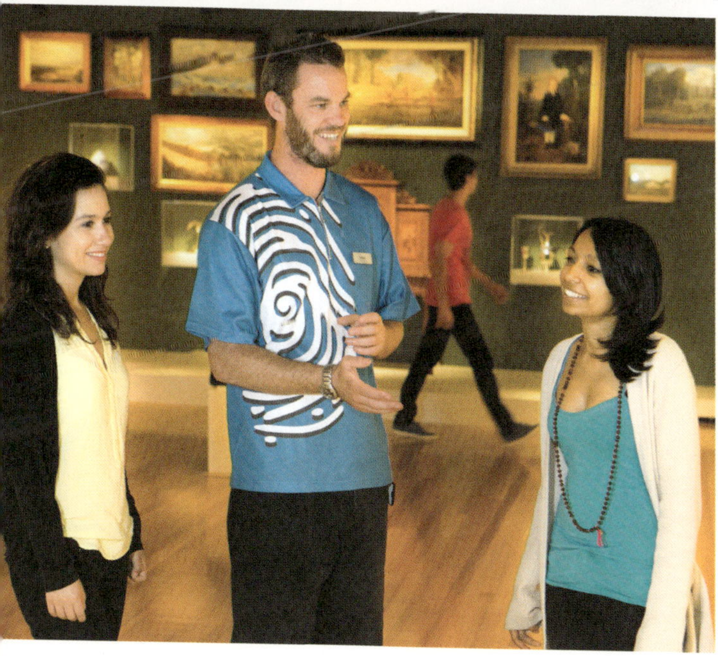

2.

1\.
The history exhibition *Exhibiting Ourselves* on level four.

2\.
Visitors at an art exhibition on level five, *Ngā Toi Arts Te Papa*.

This 'dream team', as it was known at the time, was kept in line by able project manager Alison Preston.[54]

For Phillips, who headed the Historical Branch of the Department of Internal Affairs, working at Te Papa part time was 'three days of despair' followed by 'two of ecstasy' back in the 'ordered calm' of his office. He found there were many challenges: the long hours, the politics, the endless meetings, the reporting; but also many valuable lessons: teamwork, interdisciplinarity, the value of planning and the requirement not to do history through a book. History in a museum was different because 'it meant presenting our past to diverse audiences,' he argues, 'young and old, Māori and Pākehā, locals and overseas tourists, and to do it using film and sounds and images and objects and computer games.' This was a valuable lesson for Phillips:

> This focus on diverse audiences and the need to make the exhibition experience work for all of them was a huge learning curve for me but one that I came to treasure. It was a particular privilege to work with the writing team . . . who turned 'our bald meat-and-potatoes' briefs of facts and figures into labels which were both accurate and informative, yet also, through clever analogies and wit, captured the imagination. This was, in my view, one of Te Papa's great achievements.[55]

As we saw in the previous chapter, three history exhibitions were linked in an overall plan: how people came here (*Passports*), the culture they created once they got here (*On the Sheep's Back*), and how they thought about themselves and their identity (*Exhibiting Ourselves*). Of the three shows, the last (and unfortunately the first to be de-installed) was the one that most clearly addressed national identity as a question and not a natural given.

In an interview at the time, Phillips said that 'we had to get people thinking about what it is to be a New Zealander', and that the displays were arranged to question rather than define New Zealand identity as 'an artificial creation'.[56] This deliberately 'subversive'[57] approach appealed to academic critics, who found the artificiality of the exhibits drew attention to the constructedness of identity formation. One called it 'a quintessentially postmodernist display'.[58]

Recently Phillips reflected that he always regarded *Exhibiting Ourselves* as 'the most successful history exhibition', partly because they 'really did attempt to integrate art works and history objects — particularly in the 1992 Seville Expo section'.[59]

In an article where he reflected on his experience, Phillips wrote that there was certainly a lot of pressure on the staff in the project office to produce 'feel good' exhibits that did not make Pākehā feel bad about themselves. They were required to explore and affirm national identity, 'for that is what society wants', but in a way that takes account of the 'very genuine concerns, both intellectual and social, about that notion'.[60] Staff therefore set out not to prescribe but to provide the means for people to make up their own minds, as part of the idea of the museum as a forum for the nation.

Phillips was aware of the 'clamour for simple nationalist affirmations' but was not prepared to do a 'hall of fame'. He recognised the need from a mass audience to search for a recognisable sense of belonging, but was determined 'not to give simple answers'.[61] The general approach to the history exhibitions was, like the other zones, accessible, interdisciplinary, and multi-media. Phillips looked at lots of exhibitions overseas, where different forms of presenting the past were being explored. 'I think the idea of people standing passively and looking at glass cases is no longer acceptable to people,' he said in 1998.[62]

This engaging style of public history can be seen in *Passports*, usually the first history exhibition visitors encountered, which told the story of migration. Here the objective was 'to take people on a journey themselves', as Phillips put it.[63] This was achieved, as we saw in the previous chapter, in the layout of the exhibition, where visitors moved through sections dealing with leaving, crossing and arriving. One of the most effective mechanical interactives in the museum could be found in the crossing section, which was developed by Jane Martin. In what felt like the dark, cramped confines of a sailing ship, visitors looked through a porthole and turned a lever that gave them different views of the old country they had left behind, the ocean passage around the world, and glimpses of their new home.

The passports that visitors took and had stamped, and the drawers with real stories of migrants who came to live in New Zealand, were other very successful interpretive devices that conveyed complex ideas in simple form. In total there were 95 such stories in the exhibition. The power of these personal stories was attested to by one visitor, 75-year-old Glenys McGrath, who found the passport of her grandmother Mary Player, who had immigrated from County Kilkenny, Ireland, in the nineteenth century. Seeing her grandmother's face in the national museum was a moving experience — it was a 'passport to the past'.[64]

But *Passports* set out to do more than simply give Pākehā people a sense of nostalgia about their settler forebears and was anything but a celebration of foundational myths about the 'hardy pioneers'. The exhibition included stories of privation, failure and conflict, including the grisly tale of whaler Jacky Guard and his family and their violent interaction with Taranaki Māori. Wanting to challenge the Anglo-Protestant bias in New Zealand's European history, Phillips also set out to show that migrants were not just from England and Scotland, but also came from a diverse range of nationalities and social backgrounds. New Zealand was, he argued, 'multi-cultural even then'.[65]

This message about cultural diversity was important in the 1990s, when there was a national debate about Asian migration. It was therefore not surprising that the first community gallery adjoining *Passports* was devoted to the Chinese. Developed in partnership with various Chinese communities, from Cantonese families who had arrived in the gold rushes of the 1860s to recent migrants from Malaysia, Singapore, Hong Kong and Taiwan, this was the first of several ethnic groups featured in the space, later followed by Indian, Italian, Scots and refugee communities.[66] As curator Michael Fitzgerald explained later, a community gallery took about two and a half years to develop, with the staff 'working hard to ensure that it is the community's own stories that are presented'.[67] *The Making of a Chinese New Zealander* talked about the difficult side of their history — the poll tax, opium and discrimination — as well as the successes. One telling snapshot of cultural hybridity was the story of a family sitting down to eat a meal of fish and chips, with chopsticks.

The community gallery was greeted enthusiastically by Chinese visitors and critics, despite the inevitable tensions between different sections of the community about how they were being represented on a national stage.[68]

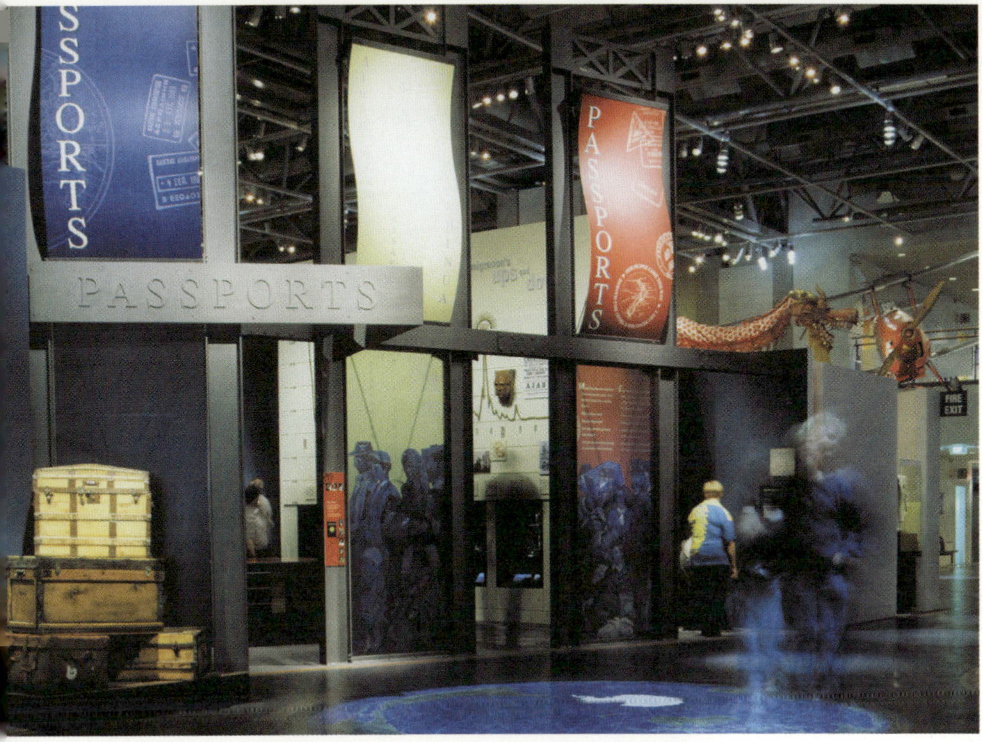

1.

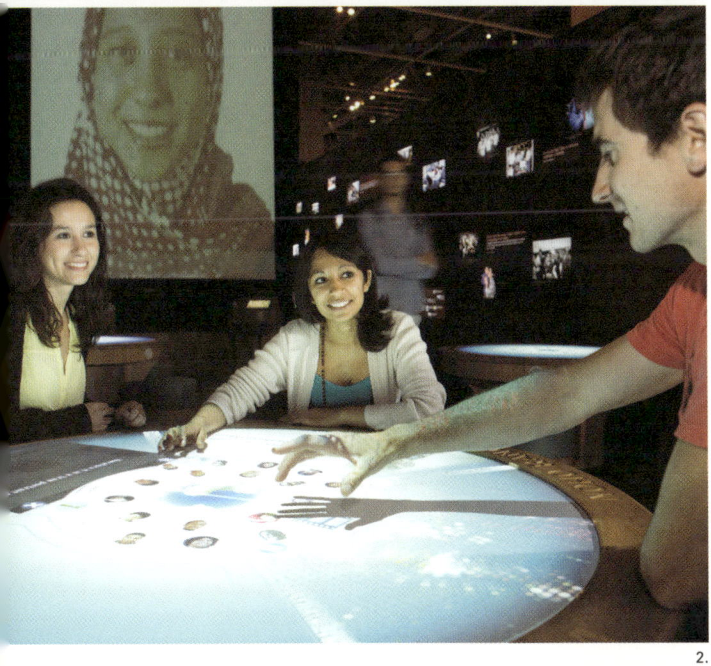

2.

1.

The *Passports* exhibition entrance.

2.

Visitors in the latest community gallery, *The Mixing Room*, which tells the stories of refugees.

Chinese historian Steven Young wrote that the Chinese community in Wellington was 'delighted' with the show. He added that he was particularly pleased to see the Chinese 'at long last recognised as an integral part of New Zealand'.[69] However, more recent research on *Passports* suggests that community 'migration' exhibitions framed by ethnicity fail to explore the complex lives of Asian people in New Zealand today.[70]

Generally the reviews, as well as visitor surveys, were very positive about *Passports*. Journalist Ann Bailey said the displays were 'carefully crafted', and that the migration stories had strong 'pulling power'.[71] Historian Paul Hudson wrote that *Passports* was 'well conceptualised and beautifully constructed'.[72] Summative evaluation in 2002 showed that almost half (47.5 per cent) of all adult visitors to Te Papa had visited *Passports* since the museum's opening, making it the sixth most visited exhibition. It was also ranked as the sixth most popular long-term exhibition. Specific highlights included the *Voyage Out* and *Promised Land* computer interactives, and learning about immigration and entry criteria into New Zealand.[73]

Nevertheless, despite the good feedback formally and informally, staff *were* conscious of various conceptual and historiographical issues with these exhibitions, and continued to experiment with new approaches to collecting and exhibiting New Zealand history in later work.[74] Jock Phillips for his part was pleased with how the history exhibitions turned out but frustrated that serious historians did not engage more with them, and was disappointed the planned integrated spaces did not eventuate.[75] Historian Bronwyn Labrum, a curator who worked on day-one exhibitions, wrote later that in hindsight there was probably too much focus on national identity, that Māori-Pākehā relations tended to be separated out and should have had more sense of interaction, and there were not enough everyday objects.[76] Some of these issues were addressed in the later history exhibition *Slice of Heaven*, which opened in 2010, and in 2017 there are plans to experiment with different and more integrated approaches to all the history and culture exhibitions on level four.

In reflecting on the day-one art and history exhibitions, Ken Gorbey has commented that they perhaps failed to achieve the interdisciplinary synthesis sought in the original concept because once staff started working on the exhibitions they tended to default back to their disciplinary poles and did not mix up objects and stories as much as they could have.[77] In part, however, this was due to the fact that the central integrated exhibit where everything was supposed to come together, what is now occupied by the level four cafe, did not materialise.

The strongest reaction to the original layout of level four, which preserved the traditional boundaries between disciplines and collections, comes from Sean Mallon, now Senior Curator Pacific Cultures. 'If I had my way,' he told a museum studies class in 2006, 'I would bulldoze level four and start again.' That, indeed, is not far from what staff are now thinking for the proposed new exhibitions on level four. Early conceptual planning suggests a radically different interdisciplinary space that breaks down the divisions between Māori, Pasifika and New Zealand history and culture. It may be that, 20 years after a holistic vision of New Zealand life was conceived, it will finally be achieved.

ART APART? PARADE AND ITS DISCONTENTS

As it turned out, the art exhibitions were to be the most controversial of Te Papa's opening displays in terms of stakeholder and visitor reaction, although this could be seen in hindsight as a storm in a teacup. There were indications early on that whatever happened with art at the new national museum would receive close scrutiny from those who felt disenfranchised by the integration of the National Gallery into Te Papa.[78] Nonetheless, most of the art offerings in February 1998 were actually fairly conventional: the touring gallery with international art shows that pulled in big crowds, The Boulevard where *Dream Collectors* received warm although mixed reviews,[79] and contemporary installation spaces such as *Facing IT*.[80]

Concept leader Ian Wedde describes the overall plan for this suite of exhibitions thus: '*Parade* investigated the broadest possible range of visual cultures, *Facing IT* some recent developments in what was then termed new media art, and *Dream Collectors* a conventional picture-hang where the implicit message was that the "national collection" is cared for nationally by many institutions and individuals.'[81]

The museum made overtures to art lovers with a lot of prominent floor space devoted to art and a PR campaign to woo them into the building. It was repeatedly pointed out that there was much more space for art than there had been at the old National Gallery, and it was a great opportunity to see works from the art collection integrated into the museum; in other words, to see art as part of the wider visual culture of the country.[82] With some hard-core fans, who were clearly not interested in anything other than seeing art by itself in an art gallery, it need not have bothered. This exceptionalism was expressed by one board member who made his preferences clear: 'All I need to know is where the door to the National Art Gallery is.'[83]

The main point of contention was the exhibition *Parade*, which was an interdisciplinary mix of objects from art, design, fashion and photography, along with some taonga Māori. The team who worked on it included concept leader Ian Wedde, concept developers Tim Walker and Megan Tamati-Quennell, and interpreter Paul Rayner. At the time the links between art galleries and social exclusion were well documented in research locally and internationally, and in response many argued that galleries needed to appeal to a broader audience.[84] Walker remembers that a 'key issue', which arose from the strategic purpose of Te Papa as a 'museum for all New Zealanders', was the philosophical response to the question of 'whose art?' was on display; in other words, 'which traditions of art and creative endeavour were typically privileged in a "national art gallery" and whose were excluded.'[85]

Driven by this philosophy and sense of enquiry, the team set out to orchestrate an engaging display of art and visual culture for a broad audience using all the strategies available to them. Walker felt that the exhibition sought the 'braiding together' of 'complex interplays of traditions and values' on the one hand, and on the other 'a sense of generosity to audience(s)'.[86] As the interpreter, Rayner employed a similar style of visitor-centred interpretation as elsewhere in the museum. I recall him telling me at the time that his aim was simply to do a 'family friendly' art exhibition. In order to broaden their appeal to a wider range of people the conventions of display — works of art isolated against plain walls with minimal labels — were overturned, and greater levels of information were provided for those visitors not already familiar with art.[87]

Intellectually, the critique of art 'set apart' from other objects and their wider social context in art museums was nothing revolutionary, and indeed the analysis of art as a social product was current at the time in the new art history, literary theory, museum studies and other academic fields.[88] But the thing was that nobody had yet tried to implement these ideas on this scale in a national museum. *Parade* was one of the first experiments anywhere that attempted to do something different. In contrast to the usual temple of culture, *Parade* 'bombarded' people with art in a way that was diverse, colourful, eclectic and, *quelle horreur*, fun. Moreover, developers wanted to confront visitors with different 'ways of thinking about art', Walker remembers, and reveal its connections to history, power, class, culture and identity, etc.[89] When Walker showed a journalist around the show before opening, he seemed to sense a negative reaction. If visitors are open to 'aesthetic stimulation' then the exhibition 'opens up new areas of enquiry'. But, he added, 'if you resist it, you'll come back quite tense . . . because there's a lot to be tense about.'[90]

That was just a foretaste of the reaction that was to come. The month before opening, Anthony Hubbard wrote after a sneak preview: 'There are shocking scenes at Te Papa. In one corner a masterpiece by Colin McCahon hangs near an advertising poster for a 1959 Kelvinator fridge: High art and the kitchen sink.'[91] Wedde, obviously trying to explain, is quoted in the same review as saying that by putting things usually kept apart, like design and art, side by side, we can reconsider their comparative values. Pressed to say what he thought of a bright plastic interactive eliciting visitors' responses, likes and dislikes, Wedde responded that the exhibition is 'relativist'; it encourages you to make up your own mind.

When Hubbard was confronted in the exhibition with the juxtaposition of *The Northland Panels* and a Kelvinator Sheershape, Wedde commented, 'remember that both objects grew out of the same time, and only later were they separated'.[92] Both items signalled a radical shift from New Zealand's predominantly English-centric aesthetic and design world view to one dominated by American values. Hubbard conceded that *Parade* was a 'cunning mixture of high art and kitsch, taonga and television', but perhaps missing this rationale for their dual inclusion, concluded that it was 'artistic blasphemy to hang Colin McCahon in the kitchen'.[93]

At the time, Ian Wedde responded that *Parade* deliberately mixed art, design and popular culture in a postmodern 'bricolage'.[94] Twenty years later he reflects that, despite the adverse reaction, it 'was one of the opening exhibitions at Te Papa that found an audience that didn't know it existed until it met itself in *Parade* (and elsewhere).' Of the infamous McCahon/fridge pairing, he comments: 'Had we shown McCahon paintings in the combined company of Raphael, comic strips, geomorphological diagrams, roadside vege stall signage and Bernard Roundhill labels (we later acquired the Roundhill archive for Te Papa's collection) it might have generated thoughtful frowns rather than outrage, but I doubt it.'[95]

Subsequently, this image of a McCahon next to a fridge (which is not strictly accurate in terms of the layout of the exhibition) became a *leitmotif* in a torrent of criticism from art critics, art historians and artists, who complained loud and long. Mark Amery wrote that *Parade* was 'overtly provocative to the point of being disturbing'.[96] Even Prime Minister Helen Clark weighed in.[97] Critics claimed that art was treated with disrespect: it should not be 'dumbed down' with labels and interactives, and it did not need interpretation because it 'speaks for itself'.[98] A related complaint was that not enough art was on display, that it was somehow being 'hidden away' — an old chestnut that surfaces every now and then in ignorance of the realities of stored collections in which, on average, less than 10 per cent of any collection anywhere is on public display.[99]

The reaction to the exhibition can be evaluated within a longer view. It has to be said that much of the commentary was, surprisingly, rather conservative on a theoretical and political level. Critics such as Hamish Keith evoked an idealised model of public art galleries that overlooked their historical roots in bourgeois taste and social exclusion.[100] Today Tim Walker feels that, whereas hanging a McCahon next to a fridge was called a 'blasphemy' by critics at the time, the intended blasphemy in *Parade* was its challenge to, and violation of, art museums as bastions of middle-class power and privilege. Four decades after Pierre Bourdieu's social critique,[101] and two decades after *Parade*, he wonders, are we any closer to a 'transformative vision' for art museums?[102]

Putting aside these questions, it is fair to say that given generally positive summative evaluation, and good responses from most visitors, including school programmes, the criticism of *Parade* seems out of all proportion to the target.[103] The most balanced reviews were those from critics outside the caustic confines of New Zealand's art world. An example is Virginia Fraser, writing in *Art Monthly Australia*, who described the displays as 'discursive, theatrical and celebratory', and *Parade* as a 'collage' of different objects 'snaking colourfully' through level four.[104] Aspects of the exhibition were '[b]ig, bright, controversial . . . attention seeking'. Clearly, she wrote, it '[i]nfuriated some New Zealand art professionals' by 'juggling conventions', and its 'perceived insults to works usually treated reverentially'.

Even before opening, Fraser noted, Te Papa was criticised for 'practically everything', but despite an 'avalanche of blame' it is 'unmistakably of New Zealand', and has proved enormously popular.[105] 'Almost everything people say about Te Papa is true,' she concluded. On the one hand it can be seen as 'gross, cluttered, parochial, distracting, loud', but seen from other angles it is 'accessible, visually and aurally exciting, and novel in its presentations'.[106]

THE REVIEWS ARE IN

So, what did people think of Te Papa when it opened, and in the months and years that followed day one? Below I survey the popular response judged by audience research. The critical reception was more mixed than the public response, which was overwhelmingly positive. 'Everybody hates Te Papa,' commented the *Evening Post*, 'except the public.'[107] Reviews of the science, history and Māori exhibitions were mostly very good, but those from art critics and academic commentators were more negative. 'If you are unaware that the new Museum of New Zealand . . . is open you are probably dead,' wrote reviewer Paul Hudson.[108] He continued: 'The journey through the Museum of

New Zealand — for it is a journey — allows an outsider a glimpse of the hopes, aspirations, problems and fears of New Zealanders.'[109]

The reviewer for the monthly *North & South*, however, clearly used to art gallery spaces, lamented that she did not feel 'at home' till she got to The Boulevard on level five 'with its long, white sterile gallery'.[110] Others praised this very lack of temple-like atmosphere. Columnist Joe Bennett wrote: 'Gone is that austere oppressive reverence that one associates with colonial New Zealand, traditional museums and church.'[111] A regional newspaper declared that Te Papa was '[m]ore about Disney than dinosaurs', adding that, 'it is not intended to be just a meeting place for the cappuccino-sipping culturally elite.'[112]

What is striking now, in rereading the reviews of Te Papa from 1998, is the way they circle around notions of democratic access versus dumbing down, or elitism versus populism. A common theme in comments at the time, which now appears rather old fashioned, is the complaint that the style of display was an assault on the senses: the noise, movement and colour of interactives, for example. Neil Cossons, Director of London's National Museum of Science and Technology, told one journalist that sometimes hands-on meant minds-off. 'However,' he continued, 'interactivity in the right context in relationship to the right message is excellent, and that's what I believe this new museum has done.'[113]

Others defended the museum against criticism. After a critique by academic Denis Dutton, historian Peter Franks in turn attacked his 'intellectual arrogance'. 'Stuck in his dugout of dogmatism, Dr Dutton cannot understand why hundreds of thousands of people are flocking through the doors,' Franks wrote; '. . . perhaps he is just a sophist.'[114] Wellington's deputy mayor Kerry Prendergast responded to Prime Minister Helen Clark's criticism of the art display. 'Is it a way to put ordinary Kiwis in their place,' she retorted, 'because "Our Place" is not high-brow enough for her and her academic and acolyte friends?'[115] After an exchange about Te Papa in the *Listener* that was critical of its art exhibitions, the following letter appeared:

> So the white folks at the *Listener* are getting antsy about Te Papa's success? What a surprise! We know it may be hard to bear, but New Zealanders

> are well travelled and well educated and we vote with our feet . . . But, of course, what really upsets the snobs and the cynics is seeing so many of us brown faces visiting the place. Such a change from the usual gallery experience, where a token Māori is employed as a curator or guard and the small coterie of visitors are a nice, safe pale colour.[116]

In the last of a series of reviews, the *Evening Post* concluded: 'Here is the core of the debate over Te Papa. Is it a museum for the people or the experts?'[117] Te Papa's own response, articulated by CEO Cheryll Sotheran a few months after the museum opened, was firmly on the side of the people.[118]

Considered in a wider frame, conflict over museum display was part of the 'culture wars' of the 1980s and 1990s, a debate that was about the ownership of culture. Te Papa was often cited in this respect.[119] 'Culture isn't dumbing down,' stated museum professional Philip Dodd in response to the accusation of lowered standards in art museums in the UK. In his view it was simply 'being wrested from the control of a very small body of people who used to think culture was theirs'.[120] According to American historian Neil Harris, museums were no longer 'self-defining, socially aloof places that maintain transcendent categories', but could be seen as 'demilitarised zones in the culture wars, places where all the arguments should be heard'.[121]

'Never attempt to run an exhibition on its educational merit. Instead, provide the public with plenty of good, healthy entertainment,' declared G.S. Munroe, Superintendent of the New Zealand International Exhibition in Christchurch, in 1906. He had a point. Much of the negative reception of Te Papa's opening exhibitions assumed, almost one hundred years later, that education and entertainment should somehow be kept separate, as if it is not proper for us to have a good time in the museum. In common with other new national museums around the world, critics were unhappy with what they saw as paradoxical elements (commerce/culture, sacred/profane, nation/native), often figured in a black and white dichotomy of good/bad, old/new, etc.[122] But, as sociologist Nick Prior has argued, new museums are really not that new, and many of these populist and commercial elements have always been there right alongside the more refined scholarly ones. Although museums struggle to reconcile these tensions, they generally manage some kind of compromise in 'muddling through', and should therefore be understood as 'double coded', with contradictory elements ever present. Museums are far more flexible, and durable, than we realise.[123]

Whatever the critics thought, what the visitors did is plain. The initial figures were quite astonishing. By the end of the second year, 3.5 million people had visited the museum, a number equivalent to the country's total population. But long after the typical 'honeymoon' period for new institutions, Te Papa continued to attract huge numbers, an average of 1.3 million a year.[124] Total visitor numbers reached 5 million in 2000, 10 million in 2004, 15 million in 2008, 20 million in 2012, and 25 million in 2016 (see Appendix A).[125]

As shown in the chronological highlights in Appendix A, Te Papa achieved a record high of 1,578,292 visitors in 2016/17. By the end of June 2017, a total of 27,591,143 people had visited the national museum. As Te Papa approaches its twentieth birthday, the high numbers are impressive, although they can mainly be attributed to the success of the popular *Gallipoli* exhibition. These figures are obviously far larger than those achieved by the former National Art Gallery and National Museum in Buckle Street, although of course those institutions were on a much smaller scale, and with fewer staff and less funding.[126]

Who was coming? It was a striking feature of the statistics that a broad cross section of New Zealand visited Te Papa. The 1999 annual report declared that the museum had 'succeeded in expanding the core audience for museums' and that visitors typically reflected the 'diversity of New Zealand's population to a much greater extent than has been traditional'.[127] Indeed, the profile of visitors in the first year reflected New Zealand's general population. What was noteworthy was the significant reduction in the typical over-representation of wealthy, highly educated professionals.[128] By February 1999, of all the visitors through the doors, almost half were aged between 15 and 34, usually a very difficult group to attract to museums.[129] Over its first 10 years, Te Papa maintained an audience that was clearly more diverse than its predecessors and many other museums: younger, more male, more ethnically diverse.[130] Visitor numbers to the building in Cable Street remained fairly constant, but the numbers visiting touring exhibitions offsite, and the website, grew enormously.[131]

Obviously the steady growth of the physical visitation at Te Papa over the period 1998–2018 is important in terms of the core visitor experience, but there has been a huge increase in virtual visitation. This is clearly documented in the chronological highlights (Appendix A), where we see traffic to the website in 1998/99 increasing exponentially from the 2000s onward, with Collections Online and other platforms. Now museums are more than bricks and mortar, and must consider the 'offer' to users online as well as visitors on-site. This was not at all evident in 1998, when the world wide web was only a year old, digital technology in museums was in its infancy, and websites were regarded as marketing tools rather than knowledge and information channels in their own right.[132]

The diverse audience attracted to Te Papa did not go unnoticed. In surveys, other visitors often remarked on the 'real cross section of people' going to the new museum. 'The profile of visitors is amazing,' said one. 'People of all ethnicities, ages, clothing styles . . .' Parents pointed out that their children did not like going to the old museum because 'everything was dead and stuffed', but they loved Te Papa because it 'seems alive'. Another visitor compared the different audience attracted by the two institutions: 'It's not like the old museum, which was for students and scholars. This one is for ordinary people.'[133] The *Evening Post* observed: 'A point that was apparent to anyone was that the crowds thronging the building were not "typical" or traditional museum patrons: on busy days the museum's patrons seem to represent the entire demographic spectrum, from black T-shirts and tattooed forearms through to cashmere sweaters and Gucci handbags.'[134]

The area where this strong community engagement was really groundbreaking for museums internationally was Te Papa's success with Māori audiences. Historically, New Zealand museums attracted small numbers of Māori visitors, though it is not true that, as has been claimed, Māori never visited museums before *Te Maori*.[135] From the 1980s, anecdotal evidence suggests Māori did visit museums in much larger numbers.[136] But after Te Papa opened in 1998, the increased numbers of Māori visitors seemed to overturn the historical international trends — indigenous people like going to museums, at least here they do! At times, Māori constituted 13 per cent of New Zealand visitors, comparable to their proportion of the general population.[137]

A systematic comparison of the numbers of Māori visitors to New Zealand museums over the last few years suggests that Māori have taken up museum going with enthusiasm.[138] However, this new Māori museum audience does seem to be vulnerable to changing circumstances, as demonstrated by the ups and downs of Māori visitor statistics between 1998 and 2017 (see Appendix A). Evidently Te Papa has to work hard to maintain its indigenous patronage, alongside its other audiences old and new.[139]

Nevertheless, this remarkable reversal of trends leads us to consider what it was about the new museum that accounted for its success with Māori visitors? To answer this question, we have to step back of house again, and explore what was going on with staffing, policy and practice that made Te Papa so important for Māori people, and a world leader that would show the way forward for museums of anthropology.

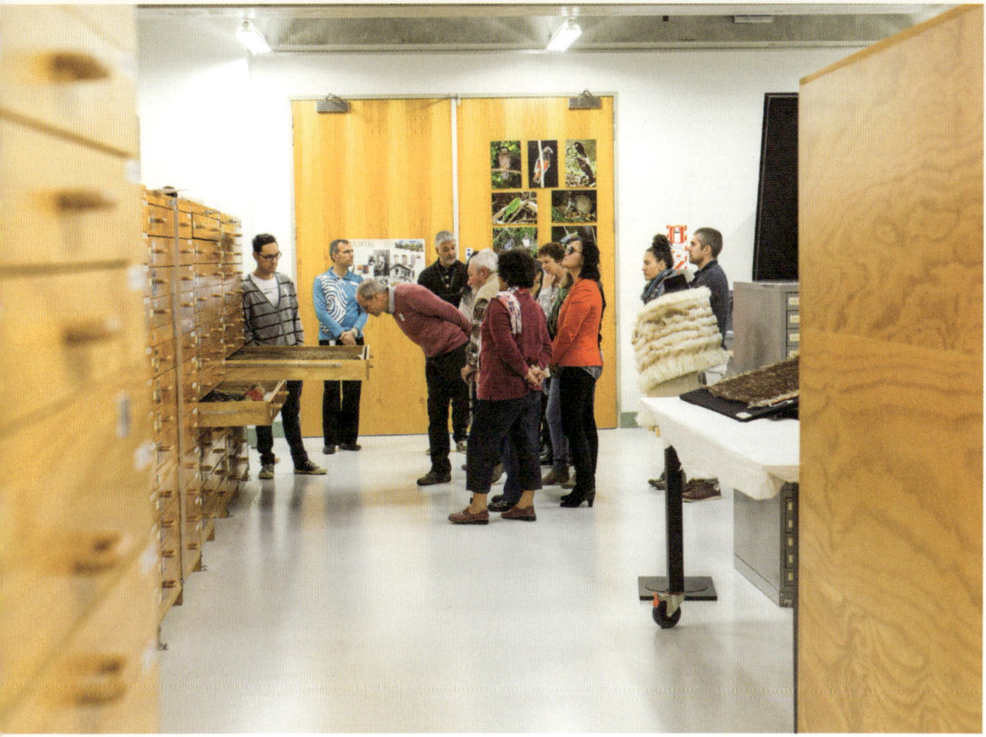

1.

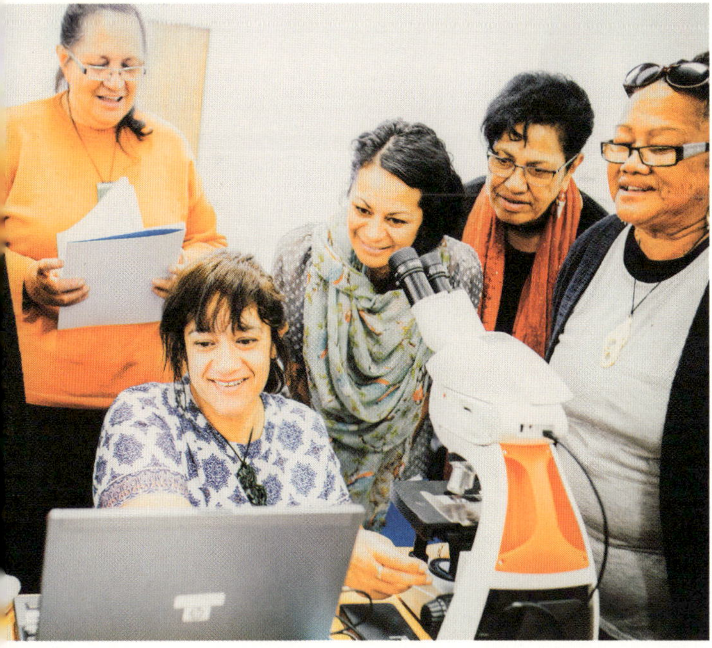

2.

1.
Te Papa open day visitors in Te Whare Pora o Hineteiwaiwa, the Māori textile storeroom.

2.
Te Papa's Bicultural Science researcher Hokimate Harwood (centre) leading a feather identification workshop at Whanganui Regional Museum, 2016.

04.

biculturalism and beyond

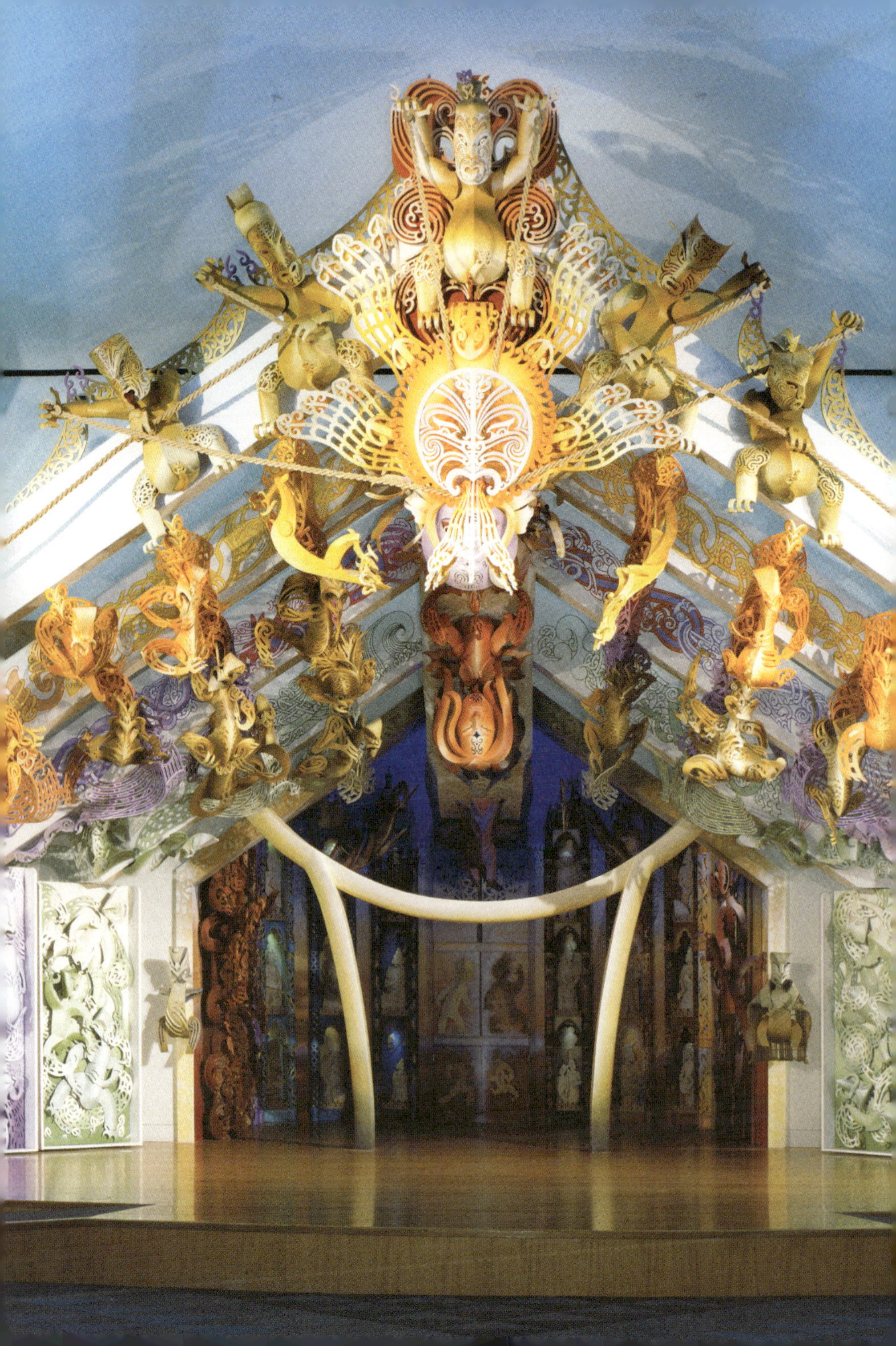

Moving on from the museum's opening exhibitions in 1998 and its success with visitors, this chapter explores what was going on behind the scenes that led particularly to the successful public engagement with Māori audiences, usually under-represented among museum visitors. Looking at the work of Māori staff in five different areas of the museum reveals where 'bicultural' museum practice was and is most active: policy, management, staff, collections and exhibitions. Throughout the text I draw on my own previous published work, primary and secondary sources including annual reports, policy statements, correspondence, documents and intranet resources, fleshed out by interviews and informal conversations with staff and my own first-hand observation while working at Te Papa from 1996 to 2000 and subsequent visits as a researcher.[1]

As noted in the Introduction, over the last thirty years the relationship between Māori and museums has been transformed: Māori have moved from being presented as colonised subjects whose captured material culture was displayed according to alien frameworks, to active audiences for exhibitions of their culture that incorporated their perspectives.

From outsiders to insiders, Māori are now working within museums as staff and board members, as well as being influential stakeholders and visitors. They have moved beyond models of consultation and collaboration to becoming active patrons, to an extent rarely seen with other indigenous peoples.[2]

This change reflects a wider shift in New Zealand society from the 1980s, commensurate with the settlement of claims through the Waitangi Tribunal, the growth of the Māori population and the strengthening of Māori political representation. This social and political context is reflected within the organisational culture of the national museum. Here I provide an anatomy of that culture, exploring the ways in which it is inflected by Māori ideas and ways of doing things. In this way, the chapter surveys developments before and after 1998, and up to the present.

POLICY MATTERS

Policy frameworks are often seen as dry and abstract, but they reflect what an organisation sees as important. Policy really does matter. At Te Papa, below the higher level where the founding Act and mission set the institutional direction, a series of policies developed over a number of years give organisational expression to biculturalism. It is one of five corporate principles, along with 'speaking with authority' (including mātauranga Māori),[3] acting as a 'waharoa' (gateway) to New Zealand's heritage, and the 'mana taonga' principle, which recognises 'the role of communities in enhancing the care and understanding of collections and taonga'.[4]

The policy of biculturalism itself has gone through several versions over 20 years. It is described as a 'partnership'. Alluding to the Treaty as well as to the international context for the rights of indigenous peoples, the policy acknowledges the 'unique' position of Māori as tangata whenua, and calls for Māori 'participation in the governance, management, and operation' of the museum.[5] Policy analyst Cath Nesus, who developed this and many of the other policies at Te Papa, has written that active relationships with iwi are the key to activating biculturalism, putting policy into practice. Biculturalism 'at work' required a commitment from staff and management, a connection to iwi, and capability in terms of skills, resources and money before it could be translated into operational practices. Connections with iwi were facilitated by four key factors: the concept of mana taonga, the iwi relationship strategy, the iwi exhibition programme, and Te Papa's 'living marae' Rongomaraeroa.[6]

When I spoke to individual staff at Te Papa in 2008–09, they came up with a variety of responses when asked to explain their understanding of biculturalism — but several conceptualised it as a Treaty-centred relationship. For example Victoria Esson, now Head of National Services Te Paerangi at Te Papa, is a Pākehā with over twenty years' museum experience, mostly in education and outreach. She described biculturalism as 'adhering to the principles of the Treaty of Waitangi — particularly aspects of equity (rather than equality), self-management/rangatiratanga, reasonable cooperation and redress'. She added: 'The partnership is between tangata whenua and tangata tiriti — all other people of New Zealand — and it is *not* multiculturalism!'[7]

However, despite widespread goodwill and commitment to the ideas of social justice behind biculturalism, it does appear more and more to be an idea whose time has come and gone (even though many Pākehā still think of relations with Māori within this framework). At the end of this chapter I consider other more recent formulations, in museums and in wider society, for articulating the relationship between Māori and Pākehā/other New Zealanders. As far as Te Papa is now concerned, the key Māori concept that has been driving policy and practice is mana taonga.

The concept of mana taonga was developed by Api Mahuika in 1989–90, when he led the Māori advisory group Ngā Kaiwawao (see Chapter 1). It was endorsed by the board in 1992, and became a corporate principle in 2003. Mana taonga is the power and authority arising from and pertaining to taonga. This word *taonga* has a complex genealogy but in modern times it has come to be interpreted as 'cultural heritage'; it refers to a broad range of tangible and intangible resources, from tribal heirlooms like carvings to natural resources such as fishing grounds, cultural practices and beliefs.[8] The word *mana* (power, authority, reputation, respect) has been added to *taonga*, resulting in a powerful idea that not only captures the efficacy of these objects in museum collections, but also encapsulates indigenous ownership and management rights to this cultural heritage.

As Kaihautū (Māori co-director) Arapata Hakiwai and former Te Papa staff member Philipp Schorch argue, mana taonga is an indigenous principle that allows museums to develop a 'structured process of engagement with its communities' by recognising the 'living relationships' between taonga and their communities of origin.[9]

According to the museum's annual reports, mana taonga 'affirms and acknowledges the spiritual and cultural connections of the people to taonga or treasures'.[10] Cath Nesus wrote that it 'provides iwi and communities with the right to define how taonga within Te Papa should be cared for and managed in accordance with their tikanga or custom'.[11] The concept was partly a pragmatic solution to the problem of enabling nationwide tribal involvement in a national museum alongside local tangata whenua (that is to say, the local iwi who have 'mana whenua' or customary jurisdiction over that particular region). It should be noted that it has been disputed by some Māori critics, who argued that it usurps a traditional practice and overrides local tribal authority with a government mandate.[12] But as Te Taru White of Te Arawa explained at the Museums Aotearoa Conference in 2005, when he was Te Papa's Kaihautū, a national museum has to respect the place of iwi and their mana whenua, but cannot have a relationship only with local iwi. As he put it bluntly, 'Te Arawa don't want to go through Te Āti Awa to get to their own taonga.'[13]

According to current Kaihautū Arapata Hakiwai, mana taonga recognises that Māori people should have access to their collections on the basis of the relationships they have with this living ancestral heritage, and they should therefore be involved in their care and management internally as well as participating in exhibitions and public programmes externally.[14] In this formulation, then, the community *outside* the museum becomes a participant *within* the museum alongside professionals. Interestingly, the concept of mana taonga has now been extended to other non-Māori collections in Te Papa, to other museums (see below), and even overseas.[15]

In summary, mana taonga effectively reverses the universal European assumption of possession, the notion that museums have the objects, and that they deal with external communities (who are on the outside) through professionals (who are on the inside). Therefore mana taonga is a fundamental challenge to the very idea of the western collection-based museum. Most museums in New Zealand now say that they merely look after taonga, which belong to the community of interest. Iwi, hapū and whānau (tribe, subtribe and extended family) now have a stake in internal management, care and interpretation of *their* taonga, and museums are having to respond to their demands for access and control.

Māori staff at Te Papa feel that the policy empowers them to do their work within the museum, and move beyond the parameters of the museum to work directly with Māori communities outside the institution. The concept continues to be applied to a broad range of activity at Te Papa, which includes collections management, exhibitions, research, events, publications and even the auction process. Its most public expression is seen in the ongoing iwi exhibitions co-curated with a number of tribes. Less well known, but equally important, is the repatriation of human remains through a special unit, Karanga Aotearoa,[16] and an ambitious global digital repatriation project that aims to reconnect taonga in overseas museums and private collections with tribal communities in Aotearoa New Zealand.[17]

Another key policy at Te Papa is mātauranga Māori. This was first developed in the mid 1990s in response to debates within the museum project while developing exhibitions such as *Mountains to Sea* and *Awesome Forces*, where Māori understandings of the natural world were presented alongside western knowledge. It was felt that Māori needed to articulate a parallel framework to support their research and interpretation in the form of exhibitions, just as Māori academics in universities were conducting research that was equivalent to that of Pākehā colleagues in a range of disciplines. In 2004 a strategy document stated that mātauranga Māori encompassed both a Māori world view and the knowledge that it contained. 'Mātauranga Māori,' it declared, 'is a dynamic and evolving system of knowledge used by tangata whenua to explain, interpret and understand the world in which they live.'[18]

In 2006–07 National Services Te Paerangi released a resource guide and discussion paper based on research undertaken by Ngāti Raukawa scholar Te Ahukaramū Charles Royal, who now works at Te Papa as Director Ngā Manu Atarau.[19] Helpfully, he explained that mātauranga (knowledge) should be distinguished from mōhiotanga (understanding) and māramatanga (enlightenment). It is a modern term that refers not just to traditional knowledge, both esoteric and common, but also to *new* knowledge actively created today within a Māori paradigm but also in response to outside influences. Mātauranga includes a range of perspectives on knowledge and knowing, and exists on three interrelated levels as: a body of knowledge (expertise), a system of knowledge or epistemology (world view), and the dissemination of that knowledge (learning).[20]

In the section on collection care and management below, I describe in the words of working professionals how these customary concepts guide the handling, storage, transport, documentation and display of taonga. These practices, or tikanga taonga, are an evolving aspect of kaitiakitanga (stewardship, guardianship) subject to debate, personal preference and regional variation. Royal warns against codifying tikanga into a series of prescriptive do's and don'ts, and recommends that understandings and applications of Māori concepts should be founded on an 'evidential base'.[21] He points to the 'contemporary dynamism' of mātauranga Māori, reminding us that tikanga are living and evolving cultural practices, and recommends further research on 'contemporary tikanga in relation to taonga in order to discover the perspectives and behaviours that are relevant to museum practice'.[22]

MĀORI MUSEUM MANAGEMENT

The reader will see from the policies discussed above that Te Papa has a regulatory framework shaped by Māori philosophies. However, at the level of governance the museum's Act does not actually mention the Treaty of Waitangi, although the board *is* required by the Act to ensure that Te Papa 'expresses and recognises the mana and significance of Māori, European and other major traditions'.[23] Although there are always two Māori trustees, Te Papa does not have a bicultural governance structure, like some museums.

Furthermore, there has been criticism that it does not recognise the local people Te Āti Awa as tangata whenua. Local leader Ngatata Love expressed disappointment that they 'have no say' at the board table.[24] Yet the board has adopted the same bicultural policy as used internally, and professes in its annual report that 'Te Papa is a bicultural organisation, and as such, the Board acknowledges the importance of the Treaty of Waitangi, particularly the partnership implicit in the Treaty'.[25]

At Te Papa, senior managers are required to demonstrate their commitment to biculturalism by attending pōwhiri, dawn ceremonies for the opening of exhibitions and events on the marae.[26] Meetings and other aspects of everyday work are usually marked by karakia (prayers), mihi (verbal acknowledgement) and waiata (song). International museum visitors often express surprise to see so many managers present at Māori events, and to witness the CEO make a speech with a short introduction in Māori, regarded as a normal part of how things are done at Te Papa. This attendance is not simply 'dial-a-pōwhiri', as Māori staff take note of who turns up to events such as repatriation ceremonies.

There is always concern that there could be more Māori staff at management level, but at various times in the 2000s there were no fewer than four Māori at senior management level: Te Taru White (Kaihautū), Jim Te Puni (Director Māori Strategy), Arapata Hakiwai (Director Mātauranga Māori) and Jonathan Mane-Wheoki (Director of Art and Collection Services).

One major aspect of bicultural leadership is the Kaihautū position (literally the navigator of the 'waka' that is the museum). In August 1995, the board approved a new management structure, with the Kaihautū engaging in dialogue with iwi in a position 'analogous' to the CEO. The minutes noted that the position 'gave substance to the concept of te tino rangatiratanga as expressed in the museum's bicultural policy'.[27] Cliff Whiting said that the agreement was that he and Cheryll Sotheran 'would work together across everything that happens in the museum': 'Cliff and Cheryll' would generally do things together, whether it was official duties, committee meetings, or social occasions. It was difficult to work out the different roles, however, and Whiting spoke of a 'tendency for everything Māori to come to me'. But he added, 'Even

Māori think that the "chief executive" is the boss person, not the Kaihautū, and go to Cheryll.'[28]

Although on the face of it this dual management structure represented a big commitment to the idea of bicultural partnership enshrined in the Treaty, there have been setbacks in the relationship, which depends to a large extent on the personal styles of the different people in these roles over the years. Current and former staff have been critical of the fact that the majority of Māori staff report to the CEO rather than through an independent management structure under the Kaihautū. However, following CEO Seddon Bennington's sudden death in mid 2009, Kaihautū Michelle Hippolite, an experienced manager, was acting CEO for a full year before Michael Houlihan arrived in mid 2010. This happened again when Houlihan left and Arapata Hakiwai became acting CEO before the arrival of Rick Ellis in 2015.

With Te Taru White, who preceded Hippolite, and CEO Seddon Bennington, it took some time to work out how the relationship would work. For his part, White felt that the Kaihautū position was a laudable attempt to give expression to the idea of partnership, but that when 'push came to shove' there was a gap between appearance and reality. While there is no doubt that Bennington was genuinely committed to working with Māori, as was attested by the tributes paid to him on the marae following his death, it was evident from my interview with him in 2008 that returning to New Zealand after twenty years abroad was not an easy thing — the country had changed radically and the reality of running Te Papa alongside an assertive Māori co-director was a huge challenge.[29]

On the marae at Bennington's tangi, or funeral ceremony, White recalled a story of the conflict between them, to demonstrate openly that they bore no grudges afterwards and had learned to work with one another despite their differences. At one point an attempt was made to draw up a 'Relationship Charter', an agreement between White and Bennington, which was signed at a public ceremony on the marae.[30] Despite all these efforts to work together, however, 'the big question was, and still is,' White said, 'can you share power?'[31]

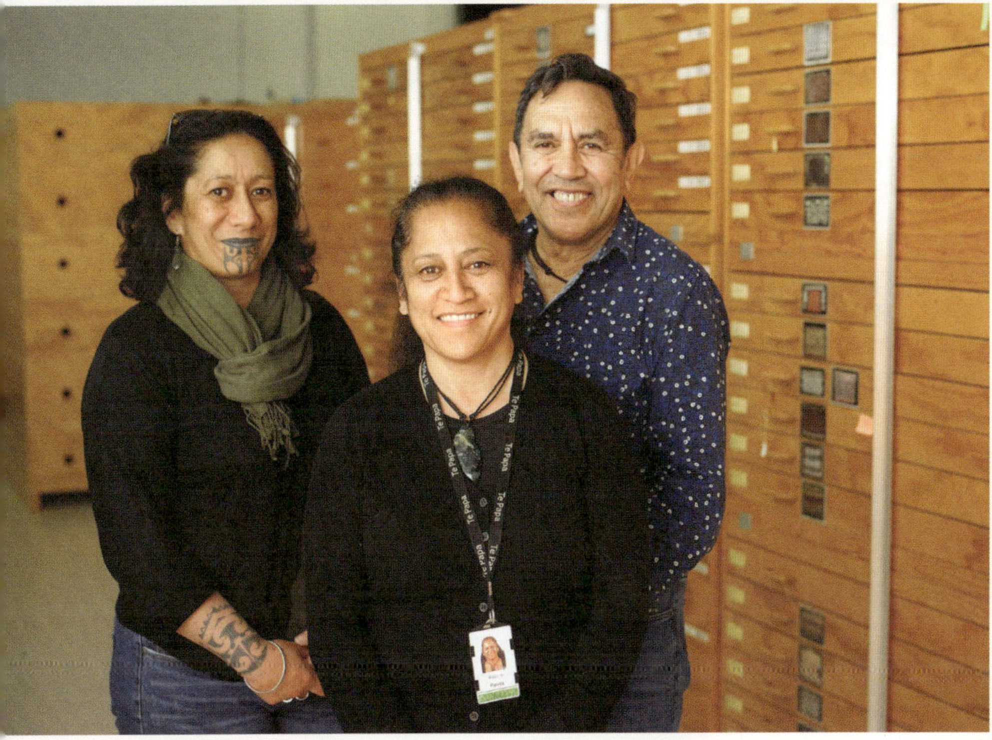

1.

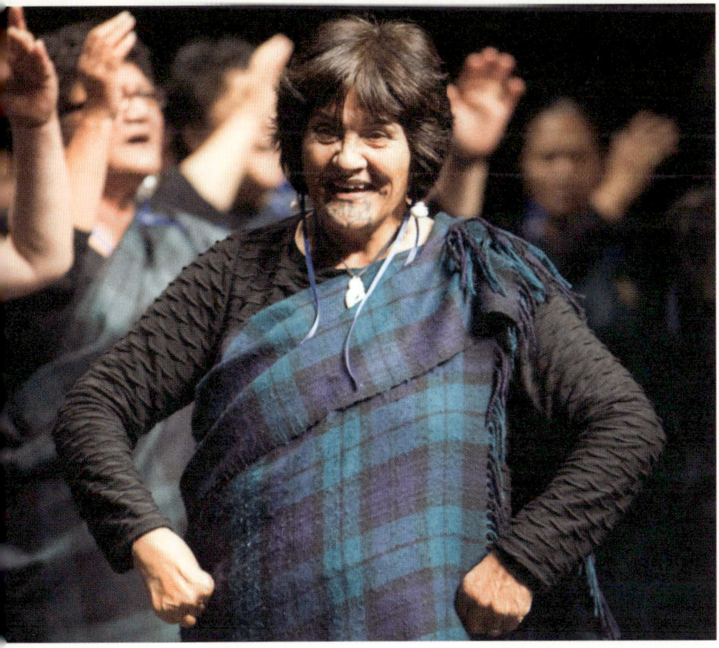

2.

1.

Kaitiaki Māori, or collection managers, (from left) Lisa Ward, Moana Parata and Mark Sykes.

2.

Ataarangi Poutapu from Waikato Taniwharau o Tainui performs at Te Papa's kaumātua kapa haka festival in 2015.

MĀORI STAFFING

I have often heard visitors remark on the high number of Māori working back of house at Te Papa, and the strong Māori ethos pervading the organisational culture. Although research suggests this is stronger in some teams than others, nevertheless Te Papa is known for being a 'Māori' space, at least among Pākehā.[32] Whether it is hearing the Māori language spoken and used in signage and documents, cultural awareness training for staff and classes to learn waiata and te reo Māori, or the active music and performing arts groups, it is immediately evident that this is a place where there is a living Māori organisational culture. All of this is expressed forcefully at the frequent pōwhiri and other events on the marae, where Māori staff come together along with Pākehā colleagues to welcome visitors, and show off the strength and vitality of oratory and the performing arts among staff and supporting iwi.

How does the staffing structure reflect Māori values? At the former National Museum in Buckle Street in the late 1980s and early 1990s, managers such as John Yaldwyn, Michael Volkerling and Alan Baker responded to calls for change by reorganising the old ethnology department and setting up an independent Māori unit (see Chapter 1).[33] This has taken various forms over the last 20 years, but today the mātauranga Māori curatorial team sits within the Collections, Research and Learning directorate. The head of this team at the time of writing is Dr Wayne Ngata, a scholar in his own right who has extensive experience working with education, tribal development and language revitalisation, often through museums.[34] Outside this curatorial team there are Māori staff across a range of units including collection management, hosts and other front-of-house staff, and those involved in learning, facilities, conservation, HR and so on.

Many of these Māori staff meet together as a group independent of their organisational areas, creating a Māori whānau within the larger structure. Some areas have few or no Māori staff. But others, such as iwi relationships and repatriation, are predominantly Māori and, while working within the overall museum structure, they are able to operate within shared values, practices and processes common to Māori communities and organisations.[35] In the next chapter, I profile some of the Māori professionals working back of house.

Much of the effort in bicultural development has gone into training non-Māori staff in Māori values, language and practices to equip them to operate in a 'bicultural environment'. In addition to this training, staff have access to resources that explain aspects of policy and practice. The intranet materials explain that not everything in the institution *has* to be bicultural, but the 'important thing is that the process by which we generate ideas, make decisions and implement initiatives is inclusive, rather than whether the output is always visibly bicultural'.[36]

As staff pointed out to me during interviews, Te Papa is unusual because the number and assertiveness of Māori staff make developing bicultural models easier than in institutions that have few if any Māori staff. In fact, for some Māori working at Te Papa the recognition of this 'staunch' Māori presence has been valuable because it meant Māori ways of operating were accepted by the whole organisation. Collection manager Moana Davey made this clear, telling me:

> I think the good thing about Te Papa is that as far as museums are concerned it's quite strong in its bicultural practice. Because there's a big team of Kaitiaki Māori [Māori guardians] there, you can just take it as second nature almost . . . most staff as far as I knew took it for granted there was going to be pōwhiri, that there was going to be karakia, mihi whakatau [welcome speech], waiata . . .[37]

For others, however, the sign that these practices had become mainstream was that they became more than a matter of protocol. They were naturalised; Pākehā not only supported tikanga but also actively observed it and participated in it. Collection manager Dion Peita felt that rather than having to 'always peg something on biculturalism, [mocking voice] because we're bicultural . . . you just want to make these things as usable as possible . . . by naturalising it, just making it more ordinary'. He gave the example of the Hau Manu group, made up of Māori and Pākehā staff, who play wind instruments at welcome ceremonies. 'So for instance, when we do go upstairs to do mihi whakatau the first thing you see is a non-Māori [woman] . . . she'll grab a putātara and we're off . . . You know that's great, it's becoming normalised as in "our way of doing things".'

It is sometimes seen as a problem when non-Māori participate in tikanga Māori, a risk of appropriation, but there is an acceptance by many Māori professionals in the sector of a role for non-Māori professionals in maintaining tikanga. When he worked at Te Papa as an exhibition interpreter, Karl Johnstone faced this head-on by hiring non-Māori for what were seen as 'Māori jobs'. On one occasion, he and Māori writer and kaumātua (elder) Te Ikanui Kapa of Te Aupōuri (aka Uncle Fisher) hired a Pākehā woman to teach te reo Māori. 'To me it is not really an issue about whether you're Māori or not,' Johnstone said. 'It's about Māori capability.' When they hired Joan Costello for this role they considered the audience (mostly Pākehā), her advanced skills, and the fact that she'd taught in kura kaupapa (Māori immersion schools). 'She had the right āhua, the wairua [feeling, spirit],' said Johnstone, 'and quite frankly was the right person for the job and has proved very successful.'

Some Kaitiaki Māori see kaitiakitanga of taonga Māori as something that is not so much based on ethnicity as on cultural competence, values and practices. Dion Peita explained that the etiquette of starting a meeting with a karakia (prayer), usually the preserve of a respected elder, could be done by anyone, including Pākehā staff. 'Although it's a Māori activity, whenever I go into a meeting with our exhibition team, Simon Garrett [a Pākehā] says, "Before we start we gonna have a karakia,"' Peita recalled. 'The next step,' he added, 'is rather than have Dion do the karakia, to have Simon do the karakia.'

For most Māori staff, it was not a problem to share their culture and teach their Pākehā colleagues in museum settings or even overseas visitors at public functions. They did not feel that this was 'selling out' at all. Te Taru White explained his role speaking to international visitors, showing VIPs around, and even participating in whakangahau or entertainment on the marae or at functions and events. In his view, he was not going along to 'poke his tongue out' (pūkana) in a superficial 'touristy' way, but aimed to present an experience that was a seamless part of the bicultural values Te Papa espoused. A skilled

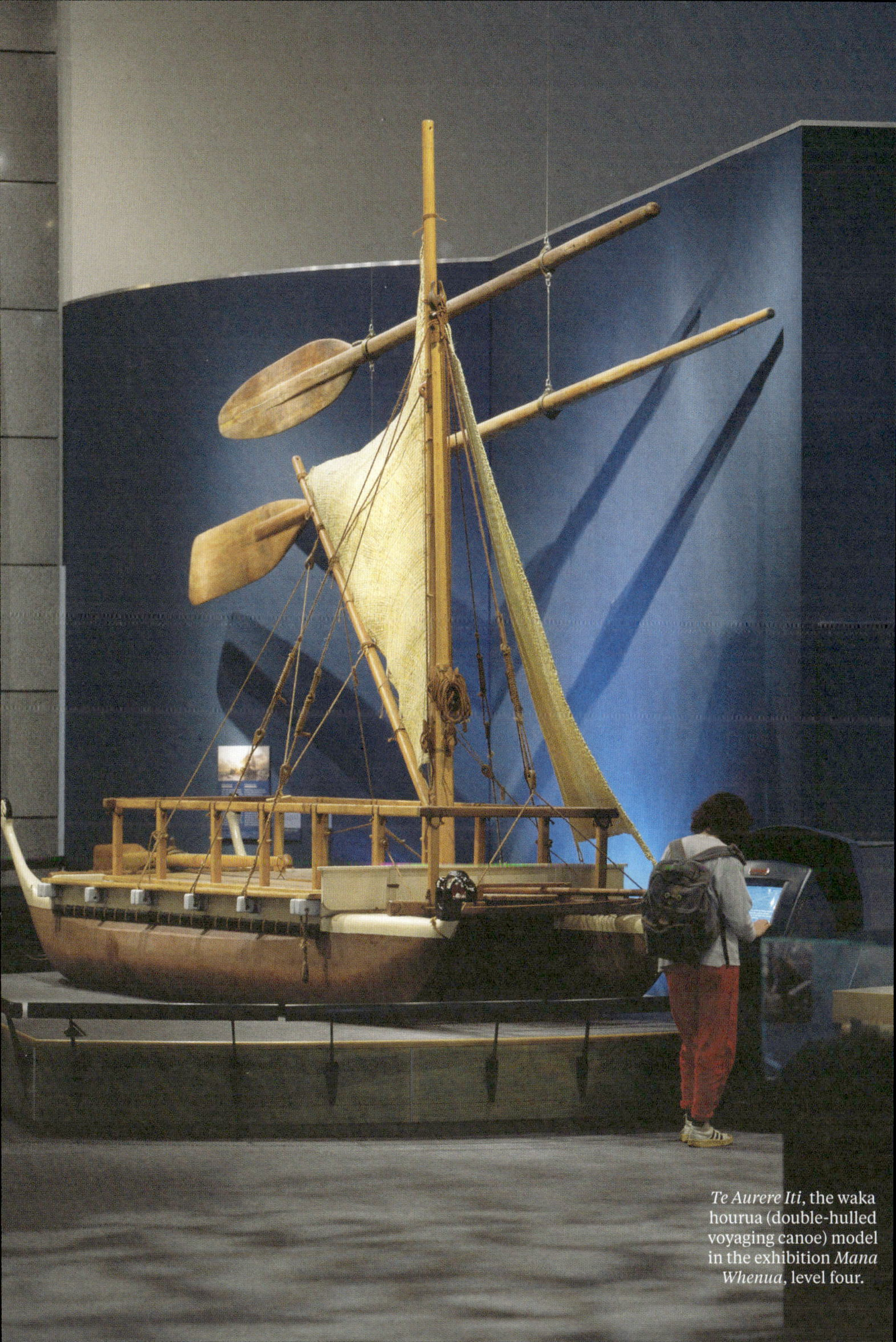

Te Aurere Iti, the waka hourua (double-hulled voyaging canoe) model in the exhibition *Mana Whenua*, level four.

multi-lingual orator, from a tribe (Te Arawa) with a long tradition of hosting visitors in Rotorua, it was usually White rather than the CEO who made speeches at exhibition openings and public events, regardless of the topic, expressing a Māori perspective as a demonstration of biculturalism. 'I was really proud as a Māori face not to be a tekoteko [carved ridgepole on a house],' he said, but to 'be able to articulate the kaupapa [topic/agenda] in both of our languages . . . to get to the heart of the exhibition'.

KAITIAKITANGA: MĀORI COLLECTION CARE

This section summarises perhaps the most significant area of museum work at Te Papa where a Māori museology is emerging. In Māori collection care and management the following precepts have been widely accepted and practised since the 1990s:

- Taonga seen as living ancestors not inert artefacts
- Collection managers understood as kaitiaki or guardians looking after taonga and making them accessible rather than being gatekeepers
- Collections managed and cared for in a culturally appropriate manner guided by tikanga Māori
- Collections classified, arranged and documented using a Māori philosophical framework
- Different approaches to handling, storage and access according to Māori values and beliefs, including tapu and noa, mauri, whakapapa
- Cultural restrictions observed in terms of water, food, blood and death (human remains)
- Ritual practices observed, i.e. karakia, mihi whakatau
- Stored collections made more accessible to iwi physically, virtually and spiritually
- As well as preservation and conservation, the overall goal of museum

collections is their reconnection with the living culture of present day communities.[38]

Former curator Awhina Tamarapa has described the changes in protocol for managing, handling and storage of objects that by the mid 1990s were universally understood and treated as taonga.[39] Staff observed restrictions such as keeping food away from taonga, water bowls were placed near collection stores to allow people to remove tapu (whakanoa), women who were menstruating or pregnant absented themselves from the collection stores, and from time to time fresh green leaves were laid next to taonga on display.

The green leaves were usually the things that indicated, to Pākehā visitors, that a different set of values was operating in Māori displays in New Zealand museums. According to the late Betty Rewi, a kuia (elder) who worked as a collection manager, this practice was derived from the Tainui custom of putting wreaths of leaves on the heads of mourners at tangihanga; they first appeared at the National Museum during the exhibition *Te Maori: Te hokinga mai* in 1986, and became standard practice in the Maori Hall from approximately 1988. At the National Art Gallery in 1991, the same practices were adopted with the presentation of the recently purchased Māori portraits by Charles Goldie, Pākehā artworks that were effectively displayed as taonga.

In collection stores, the laws of tapu and noa were recognised in the ways in which collections were managed: everyday objects were kept apart from those for ceremonial use, things connected with food or agriculture were separated from weapons and other items associated with blood and death, and kōiwi tangata and toi moko (skeletal material, preserved heads and other human remains) were placed in a separate wāhi tapu (sacred/restricted place).[40] Kaitiaki Māori at Te Papa regard tapu and noa as common sense, and are heartened that their non-Māori colleagues understand and follow these practices on an everyday level. As former collection manager Moana Davey explained, 'Banning kai from Māori collection stores is . . . in line with good conservation practice anyway, just like you wouldn't eat your sandwich beside an oil painting!' When all collection managers from every department shared a common office in the new building, it was a relatively straightforward matter to ban food and drink from the working spaces, and the adjacent photography studio, in order to make areas safe/unrestricted (noa) for taonga.

A key aspect of museum collection management is what to call things and how to organise them. Curator Dougal Austin of Ngāi Tahu was involved in the process of devising a new classification system for taonga in the early 1990s. For example, there was no detailed European classification for the Māori cloaks in the collection, and though some museums had used Māori names often they were wrong. The system Austin devised was based on the work of the late Pākehā textiles curator at Auckland Museum Mick Pendergrast, but was more culturally appropriate and intuitive. The phrase 'kaitaka paepaeroa', for example, indicated that the object was a paepaeroa within the group of cloaks known as kaitaka.

Austin also spent two years working on Māori classifications for the Ke EMu database, introduced in 2005, starting with weaponry, and going on to whare (houses), and then fishing. This last category was a huge job, with kupenga alone (nets) a huge group of artefacts in itself. Māori names were also used for storerooms containing taonga: the former greenstone room was called Tatau Pounamu, the large carving store was named Ahuru Mōwai, and the weaving area Te Whare Pora o Hine Te Iwaiwa. This renaming process 'just seemed the natural thing to do for us', Austin explained. 'Once you name it you're classifying it within a cultural framework . . . It's moving away from western academic practice, from treating it as a specimen to seeing it as a taonga in its own right.'

The identification of taonga according to iwi and hapū origin has been standard practice since it was popularised in the *Te Maori* exhibition and catalogue in the 1980s.[41] Because of this close relationship with tribes, even when the provenance of a taonga is not known, Kaitiaki Māori at Te Papa today describe their work with Māori collections in terms of 'tikanga taonga' (roughly, Māori practices for taonga). Collection manager Moana Parata of Ngāti Toa learned her job by observing what the 'aunties' did — Auntie Betty (Betty Rewi, Tainui) and Auntie Bessie (Irihāpeti Walters, Ngāti Porou), the elderly kuia who worked at Te Papa with the collections. In her work with professionals and university students of museum and heritage studies at annual wānanga (workshops) at Hongoeka Marae, Parata explains how she cares for taonga and engages with iwi who visit the collections, often referring back to the advice and guidance of 'the aunties'.

In the same way, Moana Davey learned tikanga taonga from Aunty Bessie when she worked at Te Papa. 'That's something that's hugely important to any major institutions that have taonga, because kaumātua give that foundation of security and knowledge,' Davey recalled. 'Basically they're like the ultimate in guardians, they safekeep not only the taonga but the staff, [especially] junior staff.'

Kaitiaki maintain strict observances in the presence of taonga. Collection manager Lisa Ward explains how she observes tikanga every day through karakia (prayers) to clear the way for her work with the taonga. After handling them she sprinkles herself with water to remove any residual tapu. 'Karakia is always first on my list,' she told me. 'I am the first to arrive in the morning just before 7 o'clock. I come straight up here and I have karakia in here, in the dark . . . when the building is still quiet. So that is my way to start my day, setting everything in place for me.'

Ward showed me how she handles taonga. 'Personally myself I try and put as much care and aroha into the moving of taonga from A to B,' she said. Here the word 'aroha' refers to the loving compassion and affectionate regard that Māori feel for their loved ones and for taonga as living things. Dougal Austin listed the procedures that he followed on a daily basis when working with taonga: don't step over or disrespect taonga, don't swear, if you cut yourself and bleed then clean it up quickly, and always use water bowls when leaving storerooms, sprinkling yourself with water to remove tapu. He explained how tapu 'can be transferred from an object to a person through contact', and that water 'neutralises and normalises' you back to an ordinary state and 'makes it safe'.

The adoption of tikanga in museum collection management not only enables Māori staff to work with collections within what are considered the bounds of 'cultural safety', but it has also had the positive effect of making Māori visitors more comfortable with the way the museum goes about storing and looking after taonga. Large numbers of iwi groups go on back-of-house tours of the Māori collection, and according to the kaitiaki I spoke to they like seeing 'their taonga' and are reassured that they are being 'kept warm'. This notion of warmth is regarded as an essential element in the care of taonga, and refers to the bond between people and treasures that is activated and maintained when they come together.[42] Lisa Ward reflected on how attached to the taonga she had become. Once she discussed this with Aunty Betty. 'One thing she did say to me was that "You'll find, dear, that when you're in that position you'll become very, very protective of the taonga." I said: "Really?" and she goes "Yeah". And I *have* [laughs], I really, really have!'

Over the 20 years, collection managers at Te Papa have made collections more accessible and visible for visiting groups, not just through culturally appropriate care and safe handling but through improved space and layout in the storerooms. Certainly the shift from substandard storage in the basement at Buckle Street to the state-of-the-art facilities at Cable Street in the late 1990s made this kind of access possible. However, conservators sometimes complain about this public access because of the risk of tours in storage areas leading to damage, and insect and mould infestations.[43] Another problem has arisen when taonga from the collection are used in ceremonies on the marae and other public activities such as outreach, loans for tangi, graduation ceremonies, Waitangi Tribunal hearings, etc. The tension between use/reactivation of tribal links and preservation is acute, but most Māori professionals feel this is part of the natural process of 'performing' taonga to revivify connections to whenua and whakapapa.[44]

What are taonga? Much ink has been spilt trying to describe this most complex and elusive of Māori concepts. For this book it is appropriate to express the views of current Māori professionals who work with taonga on an everyday basis at Te Papa.[45] Former curator Huhana Smith defines taonga as: 'Anything tangible or intangible to do with accumulated value with regards to people's relations to it, including objects, stories, whenua, awa, in a whole of person, whole of entity context . . .' She adds that Māori notions of taonga are 'in line with international standards of indigenous cultural property'.[46] Dougal Austin has an equally expansive usage: 'A taonga is something that you hold as being precious . . . It's not just a physical treasure, it can also be intangible such as genealogy, traditional stories, that have been passed down from ancestors.'

Curator Matiu Baker defines taonga broadly as everything 'from personal possessions to land', which are 'all bound up with identity'. Compared to a non-Māori curator working with these objects, he felt that Māori understand that dealing with taonga means that they have a 'tapu aspect' that makes them 'more than historical artefacts'. Taonga are beautiful things, and have aesthetic values, but are also 'associated with people', and are 'locaters in time and space'. According to Baker, 'Māori curators see stories and people and not just things.' He gives the example of his Ngāti Toa ancestor Te Rauparaha's renowned taiaha *Kimihia* (housed in the taonga Māori collections), which often produces a 'powerful internal emotional reaction' in him and other descendants of the famous warrior chief.[47]

EXHIBITIONS, REPATRIATION, CURATORSHIP

I have dealt in an earlier chapter with the collaborative process of developing the Māori exhibition *Mana Whenua*. This was the result of Māori curators working *with* Māori communities, becoming facilitators of a process of community engagement rather than authoritative experts on an academic discipline. Since the museum's opening, Māori staff at Te Papa have been involved in other large temporary or touring exhibitions such as the natural environment exhibition *Blood Earth Fire: Whāngai Whenua Ahi Kā* on level three; the contemporary art exhibition *Taiāwhio: Continuity and Change*; *Mauriora: Treasures from the Museum of New Zealand*, which toured to Japan; *Whales / Tohorā*, which toured the US; and *E Tū Ake: Māori Standing Strong*, which went to France, Mexico and Canada (see Appendix A for additional exhibitions).

The iwi exhibitions follow this same process, with key museum staff in the positions of concept developers, interpreters and designers working with designated iwi representatives, and the internal museum review process being matched by an iwi steering group. Whereas *Mana Whenua* was organised in consultation with different iwi around one major taonga, reflecting the relationships forged at a higher level through Kaihautū Cliff Whiting and Ngā Kaiwawao, the iwi exhibitions resulted from a more extensive collaboration between the museum and iwi. Iwi exhibitions include: Rongowhakaata, opening in late 2017; Ngāti Toa, 2014–17; Tainui, 2010–13; Ngāi Tahu, 2006–09; Whanganui Iwi, 2003–06; Tūhoe, 2001–03; Te Aupōuri, 1999–2001, and Te Āti Awa, 1998–99.[48]

In 2004 Kaihautū Te Taru White described the *Whanganui Iwi* exhibition as a partnership. 'They contributed the mātauranga,' he commented, 'we contributed the infrastructure and exhibition support.'[49] The exhibition *Mō Tātou*, which dealt with the Ngāi Tahu people of the South Island, was another successful partnership for museum and iwi, according to research.[50] With themes such as 'tenacity' and 'innovation', the display was diverse, contemporary and forward-looking, featuring a range of contemporary art as well as old taonga. More than 2000 people turned up to the opening of the exhibition, and joined in a celebration of their culture in a full programme of events and activities. As Arapata Hakiwai's own research shows, through programmes like this museums can help iwi by actively supporting their cultural and social development.[51]

Each iwi exhibition in the last 20 years has been different, in part because the experience of tribes around the country is so diverse. More recently the Ngāti Toa exhibition *Whiti Te Rā* was staged at the national museum at the same time that the tribe's claim was going through the Waitangi Tribunal, and this meant a strong emphasis on identity and politics in their exhibit. A small tribe with a famous history and a very rich legacy of material culture, much of it in private collections, Ngāti Toa were able to display a wealth of treasures such as the greenstone mere *Tuhiwai*, which belonged to their illustrious and feared leader Te Rauparaha in the early nineteenth century.[52] Next up in 2017 was the Rongowhakaata people of Gisborne, whose famous meeting house Te Hau ki Tūranga, currently in the *Mana Whenua* exhibition, will return to their region at the close of the exhibition.

This issue of repatriation is a complex one. Internationally it is sometimes figured as a negative spectre that puts the future of museums at risk, but Māori staff at Te Papa see it as an opportunity not a threat. In this case the famous meeting house, the jewel of the collections since it was confiscated during the wars of the 1860s, was the centre of Rongowhakaata's claim to the Waitangi Tribunal. Lodged in 1989 and heard in 2002, a report on the claim was issued in 2004, and a heads of agreement was signed between Crown and iwi at Te Papa in 2011.

Arapata Hakiwai is positive about the situation despite losing the house, and believes Te Papa has learned many lessons, namely that the long-term and ongoing relationship with the tribe is the most important thing. While the whare has important aesthetic and historical values for the museum, for Rongowhakaata today it is also a platform for the future, articulated in their vision of 'restoration, revitalisation and return'. Plans include a cultural centre and the revival of carving using Te Hau ki Tūranga as a template. This will obviously be a major attraction for cultural tourism, which will provide an economic base for an impoverished and relatively isolated part of the country. While some in the museum world are fearful of what repatriation may bring, Hakiwai argues that, 'We should not be afraid of change . . . Iwi will get stronger economically, culturally, and will be creating their own structures to present themselves and their taonga to the world. I would like to think that enlightened museums can *assist* that process.'[53]

Importantly, Hakiwai sees this process within the larger context of tribal economic development. In the museum's 2016 annual report, he articulated a vision of cultural futures that put museums at the centre of social transformation:

> Helping to build stronger whānau, hapū and iwi primarily through the foundations of culture and identity will not only contribute to a stronger Māori world, but will also help our nation in our understanding of each other. We look forward to working with iwi on their Waitangi claims journey to help build a stronger and better future.[54]

Another hot topic is the repatriation of human remains from international museums, which has been spearheaded by Karanga Aotearoa, a special unit that was set up by the government in 2003 for this purpose.[55]

Guided by an expert group of elders, and working with Māori staff, Karanga Aotearoa works very hard to facilitate the repatriation of Māori and Moriori toi moko and kōiwi back to Te Papa, where they are welcomed home in emotional ceremonies on the marae. If the provenance is unknown and they cannot be returned to iwi for burial, they are respectfully stored in a secure repository for sacred objects. According to Te Herekiekie Herewini, the director of the programme, it is important that the whole process is managed very carefully, from the delicate negotiation with institutions to the handling of the remains, which are regarded as people, not scientific specimens, and as such are accorded the full respect due to revered ancestors.[56]

It should be obvious from the range of things with which Māori staff deal that their brand of curatorship is not confined to the traditional set of skills in scholarly connoisseurship and artefact preservation. They are, at various times, facilitators, cultural workers, social workers, entrepreneurs and project managers. It is only natural that in order to support the quest for tribal self-determination indigenous museum curators cannot operate as disinterested academic observers, who typically reserve the right to select and arrange objects for exhibitions over and above communities. Rather, they must become intimately involved in co-curation of what are effectively political projects aimed at the betterment of those communities. The experience of Māori curators who have been working over the last 20 years at Te Papa reinvents the concept of curatorship as kaitiakitanga, as stewards and guardians in service to their people. As Arapata Hakiwai puts it, Māori see their taonga in museums not as disconnected from the past but rather as enduring symbols of cultural identity that connect the past with the present and future.[57]

Māori curators are also breaking new ground in other areas. Those I interviewed have been keen for a long time to replace *Mana Whenua* and experiment with more diverse, challenging and risky displays. They felt *Mana Whenua* was fine as a cultural and political statement in 1998, but that things have moved on and they need to explore a more contemporary Māori world view — what it means to be iwi, hapū, whānau in the twenty-first century. This redevelopment has been delayed, but plans suggest a range of exciting new approaches that aim to 'mix things up' a bit more.

Former curator Huhana Smith, interviewed in 2009, suggested a community-based research model for a new exhibition that could recreate different 'cultural landscapes' at different sites, an approach that would get away from the constraints of cultural collections and explore the natural world. Other fresh ideas among young curatorial staff include opening up the collecting of contemporary social history and material culture, creating a wider range of objects that would reflect the experience of the predominantly young urban Māori population of today, including everyday things and digital media.[58] Curator Matariki Williams, mindful of the Latin root of the word curator meaning to 'care', sees her task as 'healing' gaps in the collection by acquiring a broader variety of things from Māori life today:

> You can see with our taonga Māori collection at Te Papa the huge influences that previous collectors had. A lot of them have been Pākehā men, and I see these gaps in the collection in relation to children, young people, women, everyday objects from the 20th and 21st Century. So for me as a curator it's those gaps that I want to 'heal', by collecting contemporary culture, collecting born digital objects. By 'healing' I mean that [in the past] Māori were prolific writers, and now they are prolific online, so to not repeat these mistakes from the past is to proactively collect where I see there could be future gaps.[59]

Senior Curator Mātauranga Māori Puawai Cairns has been active in contemporary collecting, including things as varied as Bishop Brian Tamaki's suit, a microphone from Māori Television, and gang patches. She has this to say about future plans:

> I'm always looking for opportunities to transgress those artificial knowledge / discipline boundaries that a museum intuitively guards. The curatorial challenge, in my mind, is to break out of the confined space that is *Mana Whenua* gallery on level four, and to colonise *all* the spaces at

Te Papa and beyond — with loud, distinctive, contradictory Māori voices and stories, that cross time and space. I also want to look beyond biculturalism as an exhibition model, and move towards what I call 'sovereign space', a space that reflects the principles of tino rangatiratanga, where the dialogue is not between Māori and Pākehā but between Māori and Māori.[60]

POST BICULTURALISM

This chapter has documented the innovations in indigenous museology within New Zealand's national museum over more than two decades. More than any other part of the institution, these innovations are world leading in terms of the indigenising of professional practice through Māori concepts like kaitiakitanga and mana taonga.

Te Papa has shown all museums everywhere that there is an opportunity, and a responsibility, to develop closer relationships with native and tribal peoples through better management of their cultural heritage. They can do this, as Te Papa has done, by using indigenous frameworks of art, culture, history, time, space and knowledge. The lessons of Aotearoa are relevant to museums worldwide, not just in post-settler societies. In allowing museum collections to 'make connections' from the outside in, and by putting communities at the centre of institutions, museums can overturn traditional power relations and democratise museology.[61]

While Te Papa has been significant in the museum world, it has also played a crucial role in the Māori world. Arapata Hakiwai argues that the large Māori events and functions that are held at Te Papa are an endorsement from the Māori world of the museum's work. Te Papa was chosen as the venue for the Māori Economic Summit in 2004, and in 2008 a heads of agreement between the Crown and iwi (the 'Aquaculture deal') was signed at Te Papa with 10 iwi, the prime minister and a number of Cabinet ministers. This is a 'huge statement of support and endorsement' from Māori, a recognition that Te Papa is a forum for the nation, and certainly something in the way of a national

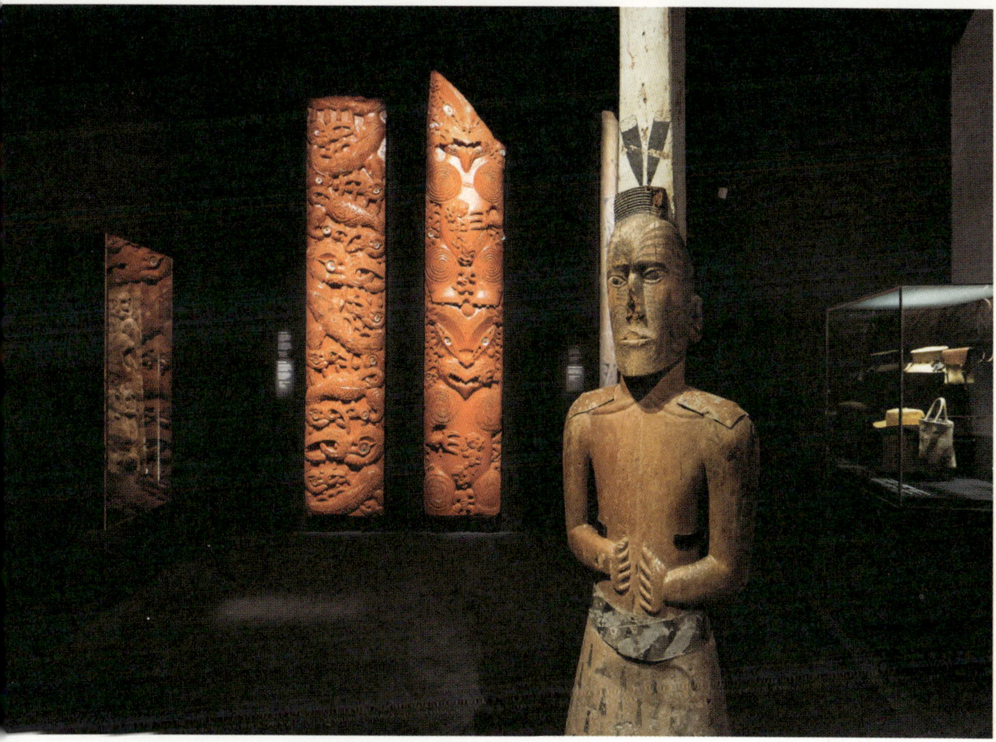

1.

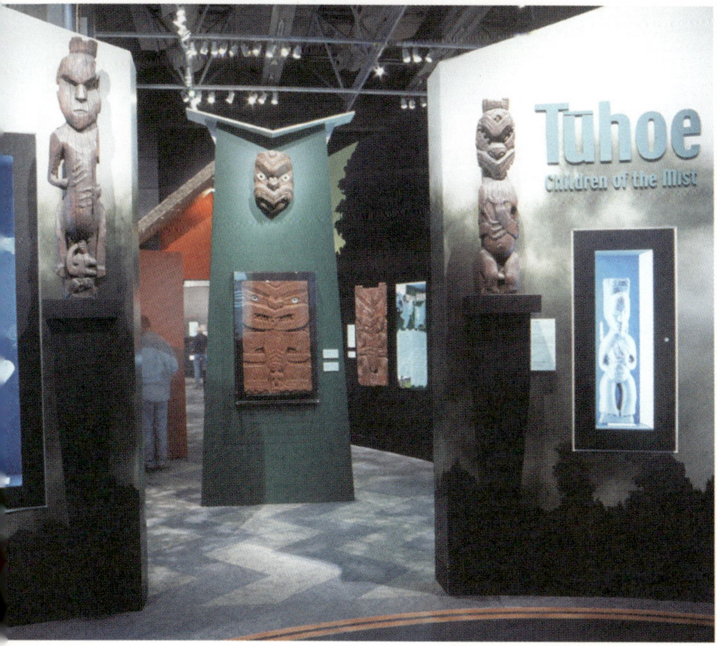

2.

1.
The iwi exhibition *Ko Rongowhakaata: A Story of Light and Shadow*, which opened in 2017.

2.
The iwi exhibition *Tūhoe: Children of the Mist* on display from 2001–03.

marae. Hakiwai points out that 'the way Māori interact with, use and adopt Te Papa, I think shows they are very comfortable with this place . . . in respect to who we are, who works here, our policies and what we stand for as a bicultural museum'.[62]

Many outside commentators see Te Papa as the exemplar of biculturalism, whether they regard that as positive or a somewhat dated paradigm. On a positive note, academics Brigitte Bönisch-Brednich and Richard Hill have described Te Papa as 'biculturally conceived, executed and operated'.[63] Māori staff inside the building are more cautious. Hakiwai has often said Te Papa is bicultural 'in intention', or that it is 'becoming bicultural'.[64] Academic critics, for whom biculturalism is virtually an industry in its own right, often see it as a state ideology imposed on the population in the service of nation-building.[65] Writer Dominic O'Sullivan concludes that biculturalism is 'a colonial relationship' whereas self-determination, which is 'an expression of tino rangatiratanga', aims to 'decolonise Māori/Crown relationships'.[66]

In response to the hybrid urban Māori identity that has sprung up in the cities, Māori academic Paul Meredith argues that bicultural politics needs to be reconceptualised so that there can be a focus on 'inclusionary and multi-faceted identity politics' within 'an alternative space that blurs the limitations of boundaries and engenders new possibilities'.[67] But in my view, neither fans nor critics have really done justice to the multiple biculturalisms operating within Te Papa, which range from 'soft' to 'hard' to something altogether post-bicultural.[68]

So what will come after biculturalism?[69] Within the organisation, management, staff and stakeholders are constantly debating policies and practices and how they might be improved or changed. Many argue that biculturalism is relatively constrained by its mainstream setting within a government institution, and that Te Papa now needs to go beyond the limited parameters of biculturalism and beyond the walls of the building itself in supporting iwi to set up their own cultural centres.

When I interviewed Rhonda Paku in 2009, while she worked for National Services Te Paerangi, she congratulated Te Papa for 'stepping out' with a bicultural agenda when it was politically unfashionable in the 1980s and

1990s. However, she had reservations about the ultimate limitations within a Crown agency of 'tēnei taniwha e kīia nei ko biculturalism' (this monster called biculturalism). 'Māori are clearly saying that they want to tell their own stories,' she said. 'They are not necessarily seeking a bicultural arrangement with museums.'

Research by David Butts concurs with this, arguing that biculturalism was a Pākehā idea for which Māori increasingly had little enthusiasm, and that the time had come for more independent models.[70] Other scholars call for new paradigms, such as *bi-nationalism*, which recognises two nations within one country, and acknowledges Māori claims to sovereignty (tino rangatiratanga), or *interculturalism*, which allows for a more creative and cosmopolitan sharing and exchange between cultures.[71]

Whatever the future may hold, it is a safe bet that Te Papa will still be a forum for debate about the future of museums, and the future of Aotearoa New Zealand, and that Māori professionals will continue to explore new pathways to an indigenous museology that will not only lead their profession in this country, but around the world.

05.
the museum at work in 2017

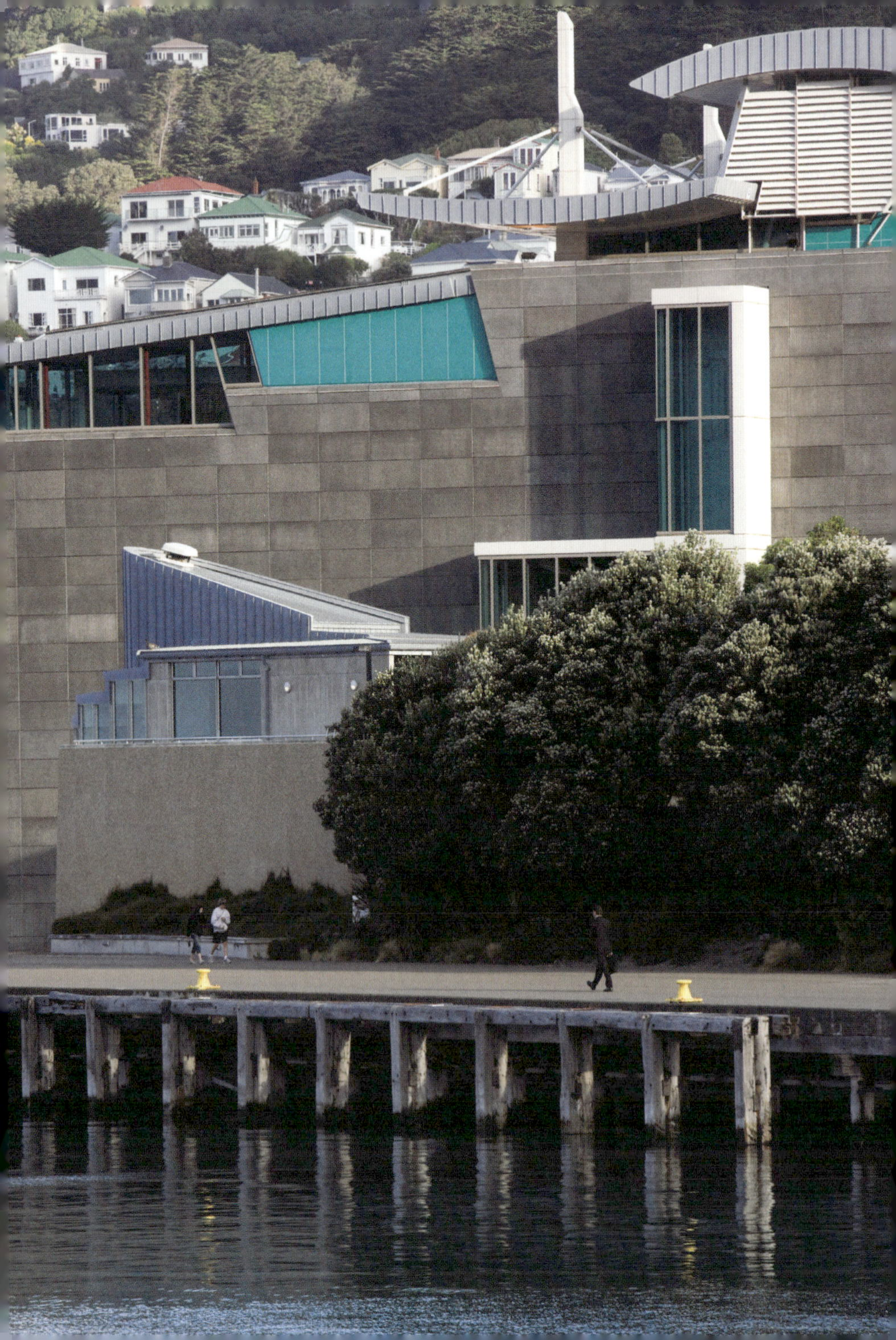

A well-known Māori pepeha or proverb asks:

> He aha te mea nui o te ao?
> Māku e kī atu: he tangata, he tangata, he tangata.
> What is the most important thing in the world?
> I say: it is people, people, people.

This chapter introduces the people behind the scenes at New Zealand's national museum and their day-to-day work. The value placed on people in Māori culture is a good reminder that, in studying the history and culture of organisations, staff matter just as much as policy, governance, money or 'outputs' reported in documents, as they are the ones who put the vision and plans into practice. While there has obviously been much useful academic research on what museum professionals do, there is not much direct writing about museum practice in the literature of museum studies, which has been concerned rather more with academic theory than with the everyday work of museums and galleries. Unfortunately, some histories of museums focus on the architecture, the public display or the 'discourse' of the museum without bothering to talk to the staff. But in the end, it is the professionals inside the organisation who do the work, and their experiences and reflections provide an invaluable insight into how museums today do what they do.

Many people have little idea of how a museum actually works. Often museums themselves are not particularly good at explaining what they do, even in core functions such as collections.[1] Studies of museums need to reveal the inner workings of professional practice and open them up to public understanding, self-reflection and critical analysis.[2] This chapter seeks to provide just such an analysis of current professional practice by using oral history methods, in addition to other sources, to provide a biographical profile of current staff at Te Papa. I have selected a cross section of staff, from those front of house to those behind the scenes who the public rarely see. Their thoughts, experiences and insights provide a snapshot of the national museum at work in 2017,[3] as they reflect on the past, present and future of the institution in which they work.

RANGIMOANA TAYLOR, HOST

Ko Hikurangi te maunga
Ko Waiapu te awa
Ko Porourangi te tangata
Ko Ngāti Porou te iwi
Ko Rangimoana taku ingoa

When I interviewed Rangimoana Taylor for this book, he introduced himself in the mihi above, which describes his tribal mountain, river, and the founding ancestor of his tribe Ngāti Porou. Rangimoana is well known outside Te Papa for his work over many years in theatre, television and film. He trained as an actor at the New Zealand Drama School, and later worked as a director in Wellington's lively Māori theatre scene. In the 1980s he had a career shift after some theatre productions at the National Museum in Buckle Street led to work as a kaiārahi (guide) working on the *Taonga Maori* exhibition alongside other Māori students from Victoria University. Later part of the education team, Rangimoana worked on school and public programmes for all the exhibitions at the National Art Gallery and Museum as it was integrated into the Museum of New Zealand in the early to mid 1990s.[4]

Rangimoana remembers this as 'one of the best experiences I have ever had', learning from knowledgeable elders like Aunty Bessie (Irihāpeti Walters), Hema Temara and others. Although raised speaking Māori, he had

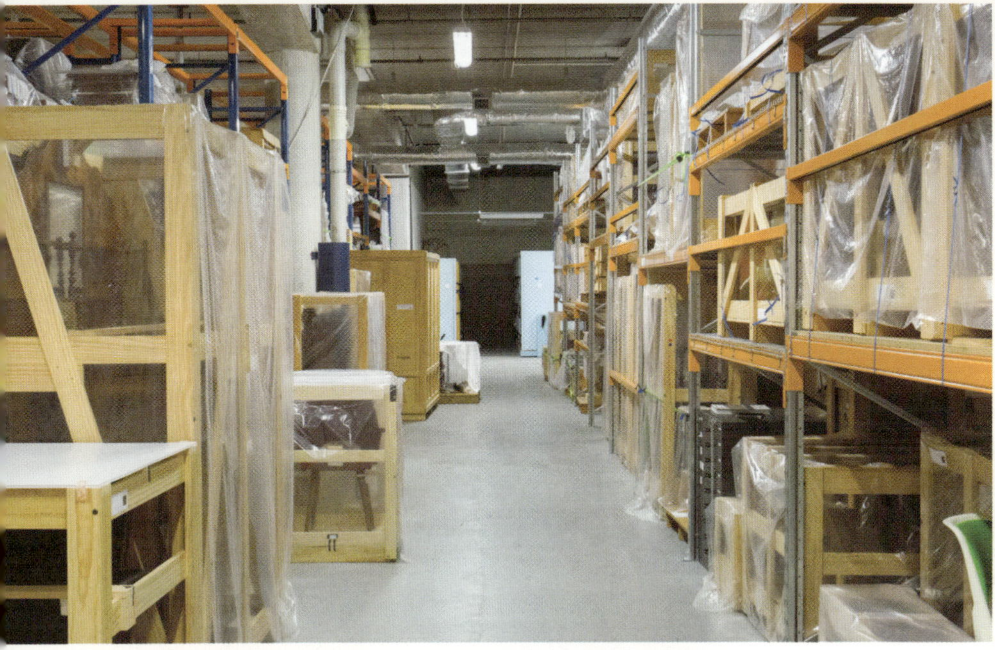

1.

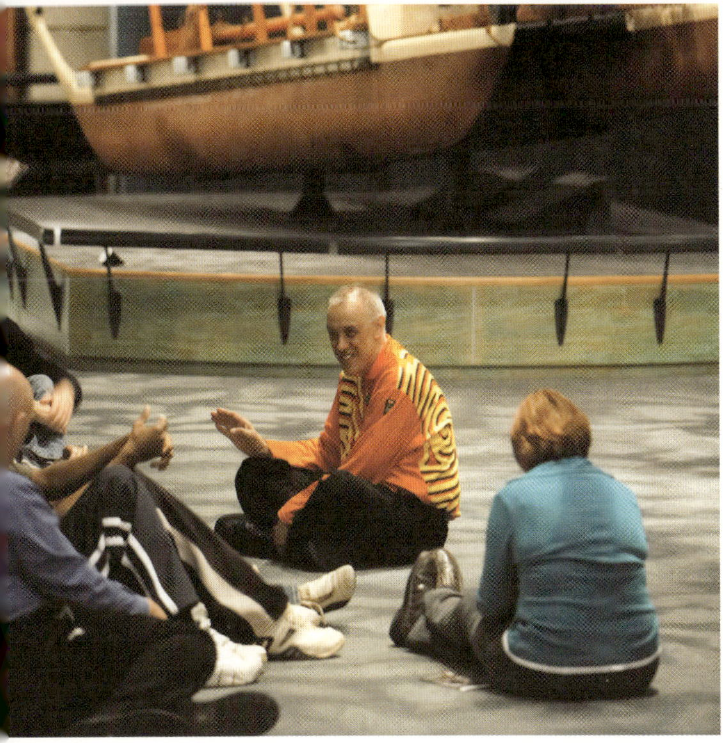

2.

1.

The storeroom for the history collection at Tory Street.

2.

Host Rangimoana Taylor takes a guided tour of the exhibition *Mana Whenua*.

lost much of his first language after living in the city most of his life. At the museum he appreciated the opportunity to strengthen his Māori by working every day among native speakers. He recalls being scolded by esteemed elder Amiria Stirling at Victoria University for neglecting te reo Māori. Thereafter he resolved to develop his language skills (which he likens to climbing up the stairway to heaven, the poutama pattern depicted in the latticework panels of the meeting house), *and* to pass this knowledge on to other learners coming after him: 'Kua pakeke haere tonu nei taku reo, ka piki ake pēnei i ngā poutama, arā, ko te āhua o te tukutuku ērā. Engari me hoatu te mātauranga ki a rātou kua eke mai nei kei muri i a koe.'

Now Rangimoana works in the Host team at Te Papa. The hosts are a large and diverse group, many of them casual or part-time staff on a roster, who do the demanding daily work of greeting visitors. They are the first staff you see when you arrive at the building and, far from looking like stern security guards in blue uniforms (as they used to), their dress, demeanour and approach are all designed to provide a friendly welcome and first line of interpretation. They come from a range of different backgrounds, but several have worked in the arts, media or broadcasting. A large proportion are Māori and Pacific Islanders. With his background and skills, Rangimoana has a specific role as a translator for visitors during pōwhiri, explaining what the speakers are saying in Māori, the gist of the songs and other aspects of the ceremony.

Asked what a host does, Rangimoana replies: 'Ko te kaimanaaki o te tangata, ko te kaitiaki i ngā taonga' (looking after people and caring for taonga). He is a guide, teacher and communicator, but also a mediator, who 'smooths the pathway for our visitors'. He is also responsible for training front-of-house staff. What makes a good guided tour? 'Tell a story, have a laugh,' he says. 'Tell another story, issue a challenge, have another laugh (at yourself), keep mixing it up — it's like the art of whaikōrero [speech-making].'

Working at Te Papa, which obviously has a very strong public image as a Māori space, he feels it is important to embrace Māori *and* Pākehā *and* international cultures. It is easy for some of us to 'ghettoise ourselves' and stay within the Māori kaupapa, he says, and he therefore makes a point, even when he is doing a tour in Māori, to show people *other* areas of the museum.

Everything in the world (on display in the museum) has a connection to Māori people, and not just those things made or used by Māori in Aotearoa in the past — and it's important to demonstrate that to visitors, whether they are local or tourists from overseas.

When he is narrating Māori 'myths', which he prefers to call 'stories', such as the story of Rangi and Papa (the Māori creation), he is careful to present them as another way of understanding the natural world, alongside the Bible or science. Also, he deliberately avoids presenting Māori culture in an idealised or exclusive fashion and tries to embrace all of his diverse European ancestry. In doing the background research for his role, Rangimoana is interested in learning about *everything*, not just the Māori content. To him, learning about Pākehā art or other topics associated with exhibitions is 'part of the bicultural journey'.

Guided tours, a much undervalued aspect of the museum visitor experience, have a basic script with information about the objects on display but there is room for extemporising.[5] Rangimoana's guided tours do not shy away from the harsh realities of New Zealand's colonial experience, and he is quite prepared to talk about the similar situation of indigenous peoples in other settler colonies where Anglophone tourists come from. This frank debate can have a profound impact on the audience, and research shows how the public interaction with hosts, as well as the exhibitions, can lead people to reflect critically on issues of race, identity, culture and history in the months and years that follow their visit.[6] In this sense, hosts cross cultural barriers, in Rangimoana's case using highly developed communication and cultural skills. But central to his professional practice is a sense of concern and empathy for people, what Māori call aroha (love), but not in a gushy New Age way. 'Aroha is a discipline,' he insists.

After working at Te Papa over 20 years, what does Rangimoana think about how the organisation engages with a broad audience? He replies that though the back-of-house staff do 'an incredible job' developing exhibitions, when it comes to way-finding, interpretation or labels they have all the theory but 'they don't understand the common person'. 'People need to be guided,' he adds; they can't necessarily figure out everything for themselves. Hosts, who work with visitors front of house every day, would like to have more input than they do into the creation of the visitor experience.

What does the future hold for Te Papa? Rangimoana would like to see in the years to come that Te Papa is a Māori-speaking space, a key part of the revitalisation of the language, and that hosts and other staff who work here are 'recognised and compensated for their linguistic ability'. 'The bicultural goalposts are shifting,' he continues. 'We have a Pākehā taking Māori classes,' who is a 'wonderful teacher', a model for and enabler of other Pākehā to speak Māori. 'As a gay man,' he says, 'I don't want to have to keep teaching straight people about gay politics! I want to teach my straight friends and *they* teach them about those politics.'

CAROLYN MCGILL, COLLECTION MANAGER

If hosts are the front line of the visitor experience at Te Papa, it is the collection managers who are the grunt workers dealing with the collections back of house. They are responsible for collection care and management, and do most of the handling, storage, documentation, transport and processing of objects. Collection managers deal with the *physical* side of the collections, whereas curators (see below) attend to the *intellectual* aspects of collections in terms of acquisitions, exhibitions, research and publications, and other outputs (although of course there is overlap). Historically all of these tasks, as well as object preservation, came under the mantle of the old-fashioned curator, who was a scholar-connoisseur, but in the last few decades the specialisation and diversification of museum operations has meant that these tasks have been devolved to other professional roles, such as conservators, registrars, designers and collection managers.[7]

Carolyn McGill did an MA in anthropology at Otago University and worked in regional museums before starting work at the Museum of New Zealand as a collection manager in 1992. Collection managers like Carolyn often describe their job as being 'the eyes and ears of the object'.[8] In caring for their collections, they don't do treatments on objects like conservators, but they do have to make sure that the objects are safe wherever they are. Sometimes this means advocating for them if they are at risk, not just from decay and degradation, environmental conditions, loss, damage or pests, but also from the public who may want to touch them, or even from enthusiastic staff members who want to make them more accessible to visitors. Often Carolyn finds that collection managers have to speak up in exhibition team meetings, and thereby earn a reputation for 'pouring cold water' on grand plans because they put objects at risk.

From the 1990s there has been a constant dialogue within the museum between those teams working front of house who want audience engagement with the objects, and staff behind the scenes like collection managers whose concern is the long-term preservation of those very objects. I asked her if collection managers have input to acquisition proposals, when the museum considers whether or not to buy objects in the first place. 'Oh, that's a "doozy",' Carolyn chuckles. Sometimes she has to say to curators who want to collect something, 'Sorry, we don't have room . . .' One of the major problems facing museums today is that they are running out of space, and they therefore have to be more strategic about planning for future collection development.[9]

A big part of the collection manager's job is the documentation of the collections. They have to know what they've got, where it is, what condition it is in, how much it is insured for, its dimensions, and so on. They may not be the experts about the object's history, but they are usually the ones who handle it, accession it into the collection, and move it around from A to B, whether that is on display, on loan to another museum, or in the conservation lab having treatment. Luckily over the last three decades the task of keeping track of thousands of artefacts has become easier through computer databases, which have replaced the old card catalogues. By the time Te Papa opened it had migrated its collection information on to a system called Te Kāhui, which in 2005 was replaced by Ke EMu, used by many large museums around the world. Carolyn thinks this system is 'wonderful' because it is searchable, can be accessed anywhere, and can incorporate images, reports, etc.

When asked what her typical day is like, Carolyn shrugs and replies that it is always different. Although she does work with objects, she spends a lot of time on the computer, and giving people virtual and physical access to the collections for research, exhibition development and other work. She has to be multi-skilled, dealing with both people and things, and must be adept at all manner of technical processes. She has a firearms licence, needs to be physically fit to lift and carry objects, and must have forklift certification and a driver's licence.

Despite the glamour of working with objects, the core of a collection manager's job is its practical problem-solving focus. In her time at Te Papa, Carolyn has had to figure out how to get a lifeboat into the Cable Street building, and how to get the Tiger Moth biplane out. At the time of writing she was about to deal with the seismic upgrade of the museum's Tory Street storage building, which meant she had to move the collections around to make way for this work (and protect them from concrete dust). Her current headache was how to move a 2.5-tonne Golden Kiwi lottery barrel out of the way.

Carolyn's particular area of responsibility is the three-dimensional history collections at the national museum, numbering some 30,000 objects in total.[10] The collection is made up of a wide variety of historical material: coins and medals, nautical and shipping, firearms, historical ceramics, furniture, technology large (cars, steam engines, caravans) and small (typewriters, sewing machines, cameras), plus the international historical collection (material from Africa, Asia, the Americas, Ancient Egypt, Greece and Rome, etc. — what was once called 'foreign ethnology'), and finally archaeo-zoology (fish bones and other fauna from archaeological sites).

The collection manager's job has diversified markedly over the 25 years Carolyn has been with the Museum of New Zealand, with the changes in technology meaning more stress on digital information, staff taking their own photographs, etc. In addition, now even staff back of house have a lot of public interaction. Carolyn estimates that between mid 2016 and mid 2017 there have been 32 visits to the collection store (totalling 123 people), which is more than one group every two weeks, in addition to several back-of-house tours. Some collection managers at Cable Street, such as those who look after textiles, art and Māori collections, do many more public tours.

There is extraordinary public interest and curiosity in stored museum collections. People love going back of house at Te Papa to see the collections on special tours. On an open day in 2016, over 2500 people turned up on a weekend to get a glimpse behind the scenes at Tory Street.[11] Unfortunately collection stores are sometimes represented as 'treasures' hidden away in dusty vaults, a popular perception that while not surprising reflects little understanding of museum history and professional management.[12] These spaces are certainly magical and alluring, with their rich and seemingly cluttered arrays of varied artefacts, but for collection managers they are specialist work areas that have to be carefully organised in a highly structured and scientific manner in order to preserve the museum's collections. In fact, public tours can threaten this very objective, because they can lead to damage, infestation with pests, and other hazards.

Carolyn tells me about her collection store in Tory Street. It is a large room filled to the ceiling with historical objects, all carefully stored and arranged. Each object has a unique number, and its location and other precise details can be traced on the CMS (collection management system). As can be seen in the photograph, there are various kinds of storage furniture and supports (racks, compactor shelving, pellets, boxes and containers) along with seismic restraints (straps around shelves, things strapped into supports, and objects nesting in foam within tubs). In fact, the Tory Street building itself has seismic joints that move in an earthquake, and the upgrade is being done to make it more resilient.

Carolyn explains that the store is carefully set up to provide the most stable environment possible to maintain the condition of the collection for as long as possible. The temperature and humidity are kept constant (20°C and 55 per cent humidity). Pests are carefully monitored. Dust is the enemy, so cleanliness is of key importance. Collection managers seem to be naturally organised people, and I have never seen an untidy collection store — here it's everything in its place. There are ladders, boxes, trolleys, forklifts and containers to move things around. Objects are handled carefully with clean cotton gloves. They are wrapped, embedded and covered with acid-free and chemically inert materials. Packaging objects for transport is nothing less than

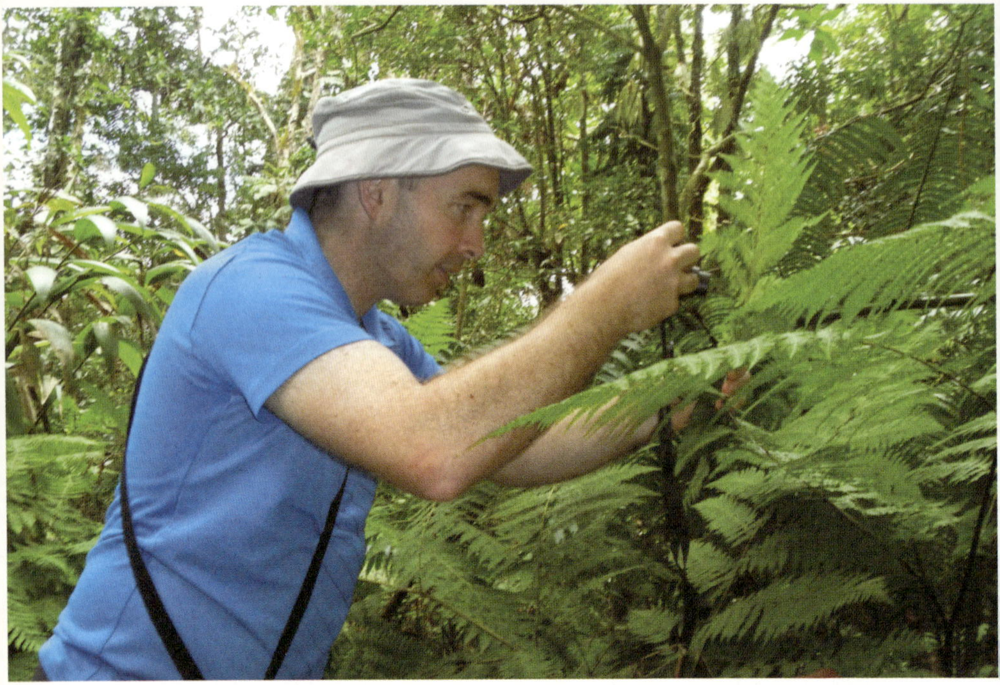

1.

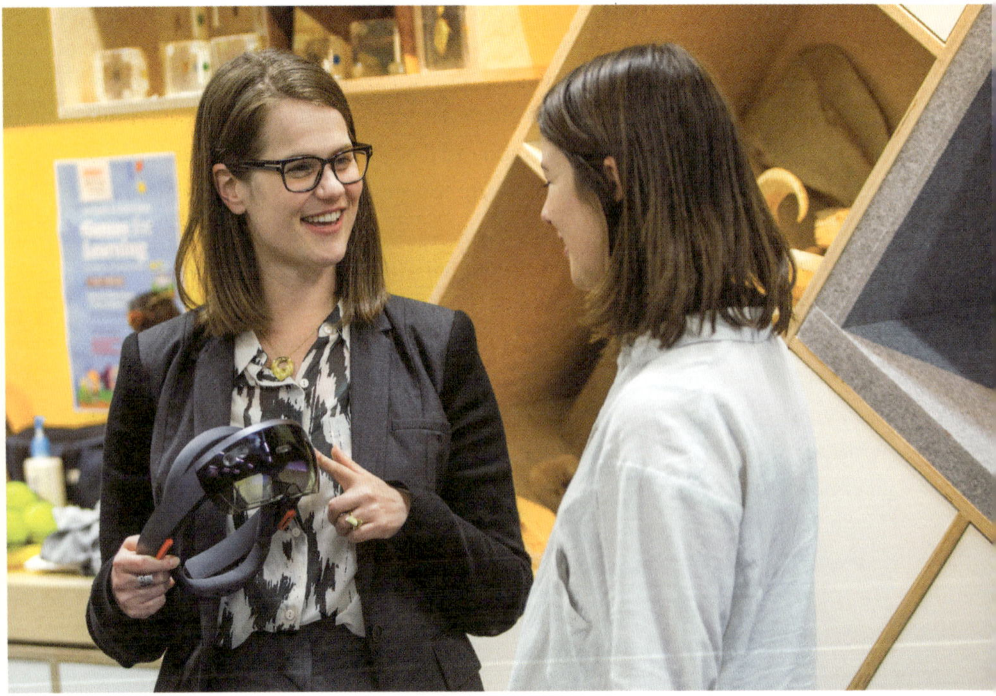

2.

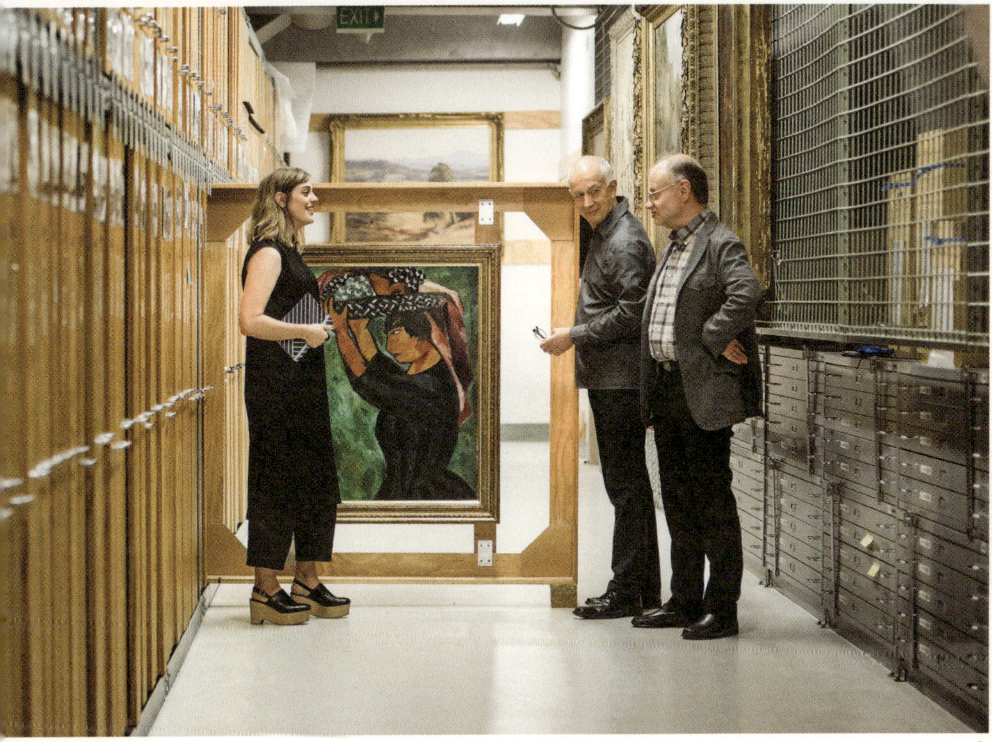

3.

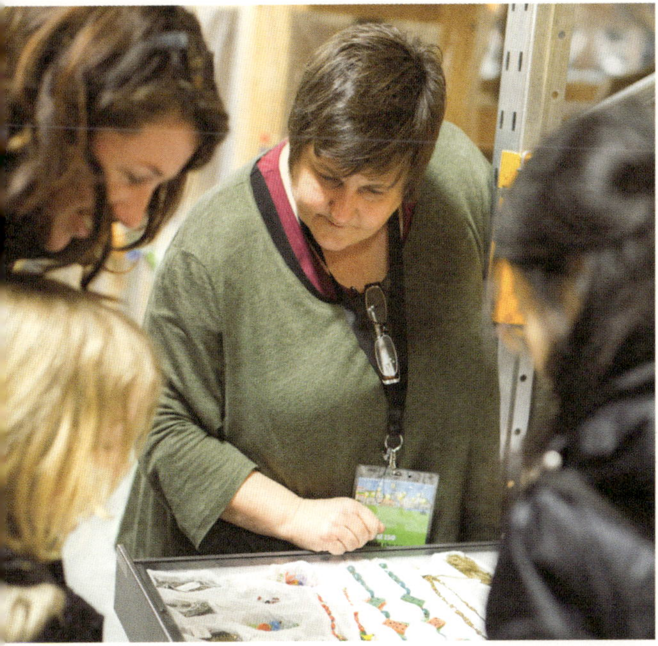

4.

1.

Curator Leon Perrie at work collecting fern specimens.

2.

Miri Young, Head of Learning Innovation, in Hīnātore, the new high-tech learning lab on level four.

3.

Curators Chelsea Nichols, Athol McCredie and Mark Stocker look at a painting by Natalia Goncharova in the art collection.

4.

History Collection Manager Carolyn McGill with visitors at an open day in the storerooms.

an art form refined over many years. Collection managers do not hurry. They move carefully and deliberately, doing one thing at a time. As my museum studies students have found on work placements, hours and days can pass in a museum collection store without their realising it — they are places where the outside world and normal time seem to be shut out.

Managing such a vast panoply of artefacts, from steam engines to cutlery, must have its challenges. Carolyn reflects on the reduction in collections staffing over the years, and feels there are not enough people to look after such big collections. But the job also has its rewards. Even though researching the objects is not her priority, she is very knowledgeable about some of them. 'What are your favourite objects?' I ask her. She does not hesitate, and names two things in the history collection that she loves. One is a beautiful piece in the studio glass collection. Another quirky favourite is a bizarre toast rack made from boars' tusks.

LEON PERRIE, CURATOR OF BOTANY

Obviously curators remain a core component in Te Papa's organisational structure. Although their role has changed over the years, especially in relation to the physical care of collections (as discussed above), the collection development, research and publishing, and exhibitions that they show are still central to the museological operation. At the time of writing there were about thirty curators at Te Papa, as well as researchers and honorary research associates, spread across the fields of history, Pacific, art, natural history and mātauranga Māori.[13] For this book I interviewed two curators, each involved in quite different projects, to get a sense of the range of activities curators are engaged in.

Leon Perrie is Curator of Botany, and specialises in ferns. After doing his PhD at Massey University, he was a postdoctoral researcher before coming to Te Papa in 2003. He worked closely with Patrick Brownsey, one of his thesis supervisors, now Research Fellow Botany, who is well known for his work on native New Zealand plants. 'What does a curator do?' I asked Leon when we met. A lot of his day is spent sitting at a computer, he explained, writing up data related to his research, which is concerned with the numbers, locations and identification of ferns. He works with a collection of dried, pressed plants that numbers some 300,000 specimens, and actively works to add to this collection, going into the field for two to three weeks every year (so far adding 5000 specimens to the total). Like the scientists who work at Te Papa on vertebrates and invertebrates, Leon does taxonomic research, or the classification of living things, which helps to document New Zealand's biodiversity. This collection, he tells me, 'is the physical proof of our plant heritage, and tells us what plants are in New Zealand, where they occur and what they look like.'

Asked about his favourite part of the job, Leon replies that discovering a new plant is very exciting. Another highlight is showing visitors some of the jewels of the collection, such as the ferns collected by Joseph Banks and Daniel Solander on Cook's first voyage in 1769–70. Leon's job as a curator is to develop these collections and also to interpret them, to add to our knowledge about them and to disseminate this information through a variety of forms, including public talks, advice to the Department of Conservation, Landcare Research and other agencies, and writing peer-reviewed journal articles.

Another way in which Leon's work is conveyed to the public is through exhibitions. He is the lead curator and subject expert on major new natural environment exhibitions that are currently in development and will be unveiled during the summer of 2018–19 as part of the museum's renewal programme. While he was not able to give away too much about the new exhibitions, he felt that compared to *Mountains to Sea* and *Awesome Forces* their objective was to get across a clear sense of how unique and special New Zealand's nature is.

Natural history museums have seen dramatic changes in the last two decades.[14] Te Papa's opening exhibitions had an ecological theme conveyed through dioramas (albeit contemporary ones), but now the display will focus on the objects themselves, complemented by images, flat-screen video and digital media (which of course was not available in 1998). The visitor experience will be immersive, creating an overall engagement with the topics through a range of media. However, in part the design will look quite traditional, and object-rich, with lots of specimens on shelves, because that style of presentation best suits the message about our special and distinctive plants and animals. 'If the message is that we have a lot of unique species,' argues Leon, 'then you'd better show me a lot of unique species!'

Another difference with the earlier exhibitions is that the new experience will place more emphasis on the interaction of people and nature, in part made possible by new technologies that allow public input. Whether it is biology or geology, the aim is to show communities relating to and being affected by natural phenomena like earthquakes. *Blood Earth Fire* on level three already confronts environmental issues, but the new exhibition will go even further and confront hugely important issues such as climate change. However, while dealing with BIG topics, the exhibition team does not want to preach, but rather to allow room for people to make up their own minds. 'If we want to change hearts, minds and lives as the mission says,' Leon points out, 'then let's see some people who are making a difference and use them as an inspiration.'

But other elements of the exhibitions will be quite similar to previous ones. Old favourites like the colossal squid will be there, as well as something similar to the popular earthquake house. In 1998 the only tactile experiences were in the adjacent Discovery Centre, but the new show will integrate interactive and hands-on exhibits. Another facet of the exhibition that builds on the day-one experience is the inclusion of Māori perspectives on the natural world. Dr Dan Hikuroa of the University of Auckland is a Māori scientist who is advising Te Papa on the integration of mātauranga Māori (Māori knowledge) and science in the exhibition's philosophy, design and development. He explains:

> As New Zealanders grapple with pressing environmental issues such as water quality, threatened species, and climate change, the integration of these two knowledges provides the potential for discovering new awareness, solutions and opportunities that could not be provided by either system in isolation . . . Mauri [life-force] and kaitiakitanga [intergenerational sustainability] are explored in the exhibition, and even though they are Māori words, they are universal concepts, reflective of the way many Kiwis feel about the natural environment.[15]

MARK STOCKER, CURATOR HISTORICAL INTERNATIONAL ART

There is sometimes an assumption that the main priority of a curator is to make exhibitions, especially in the visual arts. Our next staff member, art curator Mark Stocker, shows that this is not necessarily the case. Even though the art team of which Mark is a part is also working on a suite of new exhibitions as part of the renewal, the range of his work shows that curatorial expertise is multi-faceted.

Like other curators, Mark is a scholar in his own right. He studied art history at Cambridge and then did a PhD on the Victorian sculptor Sir Edgar Boehm, supervised at London's Courtauld Institute. His research specialities include British and New Zealand art from the late eighteenth to the mid twentieth century, including painting, prints, sculpture and public monuments, and numismatics (coins and medals). Before coming to Te Papa in 2014, he was an Associate Professor of Art History at the University of Otago. The move from academia to the museum world was a challenging but not very difficult transition, and his expertise and writing skills were soon put to work on the art collections.

Mark has been involved in a number of exhibitions at Te Papa, such as *European Splendour 1500–1800* in 2016–17,[16] and the display of the famous Te Pahi medal in mid 2017.[17] However, much of his time is taken up with building the collections, cataloguing and updating the records, or deaccessioning (taking things out of the collections to make room for new acquisitions), doing public programmes, and writing blogs and more scholarly outputs such as articles and books. He is editing one of several new art books, based on the collections, which will be published by Te Papa Press to accompany the opening of the new art exhibitions in early 2018.

Another recent book is the large memorial volume dedicated to his friend and colleague, the late Jonathan Mane-Wheoki.[18] It was Jonathan, in fact, when he was Head of Art at Te Papa in 2013, who warmly encouraged Mark to apply for his job there, and whose vision of the university and museum working more closely together is something that Mark shares. Another passion they shared was for historical European art. Although a Māori art historian and curator, Jonathan always maintained his early love of Victorian art and architecture, and Mark argues that it is very important to maintain this breadth. The Old Master prints he collects are 'a vibrant and relevant part of Te Papa's collection', and moreover figurative works such as these can be used in education programmes to help overcome the 'fear of art'.

In fact, Mark was quite critical of the display of art at Te Papa in its early years, and felt that the National Art Gallery as it was before 1992 was 'swallowed up' by the museum. Famously, he tussled in public with curator and writer Ian Wedde over the *Parade* exhibition, which he felt was 'irreverent' and contained faulty labelling, but the pair later became friends (see Chapter 3). Now that he works at Te Papa, Mark says he is not at all 'scared of populism', as he perhaps once was when writing his 'detached Olympian critique'. Indeed, he can see that the national museum's by-line 'Our place' really does work with a broad audience. However, one segment of the audience that he feels strongly could be better served is the group aged over 60, who often have a huge appetite for art, as well as leisure time and disposable income.

As an art curator, Mark is regularly asked why Te Papa can't show more of the national collection. Of course he is aware that this is a 'worldwide phenomenon', but he is determined to answer this criticism through ongoing collecting and by getting as much of the collection as possible out in the public view, either on-site, on tour or online.

MIRI YOUNG, HEAD OF LEARNING INNOVATION

From staff working back of house to acquire, manage and care for collections and to develop exhibitions, we now turn to the work of staff who are focused on the visitor experience front of house. Miri Young has a Master's degree from New York University and has worked in a variety of professional roles in informal art and Holocaust education, visitor experience, and developing new museums, including positions in the US, UK and various institutions in Wellington. The common thread in her work in museums has been what she calls 'facilitating public engagement and participation in museums and culture'.

Miri came to work at Te Papa in November 2015 as Head of Learning Innovation. In this role she leads a large team who specialise in formal education programmes, informal public programmes, and integrated learning experiences throughout the museum, which includes having input into exhibitions, visitor experience and digital products. The Collections, Research and Learning (CR&L) heads are a tier-three management role within the organisation, situated between the executive leadership team working above them and their own teams whose work includes curatorial research, collections care, learning and exhibition-making. Miri works alongside the four heads of disciplines (mātauranga Māori; science; art; New Zealand history and Pacific cultures) and the Head of Collection Services, who all report to the Director of CR&L, Dale Bailey.

This directorate is the largest in the institution and deals with the 'core' museological functions, so they often refer to themselves as 'a museum within the museum'. Other directorates are: Digital; Commercial; Marketing and Audience; Operations; Finance; Exhibition Renewal; and Ngā Manu Atarau (communities, repatriation and sector development).[19] The CR&L heads are a diverse group due to their varying disciplinary areas, and each has very different operations to manage, but they work closely together, bringing intellectual expertise to the wider museum. Heads lead thinking about how to 'best implement the vision and strategic narrative of the organisation through our curators, collection managers, conservators, and learning specialists'. As Miri explains, 'We grapple with the bigger picture of how to enable the public's access to, and understanding of, our collections, as well as at a very practical level of how to make this happen across a range of exhibitions and other channels.'

> Education is at the heart of most museums, but in recent years at Te Papa this activity has changed to a broader notion of learning rather than the

> traditional didactic idea of teaching. We recognise learning doesn't only take place at school or in formal education contexts, and we think about learning in a very holistic way. We're all learning, all the time. We talk about all our visitors and staff being learners, whether we intend to be or not.

Miri describes the Learning Innovation team as 'a combination of formal and informal learning experts who are dedicated to public engagement and social change. Our purpose is: "empowering life-long learning/he waka akoranga".'[20] One of the big achievements of day one, she feels, in addition to bringing collections together, was establishing a model of 'intergenerational learning', interactive exhibitions and hands-on Discovery Centres, and developing an institutional 'voice' in labels and text that was inviting and fun, based in research. 'We have a strong heritage in dynamic museum-making,' she says, 'and now we're at an interesting point thinking about what comes next.'

In addition to school programmes, Te Papa also engages in informal learning for a wide range of learners from young to old, taking a more broadly encompassing concept of audience engagement that is about 'sharing authority, co-creation and collaboration, and learning with others'. Rather than staff imparting knowledge to a passive audience, visitors are enabled to direct and create their own meanings. So, a part of Miri and her team's focus is audience access and reach *beyond* Cable Street — how different people can engage with Te Papa's collections outside the walls of the national museum, working with iwi, GLAMs (Galleries, Libraries, Archives and Museums), institutions and other partners. The range and variety of public programmes on offer is impressive, from talks and workshops to pecha kucha and live drone-racing, as seen in the full programme for the recent exhibition *Bug Lab.*[21]

A highlight for Learning Innovation, and a marker in this changed approach to learning at Te Papa, was the launch of Hīnātore Learning Lab in March 2017: an 'experimental learning space' for learners of all ages that replaced the previous classroom on level four next to the *Tangata o le Moana* exhibition.[22] In Hīnātore, visitors can use 'new technologies to enable more dynamic and personalised learning'. On the day of the opening I observed a range of excited children, teenagers and their parents, and all sorts of other people, participating in a variety of experiences from handling tactile objects to 3D design and printing. As Miri puts it, here the traditional, passive model of museum education is inverted — learners have agency, and direct their own learning through low-fi as well as digital technologies, such as virtual reality. Learning is still collections-based but facilitated in innovative ways.

The learning programmes in this space include a Ministry of Education-funded pilot project for kura kaupapa (Māori immersion primary schools) to provide learning experiences aligned with *Te Marautanga o Aotearoa* (the Māori curriculum) and Te Papa's collections, through Hīnātore's digital technology — delivered in te reo Māori by members of the Learning Innovation team. Hīnātore clearly exemplifies the team's objective to develop visitors' twenty-first-century competencies, skills that people need today in a fast changing world, namely creativity, communication, critical thinking, collaboration, cultural engagement and curiosity.

'We're really proud of our new approach to learning and our new space,' says Miri. 'Te Papa is investing in developing new and exciting ways into learning and we're receiving really positive feedback from our learners and our sector colleagues.' As she puts it, 'digital lets us create a whole series of new experiences where we can connect with users . . . in their homes, in their pyjamas, on the bus, in the classroom, in ways that let them dictate what that interaction is with the museum.'

Clearly the whole museum, not just the Learning Innovation team, uses digital technology to a degree far beyond the possibilities of the late 1990s. A new website was launched in 2016, Collections Online, which has gone from strength to strength, and there has been a strong emphasis on open access, or a 'collected commons', in terms of digital images and collections in GLAMs.[23]

Another bold initiative at Te Papa, which reflects the organisation's digital vision, is Mahuki, the world's first museum-based innovation incubator, which fosters business enterprise for the cultural sector.[24] Developed by the Digital Directorate under Chief Digital Officer Melissa Firth and General Manager Tui Te Hau, Mahuki sees its second intake in 2017. Ten teams of entrepreneurs spend four months developing solutions to challenges that are facing cultural institutions. The team's products, which may be taken to market, have a strong digital element: games-based learning, AR (augmented reality) and VR (virtual reality) technologies, apps and holograms, which all have applications to museums and other cultural organisations.

If museum futures are inevitably digital, what does Miri see as the challenges coming up for the national museum in the years ahead? 'As a museum our biggest challenge continues to be staying relevant and serving our diverse communities,' she says. What does this mean for Te Papa? Miri's response to this question was cautiously optimistic:

> Evolving technology enables multiple points of view, varied learning preferences and individualised meaning making, which are crucial to meeting these big challenges. We need to support this multiplicity, without losing our integrity and the trust with which museums are held. As social learning spaces, human facilitation is crucial to the museum experience. I'm confident that at Te Papa we can strike the right balance of technology and kanohi ki te kanohi [face to face] experience that will connect visitors with our collections and taonga.

LYNNE CARMICHAEL, NATIONAL SERVICES TE PAERANGI

One part of the museum that has been involved in reaching beyond Te Papa's walls for many years is National Services Te Paerangi (NSTP). Led by Victoria Esson, NSTP's mission is to 'work throughout Aotearoa New Zealand in partnership with museums, galleries, and iwi offering a range of practical and strategic programmes aimed at strengthening the sector'.[25] I have described elsewhere how this unit develops the professional capacity of museums through training and professional development, and particularly the innovative work they do with Māori and iwi to help them look after their own taonga.[26]

For this book, I interviewed Lynne Carmichael, who is a Sector Services Officer for National Services. Lynne has a background in the UK as a designer, and after completing her Master's degree in museum and heritage studies at Victoria University she joined the Visitor and Market Research team at Te Papa. Lynne says that she and her colleagues are 'brokers' who use the expertise and resources of the national museum to help museums, galleries and iwi throughout the country. In particular, she runs the workshop programme for the sector, which includes a whole range of topics (object handling, disaster management, governance, visitor research, curatorial practice, oral history, archives, etc.) and she manages the various grants that are distributed to professionals.

In addition to this work, NSTP helps organisations with institutional planning. From 1998 to 2003, for example, they helped Puke Ariki set up a new museum, library and information centre in New Plymouth (formerly the Taranaki Museum), and in 2016–17 they assisted a new Dutch-Māori cultural centre in Foxton called Te Awahou Nieuwe Stroom. The delivery of these services happens through development officers, who travel around New Zealand liaising with museums and helping them with their needs. In addition to all this, NSTP has extensive resources online, including 35 guides on all manner of museum and gallery work: cataloguing, exhibition display, writing labels, interpretation, collection policy, etc.

Several of her colleagues are on the road much of the time, but on an average day or week Lynne is mostly on the phone and email, communicating with people and getting them the help they need, usually by working with internal staff at the museum who have expertise in the relevant area. Halfway through 2017, when I interviewed her, NSTP had already dealt with over 250 separate organisations so far that year, from large institutions such as Auckland Museum to tiny museums with no professional staff. Lynne's own expertise is in visitor research, which was the subject of her Master's dissertation, exploring the 'Stowaways' exhibit in the *Blood Earth Fire* exhibition on level three. She is a strong advocate for this kind of research, and how greater understanding of the audience can underpin every aspect of museum work.

The newest addition to the NSTP team is Migoto Eria, who recently became

Manager Iwi Development Pou Whirinaki ā-Iwi. Migoto is of Ngāti Kahungunu, Tūhoe and Ngāti Raukawa descent. She worked in education and publishing before moving into the museum sector, holding curatorial positions at MTG Hawke's Bay, Otago Museum and Te Papa before taking up her current role. As a fluent speaker of Māori, and a parent with a six-year-old son in a kura kaupapa, Migoto is an energetic advocate for the use of te reo Māori in museums and as a taonga in its own right. She works with Paora Tibble, Iwi Development Advisor Kaiwhanake ā-Iwi, another fluent speaker of Māori who was previously Te Papa's Māori writer, responsible for all the exhibition labels and other text in te reo Māori.

In terms of the urgent task of maintaining and revitalising the Māori language, it is inspiring to see staff like Migoto and Paora speaking Māori in the office on an everyday basis, encouraging the use of Māori by other staff, and supporting the language in communities as an integral part of Māori cultural heritage.

HEMA TEMARA, IWI RELATIONSHIPS

In terms of outreach, the other museum department that works with Māori communities around Aotearoa is the Iwi Relationships team. The 'iwi relationship strategy' covers a range of museum work: exhibitions, repatriation, research and collection development as well as various projects such as public programmes like the Matariki festival and waharoa or 'gateway' connections with iwi through cultural and commercial opportunities.

In the museum's statement of intent, Kaihautū Michelle Hippolite described these relationships in the following way: 'Relationships with iwi are an important part of enabling engagement with a growing population that is young and more urbanised. Iwi relationships are critical for building knowledge (Mātauranga Māori) around the taonga, providing access to associated iwi, and generating respect and reciprocity.'[27]

The strategy is enabled at the operational level through a small but

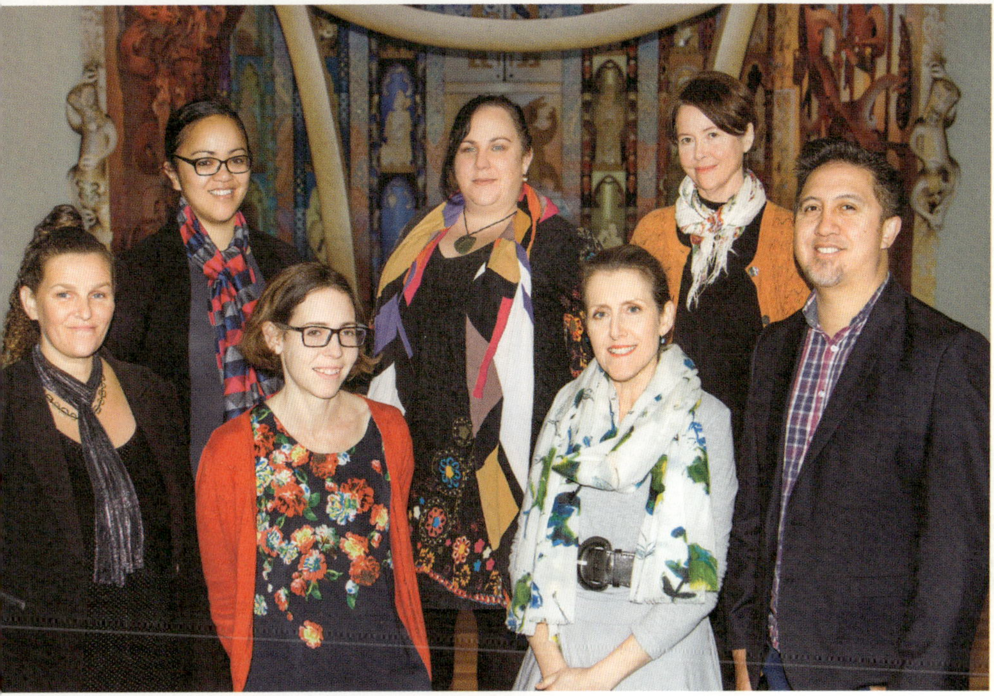

1.

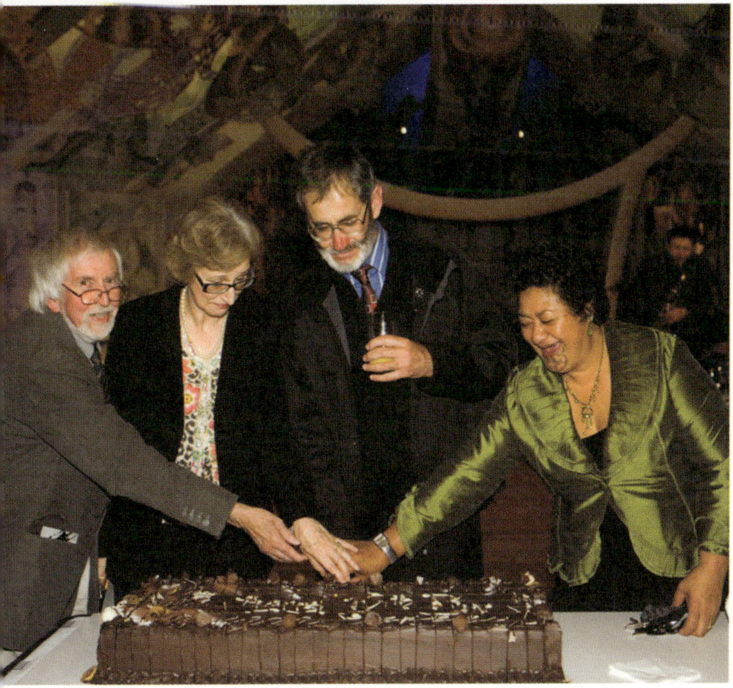

2.

1.

The staff of National Services Te Paerangi. Front row, from left: Victoria Esson, Emma Philpott, Lynne Carmichael, Paora Tibble. Back row: Migoto Eria, Sally August, Judith Taylor.

2.

Long-serving staff celebrate Te Papa's tenth birthday in 2008. From left: Ross O'Rourke, Manuela Angelo, Michael Fitzgerald and Hema Temara.

hardworking team. Iwi Relationships services the relationship with iwi in general, hosts the resident iwi kaumātua, and carries out much of the work on the marae known as manaakitanga — welcoming and looking after visitors. Currently the team's coordinator is Carolyn Roberts-Thompson, who started working at Buckle Street in the 1990s, and has worked her way up to be one of the most skilled managers in the institution.

The heart of the team until her retirement in 2017 was Hema Temara. A fluent speaker of Māori, Hema is Tūhoe and was born and raised in the Urewera. She taught Māori at high school before starting at the National Museum as an education officer in 1992. She was often sought out by staff for advice on matters of tikanga, such is her knowledge of customary culture and mythology as well as performing arts. Her staunch defence of her culture and the kawa of the marae gave her something of an undeserved reputation as a 'taniwha', so that staff often treated her with a degree of trepidation.

In reflecting on her many years of work at Te Papa, Hema feels that what they were doing with iwi was a way of expressing externally the original bicultural vision of Cheryll and Cliff, and Ngā Kaiwawao. Within the organisational culture of Te Papa the team showed the way for other staff, through a 'leadership style' that was 'transformational' in both intellectual and spiritual terms, reflecting the Māori values of manaakitanga and whanaungatanga (relatedness, kinship, family belonging). This could be seen in simple but powerful acts like the sharing of food, karakia and other ritual observances, inculcating a sense of family through group activities, and looking after visitors.[28]

Hema worked closely with the iwi kaumātua who sat on the paepae to officiate at the many pōwhiri that take place on Te Papa's marae, and worked tirelessly with everything from dawn openings and waiata practice to staff functions and concerts in order to uphold the mana of the marae. Hema and the team worked with everyone from schools to government departments, iwi and international visitors, and switched easily from working behind the scenes to stepping out in public in performance roles. A renowned kaikaranga, Hema's was often the first voice heard when visitors were welcomed on to the marae by the keening call of welcome that women traditionally perform before the men make their speeches of welcome.

TE WAARI CARKEEK, IWI KAUMĀTUA

What does the iwi kaumātua do? Alongside Rehia Kenny, Te Waari Carkeek was at Te Papa for three years from mid 2014 till March 2017. The iwi kaumātua is a member of the resident iwi, and there is a formal process to their appointment, including an interview. There's also a job description, which requires the iwi kaumātua to:

- welcome manuhiri at ceremonies on marae
- conduct blessings for the opening of exhibitions
- provide whakatau or verbal acknowledgement (not a pōwhiri, not on the marae, more informal, can use English)
- join teams of staff where required to develop exhibitions, moving taonga around, taking taonga out to iwi, etc.
- perform a counselling role
- engage in other external activities.

The key role is to 'uphold the mana of the people'. These duties are 'an expression of our tikanga Māori'. Every Thursday at 1 pm Te Waari and the kuia led waiata practice for all staff on the marae, in which they taught waiata particular to the tribe — this way the kapa haka group learn waiata from around the country from each iwi in residence. In whaikōrero (speech-making) on the marae, Te Waari felt that he had developed his 'court craft', as his own kaumātua emphasised there is an element of showmanship in speaking and also in singing, which increases the respect and appreciation of visitors. If 'wonderful food' follows the welcome ceremony, then the manuhiri feel that they are being well looked after (manaakitanga). All this meant not only perfecting his performance, but also coordinating with the marae manager and Iwi Relationships team to see that things ran smoothly on a practical level.

In their extensive use of te reo Māori the kaumātua and kuia showcase the bilingualism that is one of Te Papa's goals. There is a protocol that when staff eat, for example, the kaumātua says a karakia (grace) first. Te Waari says he doesn't do this himself at home — 'If you come to tea at my place you just tuck in!' he jokes — but it's an expectation at Te Papa. Te Waari was brought up in a strict Anglican Māori home, and even though later in life he 'left that behind', he feels fortunate that he has that background to draw on in religious ceremony and church services. In his work at Te Papa he says he consciously chose karakia Māori and not Christian prayers, but he can use Christian prayers if he needs to.

In the more informal role of listening to people in their concerns about kaupapa and personal issues Te Waari says he acted as 'the koro' [grandfather] for staff. The external duties of the iwi kaumātua include making sure Te Papa is represented at important events in the Māori world, such as hui or tangihanga for people who have an association with the museum: for example, the funeral for Jonathan Mane-Wheoki in Auckland, and then accompanying the tūpāpaku (body) to the Northland marae where he was buried. These things happen within 'an entirely Māori paradigm', which means the museum has to be flexible and allow iwi to take the initiative and manage their own schedule. On these occasions it is important that iwi kaumātua are able to engage with other tribes according to their own kawa, so as not to embarrass Te Papa and to uphold its mana in Māori communities. Te Waari says he used his own networks for this iwi engagement element of the job.

A big part of Te Waari's work at Te Papa was the development, installation and de-installation of the Ngāti Toa exhibition *Whiti Te Rā*, and while it was open he did a lot of public talks and guided tours. Originally he was on the iwi reference group who worked with staff at Te Papa to create the show. He says he found it interesting to learn how the museum designers, writers, conservators and installers worked to make their ideas a reality. Because this exhibit included a lot of taonga owned by families, Te Waari joined the team in liaising with them, asking them if they would allow their taonga to be borrowed, and finding out how they wanted them to be displayed. He remembered that, 'Most said yes, some said no.'

In other cases iwi were consulted about the stories associated with the taonga and the overall concepts and narrative of the exhibition: the journey of the tribe to the Wellington region from the Waikato, the interaction with Europeans,

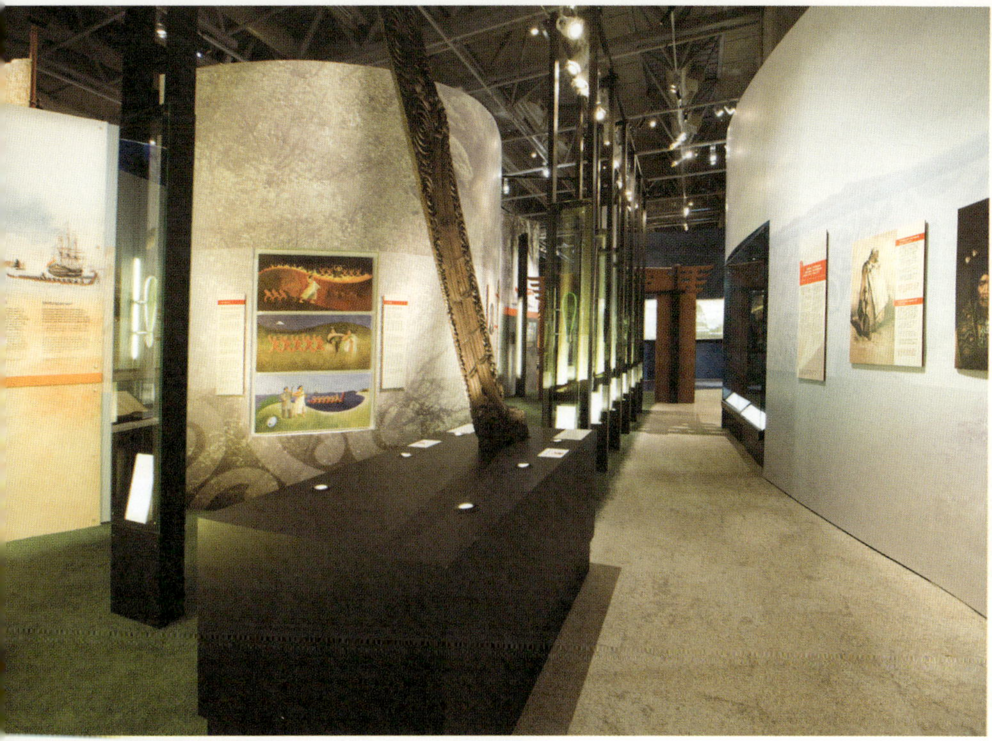

1.

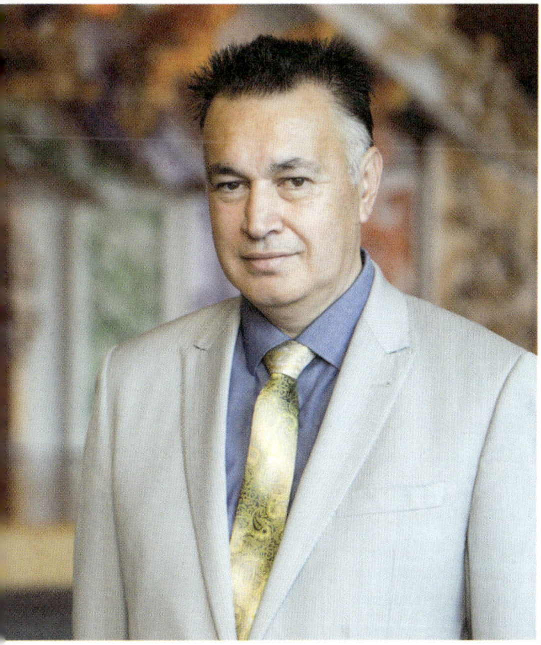

2.

1.

The Ngāti Toa exhibition *Whiti Te Rā*.

2.

Te Waari Carkeek, kaumātua for the Ngāti Toa exhibition *Whiti Te Rā* from 2014–17.

and contemporary tribal life including youth. The exhibition was focused on Ngāti Toatanga and their kaupapa (issues). It celebrated their cultural heritage and reflected their current political reality, having overlapped with the contemporaneous settlement of the iwi's Waitangi Tribunal claim (the passing of the legislation at Parliament in 2014 was featured in the display). However, the reference group was not iwi-exclusive. They chose the best curator for the exhibition based on their successes, past experiences and broad knowledge.

It is somewhat ironic that the contemporary marae, known officially as Rongomaraeroa, is one of the most public areas of the museum and yet much of the work that goes on there with iwi is hidden from public view. It is the venue for the many meetings and ceremonies associated with the iwi exhibitions, and many other programmes and events to do with iwi relationships. As policy analyst Cath Nesus put it, the marae is seen as a Māori context where the Māori language and protocol come first and the Māori voice can take precedence in dealings with iwi over taonga and other kaupapa.[29]

In mid 2009, when CEO Seddon Bennington died suddenly while tramping in the mountains, his body lay in state on the marae in the manner of a tangihanga or ceremony to farewell the dead. I was overseas at the time, and I watched the proceedings, which were simulcast on the web, including the haka pōwhiri that greeted the mourners carrying the casket, the karanga or wailing cry of the women, and the whaikōrero or speeches recounting the deeds of the deceased, which were addressed directly to the tūpāpaku or body. This went on for two hours. The scale, depth and genuine spirit of such events surprise visiting museum professionals from overseas, particularly given that they are mounted internally by Te Papa staff themselves; they are a strong riposte to the superficial and condescending criticism from some uninformed critics who claim that the marae is some kind of fake showpiece of national identity.

In February 2010, I attended a pōwhiri to welcome Michael Houlihan, the new CEO who had come from the National Museums of Wales to take up the position. Sitting in the crowd, I was struck by the confidence of the staff in the kapa haka, in comparison with our faltering efforts to sing waiata and make a barely adequate job of welcoming visitors thirty years ago at the old National Museum. I have attended tangi of former staff members, and observed Te Papa staff arriving and leaving en masse, and can see the group strength they project and the mana with which they are held in Māori communities. And here they were now, the kapa haka team, dressed in their own outfits, using traditional instruments and performing with great competence and gusto.

If this was a big occasion for staff, I can only imagine what it must have been like for the new director. Being welcomed on to the marae, having to stand and make a short speech in Māori, and touching noses with complete strangers in the 'hongi' or greeting is a rather intimidating and very public way to start work somewhere. Houlihan told me afterwards that it was certainly a bit different to 'slipping in the back entrance' on your first day, but he clearly enjoyed it and moreover understood this is what he was *expected* to do to become the director of *this* museum.

The speeches of the kaumātua, all in Māori, were very interesting. The late Lewis Moeau of Rongowhakaata referred to the whare fondly as 'te whare ataahua e whakatau nei i te Ao' ('the beautiful house that welcomes the world'). Others spoke of 'Te Papa upholding biculturalism between Māori and the other peoples of Aotearoa' ('Te Papa e whakanui i te tikanga a rua kei waenganui i ngā tauiwi me te Māori i konei'). Seddon Bennington was farewelled with respect (by now his photo was hanging on the wall along with other staff who had passed on, according to Māori custom). Finally, the new CEO was advised, with tongue in cheek, to take care if he went out tramping! These are the kinds of interactions that occur on the marae every week, sometimes every day, and they are, it seems to me, now unquestionably an integral part of the culture of Te Papa.

06. learning from the first 20 years

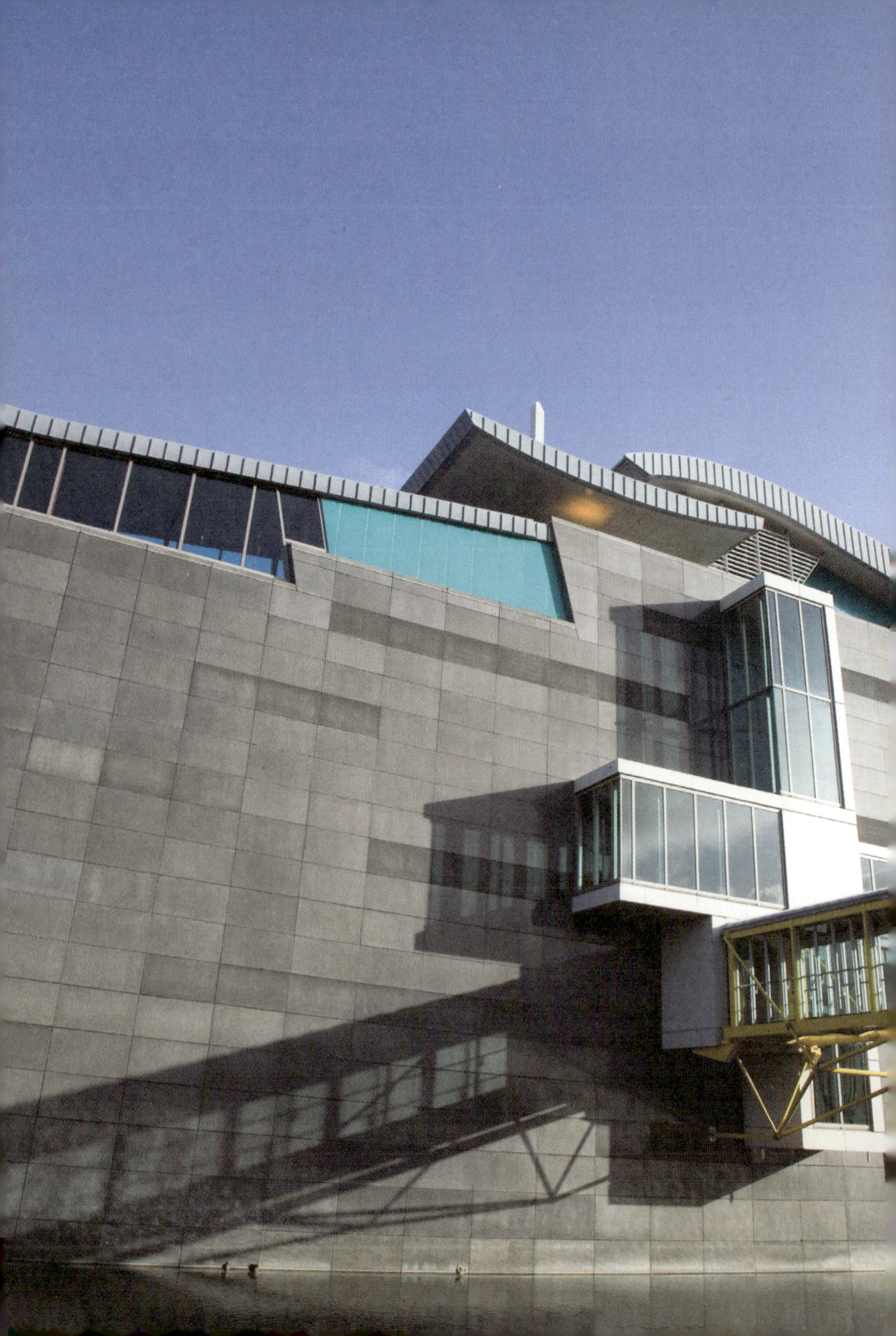

In February 2017, 19 years after Te Papa opened, crowds were still flocking to the national museum. This time the main attraction was a record-breaking exhibition about World War I, *Gallipoli: The Scale of Our War*, which had opened on 18 April 2015. In its first year, the exhibition attracted over 700,000 people, which made it the most successful in the museum's history.[1] With its giant human figures, made by Richard Taylor's Weta Workshop, it was a harbinger of things to come, a visitor experience that employed film production and digital technology developed in partnership with external companies.

Throughout 2017, major projects were underway elsewhere in the building, in what was referred to as the 'museum renewal'. This encompassed repairs to the building; upgrading the website and adding new digital channels and experiences; reviews of policy and practice; and a suite of new exhibitions, beginning with science and art opening in 2018, followed later by history, Pacific and Māori.[2] Over 2016–17 new staff were appointed at several levels, including heads of arts, science, mātauranga Māori, and New Zealand and Pacific cultures, as well as digital and learning innovation (see Chapter 5), and Geraint Martin became the fifth CEO since 1998.

As I explained in the Introduction, it is not possible in a short book like this to chronicle events at Te Papa between 1998 and 2018 in any detail, let alone give an account of current developments and future directions. But, in looking back over the 20 years described in these chapters, it is possible to consider what Te Papa has achieved, to assess its impact, and to identify aspects of its legacy. This critical historical analysis, which is, given its contemporaneity, a kind of 'history of the present', also allows me to make some broad comments about current and future directions at New Zealand's national museum, and museums more generally.

So, what has Te Papa achieved? Firstly, in the local and national context it has made museums as a whole and the national museum in particular an integral part of the social and cultural fabric at a popular level. For Wellingtonians, and for New Zealanders generally — as the visitor research and a host of other formal and informal indicators demonstrate — it has been and remains a much loved part of the everyday lives of a wide range of people from different age groups, backgrounds and ethnicities. Compared to its predecessors, it is a much more prominent and valued national institution, a vital part of Wellington's economy and cultural ecology, and a major tourist attraction. In September 2017 it was voted the nineteenth most popular museum in the world on Trip Advisor.

This last point brings me to Te Papa's second achievement: its international impact. Not only is the national museum a 'must see' with international visitors to New Zealand, it also has a global reputation among museum professionals, and has made a significant impact on museology worldwide. Travelling abroad to professional and academic conferences, I find that Te Papa is well known outside the country, and that it has generated a veritable literature in its own right. Former CEO Michael Houlihan told me that he could see 'a little bit of Te Papa' in many institutions he visited: everything from friendly hosts giving visitors a personal welcome at the front door and a commercially positive approach to events, sponsorship and retail, to its acclaimed recognition of indigenous rights. Sir David Fleming, CEO of National Museums Liverpool and President of the International Federation of Human Rights Museums, paid tribute to Te Papa as follows:

> I always hold up Te Papa as a museum that, while it may be criticised within New Zealand, acts as a beacon of biculturalism/multiculturalism to the rest of us. It may not be perfect, but it is the best example of an

> approach that tries to accord respect to the traditions, lifestyle and beliefs of indigenous people. And I always think that Te Papa reminds me that the history of New Zealand is one characterised by subjugation, oppression and inequality: the Museum does not try to avoid the unpleasant and embarrassing aspects of Kiwi history like many other museums do, especially nationally funded ones, in all nations.[3]

Thirdly, the indigenous empowerment that Fleming and many other international commentators point to is possibly Te Papa's most important legacy. More than any collection, exhibition or programme on other topics or disciplines, whatever their merit, it is the Māori dimension of Te Papa, whether it is the biculturalism of its early years or more recent formulations such as mana taonga, that the world knows, takes notice of and wants to find out about.

This overall evaluation should not detract from the many aspects of Te Papa that are significant in its history and important in their own right. Without attempting to capture all the many different projects, events and people of significance at the national museum over the last 20 years, the selected highlights in Appendix A provide an indication of the variety of activities that are worthy of brief mention. The list includes visitor numbers, finances, staffing, policy, exhibitions, collections, public programmes and other conventional indicators of performance that are described in annual reports and other internal documents. Readers who wish to find out more about particular items may follow up by consulting the annual reports, the website and other sources.

More pertinent to the aim of this book are the long-term trends evident in the chronology. Several themes emerge. The most obvious is the number of visitors, noteworthy both in its scale and its diversity, as noted in Chapter 1. The annual reports show that 25 million people have visited Te Papa in less than 20 years, which works out at an average of about 1.3 million per annum. There have been ups and downs, with some lower numbers in the mid 2000s but a recent upsurge. However, overall the numbers are surprisingly steady, and the typical 'honeymoon' period apparent in other new museums seems here to be an almost permanent feature.

In terms of the breakdown of that audience, young visitors aged between 15 and 24 are still represented strongly, and international visitors have increased to nearly half of all visitors. There is some concern that Wellingtonians and Māori visitors have declined in proportion to the total.[4] This suggests a need to drive visitor numbers with temporary exhibitions and boost repeat visits with changing programming, a challenge for museums everywhere. Meanwhile visitors continue to be interviewed on their way out the door, building up the Te Papa Visitor Profile, which now ranks among one of the largest museum data sets anywhere in the world, numbering well over 30,000. It is somewhat disappointing therefore to see that the museum's internal visitor research unit has been scaled down, and that this information is not really employed as widely as it could be to guide and underpin museum operations and programmes at all levels.[5]

Reading over the highlights of the national museum, one is struck by the importance of the commercial drive, which for many critics sits uncomfortably alongside other more traditional functions of preservation and research. In museum history, culture and commerce have often been unhappy bedfellows, but they have been and are nevertheless ever-present, despite the rhetoric about the good old days of education not entertainment, scholars not sausage sizzles.[6] Much of Te Papa's success from day one can be attributed to the way the museum embraced leisure sector techniques, particularly in the visitor experience, which helped reposition it as a dynamic attraction with a much larger and more diverse audience.[7] This can be seen in the way in which Te Papa has actively engaged in the tourist market, which, right up until the 2000s, was still seen as a slightly distasteful thing for cultural institutions to pursue.[8]

The highlights show that the organisation generated a very high proportion of its earned revenue from retail, functions, events, sponsorship and charged programmes, without imposing an entry fee. There have been problems, naturally, such as periodic funding shortfalls, touring exhibitions that lost money, and issues over the government not funding for depreciation. The annual reports document budget crises in recent years, turned around by internal cost cutting and restructuring under CEO Rick Ellis. Research suggests, however, that Te Papa, and museums in general, could be doing a lot more to raise money as a core part of their work.[9]

Another strong trend that emerges is the increasing importance of digital technology. In the late 1990s the internet was still new, but now it is ubiquitous. Gradually over the years there has been more and more emphasis on digital channels of communication and interpretation, with collections, exhibitions and other core activities being staged and managed online as well as on-site. Like most museums, Te Papa now has a website with a huge amount of content on various platforms, including blogs and databases as well as Facebook, Twitter, Instagram and so on. A digital team is devoted to making Te Papa 'a world-leading provider of digital experiences'.[10] Recent initiatives like Mahuki and Hīnātore are seen as showing the way to the future.[11]

While much of this work is genuinely innovative and exciting, it is also noticeable from the historical record that digital media, like earlier forms of 'new' technology, has slowly been absorbed into museum practices. Indeed, it is arguably no longer *new*, and as Ross Parry argues, we may be in the 'post-digital' phase.[12] This is not just a question of semantics, as the rapid change of formats, ever-present obsolescence and relentless drive for the next best thing can be problematic for museums.[13] Understanding the virtual, alongside the physical, as merely another way of managing artefacts, telling stories and engaging with communities means that museum professionals can add it to their array of tools, without abandoning the analogue, or any other method that is still useful, however unfashionable.

Something else that is apparent is the constantly changing policy framework of the national museum between the late 1990s and today. Māori policy has evolved from biculturalism to mana taonga and perhaps interculturalism (see Chapter 4). What this will mean for the way in which Māori staff do things is not clear yet, but I do sense an appetite for trying out new approaches. Certainly fresh ideas for exhibiting and collecting are being considered, as is plain from the ideas canvassed at the end of Chapter 4.

After a decade of operation there was a major policy review in 2008, and new strategies and values were unveiled in 2011 (see Appendix B). Through these Te Papa committed to: 'accessing all areas', 'being a forum for the future', 'housing the treasures', 'connecting with people', 'saving the planet' and 'mana taonga/sharing authority'.[14] In addition, a series of five bicultural core values were expressed; for example, 'Whanaungatanga/Relationships' was described as: 'caring for each other: we work collaboratively with colleagues, both internally and externally, respecting and honouring each other's mana (integrity), expertise, and perspectives'.

In 2016–17 collection development policies were also revised, reflecting a tighter and more strategic approach to collecting.[15] Despite this activity, I feel that more could be done in policy, which is not an arena many museum professionals warm to. It is a common feature of the museum sector that it updates its framework in response to shifting government priorities, but as scholars of cultural policy point out, museum professionals could be more policy literate and proactive in framing their own policies in ways that better reflect the nature of museum work.[16]

Exhibitions are a standout feature of the highlights. Often these temporary events dominate reporting documents and arguably lead collecting, swallowing up more resources than back-of-house museum functions that are less understood by the public, boards and stakeholders. There have, of course, been far too many exhibitions over the last 20 years to name individually.[17] A handful deserve mention. The *Versace* exhibition was a touring show that was successfully adapted for display at Te Papa in 2001. It was at that time the most successful charged exhibition ever, attracting 107,000 visitors, making $580,000, and contributing an estimated $18 million to the Wellington economy.[18] This shows how important 'blockbuster' exhibitions are to contemporary museums financially, but also alerts us to the risk when so much reliance is placed on a constant diet of 'turn-key' exhibitions hired from elsewhere.[19]

Of course Te Papa has its own touring exhibitions, which have been an increasingly important part of the business since the 2000s. The stand-out success is *Whales / Tohorā*, which is still touring the US years after it debuted at home in 2007. This is a classic Te Papa product, blending natural history, social history and Māori culture, and it has been a big hit with the many audiences at US and Canadian museums who have seen it over the last 10 years.

But money is clearly not everything. In other cases, successful shows did not tour that really should have. *Kahu Ora: Living Cloaks* was curated by Awhina Tamarapa in 2012 in collaboration with Māori weavers from around Aotearoa. Despite the stunning beauty of the feather cloaks on display, and the dynamic public programme that allowed visitors to observe weavers at work in the exhibition, it did not tour, not even locally.

One show that did tour nationally and internationally was *The Lord of the Rings* in 2002–03. Featuring props, costumes and models from the successful film adaptation of the Tolkien trilogy directed by Peter Jackson, it was developed in partnership with New Line Cinema. What visitors seemed to enjoy with this show, myself included, was the insight into movie magic — special effects such as CG (computer graphics), animatronics and motion capture.[20] This trend continued with the *Gallipoli* exhibition mentioned above, which similarly applied film techniques to a historical topic and created an immersive experience not unlike the cinema. Though wildly popular, and to many an emotionally effective tribute to New Zealand's sacrifice in the Great War, this exhibition raised interesting debates about war commemoration, nationalism and the relationship between film design and curatorial expertise: who had the final cut — Weta or Te Papa?[21]

Another recent example, *Bug Lab: Te Aitanga a Pepeke*, a heavily interactive and digital show, contained very few insect specimens at all, leading to the question of what made it a museum exhibition.[22] Is a museum these days really nothing more than an event centre or hi-tech attraction?

Nor is the money spent on developing exhibitions necessarily a guarantee of their success. The exhibition *Air New Zealand 75 Years: Our nation. The world. Connected* may have won a national award, but the $2 million budget should probably have discounted it from comparison with exhibitions from institutions with nothing like that money. According to one study, the most successful exhibition at Te Papa in recent years was the cheapest, quickest and simplest to produce: *The Poisoners!* The brainchild of science interpreter Eric Dorfman, this free show staged in the touring gallery in 2007 invited visitors to solve a murder-mystery or whodunnit through clues hidden among a crowded space packed with over 250 specimens and props. Playful, low-tech and visitor-centred, *The Poisoners!* suggested another way of making exhibitions that the institution has not explored as much as it could have.[23]

Lastly, a word about collections. Objects acquired for the national collections also feature in the appendix, although it is harder to get a clear picture of this activity, which is less prominent than exhibitions and perhaps harder to report on. Arguably collections have been somewhat overlooked in museum practice in the last thirty years as the emphasis has moved to how they are used in exhibitions and other public outputs. Te Papa was certainly part of this reorientation of museology, as Chapter 1 shows.

Twenty years on, the not so new museology seems a little *passé*. As its call for postmodern relativity, postcolonial reform, community engagement and relevance has been widely accepted, there is a counter trend, a renewed interest in curatorial expertise, material culture and an increased appreciation of the value of collections, not just in themselves but for society as a whole. There is an interest in the real, in physical things, and not virtual surrogates. As anthropologist Nicholas Thomas puts it, there is a 'return to curiosity'.[24] Thomas argues that 'what is good' about museums in the present is that they prompt us to be curious, and that curiosity in what is 'novel, singular or different is conducive to empathy, to a readiness to acknowledge and encounter difference'.[25] Museums can't change the world, despite what some claim, but they can help make it a better place, especially now. As Thomas puts it, 'Asking questions of objects — curiosity — is a skill which is much needed in today's heterogeneous world'.[26]

So, what does Te Papa's collecting between 1998 and 2017 tell us? Looking at the more recent acquisitions in each of the discipline areas gives a fascinating picture of the current priorities of curatorial staff and the wider organisation. Like tide marks on a sea wall, they show the ebb and flow of subjective tastes despite the objective parameters of policies. In some cases they reflect a dramatic change in thinking about what the national museum *should* be collecting in order to better reflect New Zealand society.[27] Note, for example, the trend to contemporary culture in the Pacific and Māori collections, referred to in Chapter 4.[28] Also worth noting is the wider and more inclusive range of decorative arts and photography, and the diverse material culture of childhood, ethnic minorities, refugees and migrants, and LGBT people evident in the history collections. Clearly New Zealand is a more diverse place than it was in the 1990s, with a growing Māori and Polynesian population, high Asian migration, and 'super diversity' in our cities.

Yet despite the fact that the collections reflect and materialise these long-term trends, there are still gaps. Historian and former history curator Bronwyn Labrum, now Head of New Zealand and Pacific Cultures at Te Papa, wrote the book *Real Modern* (2015) which drew on museum collections to illustrate the everyday lives of New Zealanders in the 1950s and 60s. She found that, despite the recent collecting that had incorporated a wider range of material culture, there were still a lot of aspects of life and society that were poorly represented in collections: men's clothing, schooling and gardening, food, sexuality, sport, craft, work and economics.[29] Te Papa's history collections, though relatively diverse, are also guilty of this, tending to focus on the fine, rare and beautiful artefacts of the elite rather than common everyday stuff. There is much to do.[30]

Where to from here? As Te Papa embarks on its twenty-first year, we may well ask where it is going. This history does not pretend to provide a crystal ball and gaze into the national museum's future, and I am not going to use that terrible cliché 'moving forward' to make some trite prediction about its prospects. As I have said above, there was a lot of energy and activity evident at Te Papa in 2016–17, when this book was written, which suggests it is going through another period of change as it did in the 1980s–1990s. If the new museology was the template then, another museological paradigm, yet to be fully formed, will lay down the tracks along which it will run in the twenty-first century. One thing is certain. If Te Papa shaped, and was shaped by, New Zealand society and history in the past, then this will continue in the future. That, after all, is what museums are good for.

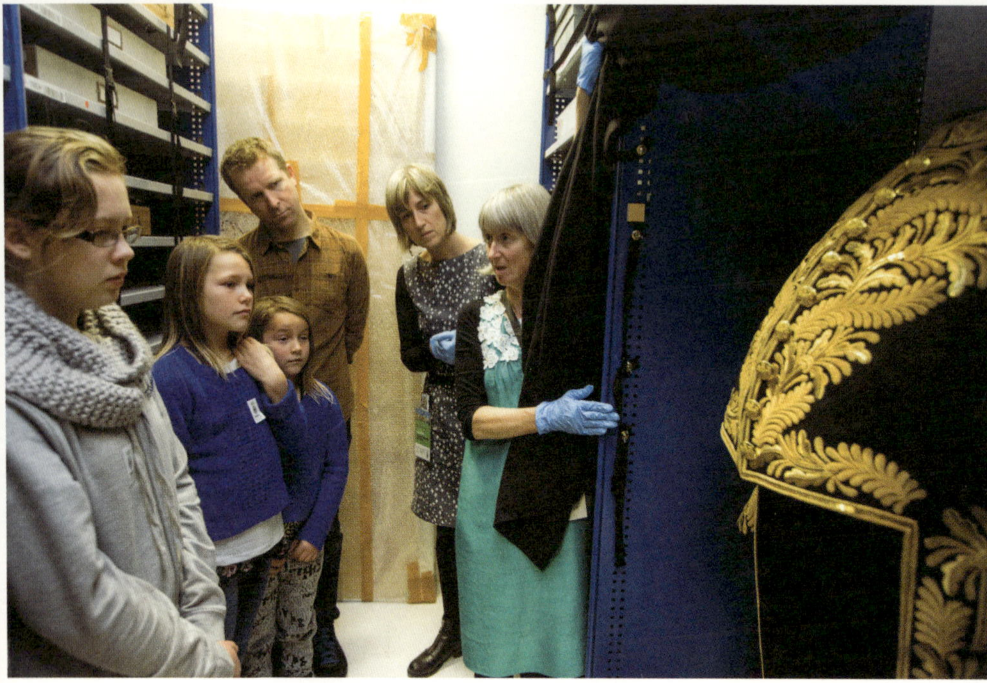

1.

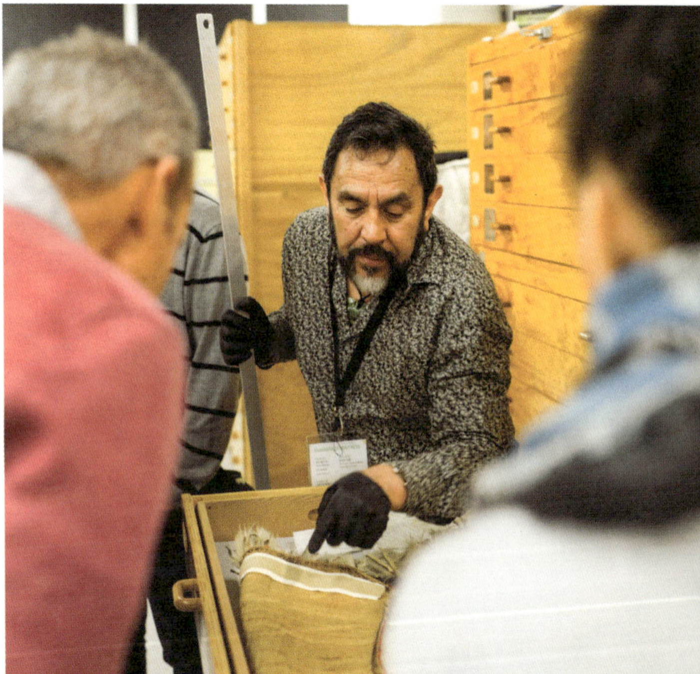

2.

1.

Curators Stephanie Gibson and Lynette Townsend show visitors Premier Richard John Seddon's waistcoat in the history collection.

2.

Kaitiaki Māori Mark Sykes shows visitors a cloak in the taonga Māori collection.

3.

The popular exhibition *Gallipoli: The Scale of Our War*, which opened in 2015.

4.

The exhibition *Whales/Tohorā*, which has been touring North American museums for several years.

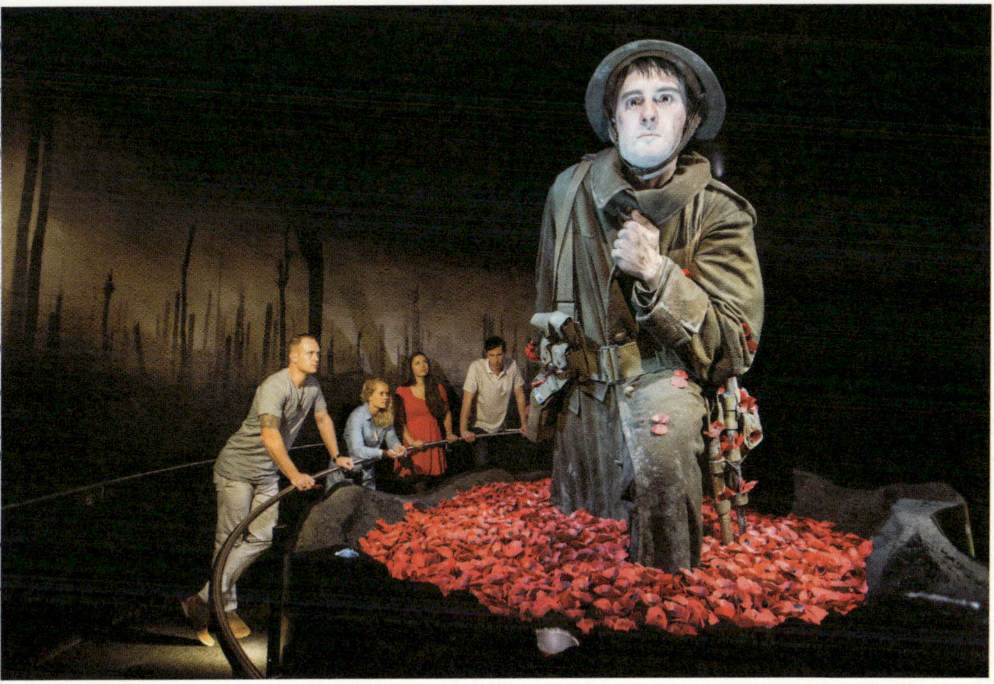

3.

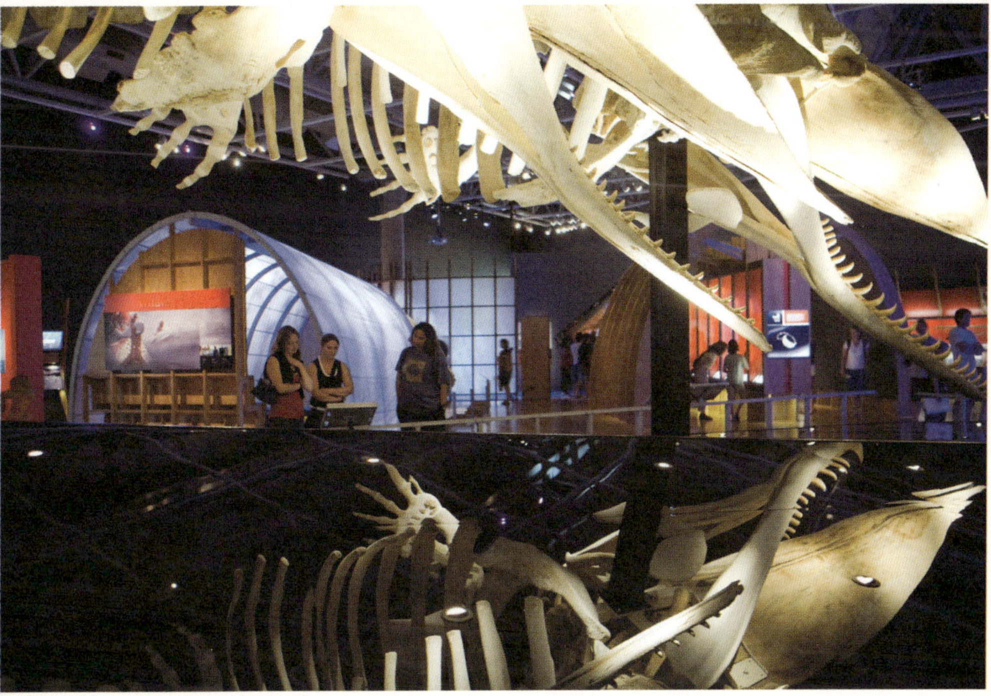

4.

appendix A

selected highlights 1998–2017

The following chronology of Te Papa's highlights is organised by financial years ending 30 June, except for 1998/1999, which covers the period from February 1998 to the end of June 1999. For more details of exhibitions, collection development, events and public programmes, and publications by Te Papa Press, see the museum's annual reports, which can be accessed on its website.[1] Thanks to Te Papa curators for the selection of significant collection acquisitions.

1998/1999

- Te Papa opens on 14 February 1998 under CEO Cheryll Sotheran.
- The travelling exhibition *Pictura Britannica: Art from Britain* (Museum of Contemporary Art Sydney) attracts controversy with protests by Christians over the *Virgin in a Condom* work by British artist Tania Kovats. Meanwhile three other temporary exhibitions are hits: photographs of the Indian monsoon by Brian Brake; Māori portraits by C.F. Goldie; and *Star Trek: The Exhibit* — the last attracts 87,000 visitors against a projected 50,000.
- National Services Te Paerangi continues its work of providing support and training for the wider museum sector, and trials the New Zealand Museums Standards Scheme in the Waikato region; this is launched nationally as a framework for professional development the following year.
- The moratorium on loans necessary during the building project is lifted, and from late 1998 to mid 1999 Te Papa loans 2500 objects to museums

around the country; three major paintings by artist Colin McCahon are loaned for exhibitions in Kassel, Germany; Auckland; and Dunedin.

- Te Papa celebrates its first birthday in February 1999 with a series of events, including sharing 'Pavzilla', a 45-metre-long pavlova cake, with visitors.
- Visitor attendance exceeds expectations, with over 2 million in the first calendar year (to 14 February 1999). Visitors to the website are calculated at 73,500.
- Te Papa art curators buy a major contemporary work by well-known artists Bill Culbert and Ralph Hōtere, *Blackwater* (1998–99).

1999/2000

- Wellington City Council agrees to sponsor Te Papa for three years at $2 million per annum. Other major sponsors include: the Earthquake Commission (EQC), Institute of Geological and Nuclear Sciences (GNS), TOWER Ltd, TelstraSaturn, Air New Zealand, Compac Computers New Zealand, Ericsson Communications, Ricoh, Carson Group, Budget Car and Truck Rentals, and Contact Energy.
- Te Papa partners with Victoria University of Wellington to teach a Master's degree in museum and heritage studies, and a strategic leadership programme for the whole museum sector managed by National Services.
- Te Papa history curators begin collecting contemporary New Zealand fashion, and in 1999 purchase a range of garments by 'the London Four', the now famous designers who showed at London Fashion Week that year (Karen Walker, NOM*D, WORLD and Zambesi). Later they began to collect garments from New Zealand Fashion Week.
- Another collecting highlight is a set of historical New Zealand photographs purchased from collector William Main, the culmination of a concerted effort to build up the holdings of historical photography in recent years, including photographs of Samoa by Thomas Andrew, and 10 photograph albums by explorer, geologist and archaeologist Leslie Adkin.
- In early 2000 the government commits for the first time to funding Te

Papa for collection acquisitions, which enables long-term collection development planning.

- In June 2000 a critical report is released on 'specific issues' related to the display of art at Te Papa; the report had been commissioned by the Ministry for Culture and Heritage and was written by Des Griffin, Rodney Wilson and Chris Saines.

2000/2001

- Staff take 15,000 children on school programmes and 10,000 visitors on guided tours, and the marae hosts 108 events for 21,000 people.
- History and Pacific collections are moved from Cable Street to a new facility in Tory Street, formerly the Wellington City Council Works Depot. The science collections previously stored at Cable Street, and the natural history unit in Taranaki Street, as well as the history collections at Tacy St in Kilbirnie, are now largely housed under one roof in Tory Street.
- Te Papa's science team help initiate an annual search for 20-million-year-old fossils near St Bathans, Central Otago. The fossils subsequently unearthed include ancestors of many birds such as kiwi, as well as tuatara and New Zealand's luminescent freshwater limpet, along with evidence for crocodiles and turtles.
- The unique programme of Māori events and performances, which eventually becomes Te Papa's signature Matariki festival, is launched for the Māori New Year in May–June.
- Kaihautū Cliff Whiting retires, and is replaced by Te Taru White.
- The art team acquires one of the last works painted by iconic New Zealand artist Colin McCahon for $2 million. The work, *A Painting for Uncle Frank* (1980), was shown in the exhibition *Dream Collectors* on level five. The history team acquire the costume of Xena: Warrior Princess, made by Barbara Darragh, Ngila Dickson and Robert Gillies in about 1995, as a gift from Pacific Renaissance Pictures.
- By the end of June 2001, there have been 1.28 million visitors to Te Papa in the last year, and 5.25 million since its opening.

2001/2002

- In response to criticism, the space for art display is expanded on levels five and six, and a new rooftop sculpture terrace is created. Meanwhile a new permanent exhibition of material and visual culture, *Made in New Zealand*, replaces the much debated *Parade* on level four.
- Prime Minister Helen Clark's 'cultural recovery' package injects $1.8 million into the national museum, but the institution is still not funded for depreciation.
- Museum staff number over 500 in total, with 300 permanent and over 200 casuals.
- Surveys show that Māori visitors make up 11 per cent of Te Papa's New Zealand audience, exceeding their proportion of the total population according to the 2001 census.
- Acquisitions include an important collection of jewellery made by Kobi Bosshard between 1960 and about 1994.

2002/2003

- *The Lord of the Rings Motion Picture Trilogy: The Exhibition*, mounted in partnership with New Line Cinema in 2002–03 attracts a record 219,539 visitors, with 3600 on the final day.
- The latest community gallery, *Aainaa: Reflections Through Indian Weddings*, opens in September 2002, replacing an exhibition on the Dutch in New Zealand. In November events are staged in association with the annual Diwali festival.
- The Karanga Aotearoa Repatriation Programme is set up with funding from the government.
- The Council of Australasian Museum Directors (CAMD) annual survey finds Te Papa the most visited museum in Australasia.
- The front-of-house bilingual database Te Papa Onscreen is relaunched as Tai Awatea Knowledge Net through the museum's website.
- Curator of Photography Athol McCredie negotiates the gift of a collection

of 37,000 photographs and archive material from the estate of New Zealand photographer Brian Brake. Comedian John Clarke gifts the outfit worn by Fred Dagg, the iconic character he created in the 1970s, to the history collection.

2003/2004

- A new bilingual website is launched.
- *Lord of the Rings* tours overseas.
- Icon restaurant is closed and the space is turned into a functions venue. Functions, conferences, retail and other commercial activity raise 27 per cent of overall income.
- A bicultural staff development programme gets underway, and the marae hosts 28 pōwhiri and 107 performances for over 60,000 visitors.
- Te Papa attracts 10 million visitors in total since 1998.
- History curators acquire stuffed toy characters from the TV series *Play School*, including Big Ted, Jemima and Manu.

2004/2005

- The long-term art exhibition *Toi Te Papa: Art of the Nation* opens in revamped spaces on level five. Temporary visual culture exhibition *Out on the Street: New Zealand in the 1970s* is also shown on level five, and the latest community gallery, *Qui Tutto Bene*, opens featuring the stories of New Zealanders of Italian descent. The first online exhibition, *Māori Showbands*, is launched on the museum's website.
- The new Ke EMu collection management system is set up.
- The inaugural National Digital Forum is hosted at Te Papa, bringing together professionals across the GLAMs (Galleries, Libraries, Archives and Museums) working with new technology.
- Seddon Bennington takes over as CEO from Cheryll Sotheran.

2005/2006

- The Collections Online searchable public database goes live.
- Karanga Aotearoa returns human remains from eight institutions in the UK and the Netherlands.
- *Lord of the Rings* returns for another season; a new multi-disciplinary exhibition, *Blood Earth Fire / Whāngai Whenua Ahi Kā*, opens on level three exploring the human shaping of the land; and a mobile exhibit about the Treaty of Waitangi, *Treaty2U*, tours the country in a bus. The exhibition *Culture Moves: Dance Costumes of the Pacific* is accompanied by an innovative public programme that focuses on intangible cultural heritage.
- International visitors pass 50 per cent of the total visitor numbers for the first time.
- Te Papa buys a portrait in oils by popular artist Charles Frederick Goldie, *Te Rahui, famed Maori carver from Rotorua* (1909).

2006/2007

- The museum's policy framework is updated and aligned with government priorities of families, national identity and economic transformation.
- The exhibition *Mauriora: Treasures from the Museum of New Zealand* opens in Japan.
- Science staff in partnership with Manaaki Whenua/Landcare Research launch a major research project on ferns, and a colossal squid (6–10 metres long and weighing 490 kilograms), one of only two specimens in the world, is caught in the seas off New Zealand. Science curators also produce two major books through Te Papa Press: *An Illustrated Guide to New Zealand Hebes* and *Extinct Birds of New Zealand*.
- Pacific Curator Sean Mallon joins a major research project, *Art in Oceania*, in collaboration with the British Museum, Cambridge University and Victoria University of Wellington. This work culminates in an award-winning book of the same name (published by Thames & Hudson, 2012) and an exhibition (Royal Academy London, 2018).

2007/2008

- Tenth-birthday celebrations are held February 2008 on a stage set up on level two, attracting over 27,000 visitors, with the highlight an outrageous performance by Auckland transvestite troupe the Queens of the Universe.
- The exhibition *Whales / Tohorā*, a successful blend of science, history and mātauranga Māori, opens in the touring gallery, and a new Pacific exhibition, *Tangata o le Moana*, opens on level four with a spectacular festival that attracts 20,000 in one weekend.
- A webcam of the colossal squid being dissected becomes an internet sensation and crashes the website.
- Significant decorative arts collections are acquired, including 12 pieces of jewellery by Warwick Freeman, made between 1984 and 2007, as well as a collection of Nigerian indigenous pottery, and British/New Zealand studio pottery (1957–1968) connected with Englishman Michael Cardew and New Zealander Peter Stichbury.
- The Pacific team continues its active collecting of a wide range of objects old and new, including a tivaevae taorei (patchwork quilt) made in the 1900s, and five T-shirts produced by South Auckland hip-hop record label Dawn Raid Entertainment in 2004. Meanwhile the Māori curators acquire a pre-contact mere pounamu, a pounamu and gold brooch made in about 1900, and a drawing of a pūhoro (thigh tattoo) by soldier artist Major General Horatio Robley dating from about 1865.
- Visitor numbers pass 15 million in total since the museum's opening, but the annual total declines for the first time, to 1.27 million. Again for the first time, physical visitation is surpassed by virtual visits to the website.

2008/2009

- Kaihautū Michelle Hippolite becomes acting CEO after the tragic death of Seddon Bennington in the Tararua Ranges in April 2009. His funeral is held on the marae, and broadcast live via the internet.
- Natural environment exhibitions are very prominent, with the display of the colossal squid on level two, while in the US *Whales / Tohorā* draws big crowds.

- The art exhibition *Rita Angus: Life and Vision* attracts over 130,000 visitors, and a touring exhibition, *Monet and the Impressionists*, draws 140,000. Te Papa collaborates with Voyager Maritime Museum in Auckland to display the America's Cup yacht *NZL32* in an exhibit called *Black Water White Magic: A Tribute to Sir Peter Blake.*
- Māori curators buy 'Tui cloak' (2004) and 'Matariki caper' (2006) from Porirua weaver Kohai Grace, and a set of tā moko equipment used by Gisborne artist Derek Lardelli. Pacific curators acquire six mu'umu'u dresses and two T-shirts made in the 1980s and 1990s from Pacific Islands women's group P.A.C.I.F.I.C.A and Helen Calder in Auckland. They also receive a gift from Mere Tapaeru Tereora of some P.A.C.I.F.I.C.A badges made by Goodwill Agencies.
- The annual Matariki festival continues in June, with the highlight the kaumātua kapa haka.
- National Services Te Paerangi launches the new national museums website nzmuseums.org

2009/2010

- New CEO Michael Houlihan arrives in February 2010.
- Te Papa's most popular permanent exhibition *Awesome Forces* is refreshed with input from GNS Science; a new twentieth-century history exhibition, *Slice of Heaven*, opens on level four; and the latest community gallery, *The Mixing Room*, an innovative exploration of the lives of young refugees using new media, opens next to *Passports*. Meanwhile an exhibition of greenstone, *Kura Pounamu*, tours to China.
- *Tales from Te Papa*, a series of short documentaries about objects in the collections, is broadcast on TVNZ's Channel 7 and on demand.
- In February 2010 annual debates on the Treaty of Waitangi are initiated and hosted by Dame Claudia Orange, and *Art After Dark*, a series of art-related events, is launched on Thursday evenings when Te Papa is open till 9 pm.
- A notable acquisition for the history collections is the chainsaw used by

Māori activist Michael Smith in his attempt to fell the pine tree on One Tree Hill (Maungakiekie) in Auckland in October 1994.

- Total annual visitor numbers rise to 1.4 million but Māori visitors make up only 8.8 per cent of New Zealand visitors (compared to 12.5 per cent of the population in the latest census).

2010/2011

- A wide-ranging review and revisioning process results in a new mission: 'Changing hearts, changing lives, changing minds.'
- Cultural diplomacy initiatives are explored with China, and a Memorandum of Understanding is signed with the National Museum of China in Beijing.
- Collections Online attracts 1.8 million viewers, surpassing physical visitor numbers to the Cable Street building and exhibitions touring overseas and at home.
- Research shows numbers for young visitors (aged 18–24) are still strong but Māori visitation falls to 8.6 per cent.
- The exhibition *E Tū Ake: Māori Standing Strong* opens in the touring gallery and starts an international tour, taking in France, Mexico and Canada. *Brian Brake: Lens on the World*, accompanied by an award-winning catalogue, opens on level five and then tours New Zealand. Meanwhile *Whales / Tohorā* is a hit in US museums, attracting more than 500,000.
- National Services Te Paerangi and Māori staff facilitate the loan of taonga for the opening exhibitions at Aratoi: Wairarapa Museum of Art and History in Masterton.
- The highlight of the year's art acquisitions is a portrait by John Webber, artist on Cook's third voyage to the Pacific: *Poedua [Poetua], daughter of Oreo, chief of Ulaietea, one of the Society Isles* (1785).
- Victoria University of Wellington donates the bulk of its herbarium, with nearly 13,000 dried, pressed specimens, adding to Te Papa's existing collection of some 300,000 plants.

2011/2012

- New strategies and values are unveiled, leading on from the new mission (see Appendix B).
- The latest iwi exhibition, on the Tainui people, opens, and a Māori weaving exhibition, *Kahu Ora: Living Cloaks*, is developed with the national weavers' organisation, along with a catalogue.
- There is a renewed emphasis on work with museums in the regions through National Services Te Paerangi's workshops and training, touring exhibitions and loans. In this spirit, Te Papa contributes to earthquake recovery in Canterbury after the fatal events of February 2011.
- Te Papa's digital offering comes to the fore: Collections Online proves to be very popular, with 100,000 images available free; the Te Papa blog (first introduced in 2008) is revamped and gains widespread interest; and artworks are available on the Google Art project.
- In 2011 Dame Margaret Sparrow gifts her large collection of contraceptive material culture dating from the 1960s to the 2000s, forming the basis of ongoing collecting in this important area of women's health. A number of decorative arts objects are added to the national collections: *Gesamtkunsthandwerk* by Karl Fritsch, Martino Gamper and Francis Upritchard (2011); archives from potters Peter and Diane Stichbury, which illustrate their contribution to the studio pottery movement; and jeweller John Edgar's *Six* works (1979–94).
- The art team buys Michael Parekowhai's *He Kōrero Pūrākau mō Te Awanui o Te Motu: Story of a New Zealand River*, which was displayed in the New Zealand pavilion at the 2011 Venice Biennale. This striking contemporary piece features a Steinway piano decorated with Māori carving and pāua shell.
- The total number of visitors passes 20 million.

2012/2013

- When Wellington City Council reviews its $2 million sponsorship to Te Papa, the museum responds by staging a public relations campaign that leads to the reinstatement of the grant.

- Visitor satisfaction levels reach an extraordinary 98 per cent, and on Trip Advisor's Traveller's Choice Te Papa comes out as the 'best museum in the region' (New Zealand, Australia, Pacific).
- Rhonda Paku becomes acting Kaihautū after the resignation of Michelle Hippolite.
- Plans are announced for Te Papa Manukau, a facility in South Auckland in partnership with Auckland Council and local museums and galleries.
- History curators start working with seven New Zealand children and their families to build a collection of objects that represent the lives and experiences of children from different backgrounds, as part of the University of Auckland's Growing Up in New Zealand longitudinal study. One of the objects acquired is a set of Mandarin-language flash cards that were used by the donor, Austin Wang, when learning to speak and read Chinese.
- A specimen of a sunfish, the heaviest of the bony fishes, is acquired via Auckland Museum. Its examination and dissection are broadcast online.
- Seismic risk assessments of buildings are undertaken after recent Wellington earthquakes.
- The 1.3 million visitors on-site are matched by 1.3 million people visiting touring exhibitions around the country and abroad, including *Kura Pounamu* in China and *Kahu Ora* at home. Back at the museum the exhibition *Ngā Toi: Arts at Te Papa* opens on level four.

2013/2014

- A financial crisis ensues after the 'poor performance' of two international exhibitions, coupled with the restructuring (that followed the new vision) failing to meet expected budgets. A PwC report leads to drastic cost reductions. In April 2014, Michael Houlihan is seconded to the Ministry for Culture and Heritage to work on World War I commemoration projects and Dr Arapata Hakiwai, recently appointed as Kaihautū, becomes acting CEO.
- Te Papa tours eight exhibitions around New Zealand and loans 2000 objects from the collection to museums, iwi and other communities.

- Education and public programmes are very active: 27,500 students take programmes, and 71,000 visitors attend events and functions.
- Te Papa raises 25 per cent of its income through commercial activities, 10 per cent through donations and sponsorship, and 6 per cent through exhibitions.
- Visitor numbers fall to 1.28 million, but there are 1.5 million visitors to the website.

2014/2015

- After a lull in visitor numbers there is a jump to 1.55 million, 20 per cent higher than 2013/2014. Hits on the website number 2 million, and 700,000 watch the examination of another colossal squid online. Trip Advisor ranks Te Papa first in the South Pacific for museums, and twenty-third in the world.
- The World War I exhibition *Gallipoli: The Scale of Our War*, developed with Richard Taylor and Weta Workshop, is an unprecedented success, with 144,357 visitors between April and December 2015, while *Air New Zealand 75 Years* attracts a total of 335,500.
- After budget deficits in 2014 there is a financial turnaround, with increased revenue and cost savings. Rick Ellis becomes CEO and focuses on streamlining operations.
- A major renewal process over the next five years is announced, to replace the permanent exhibitions and complete overdue maintenance of the building and facilities. Four discipline heads are appointed — for Mātauranga Māori; History and Pacific Cultures; Science; and Arts — in addition to a Head of Learning Innovation, Head of Collection Services, and Head of Digital.
- Te Papa's digital capacity expands: Mahuki, a digital business innovation hub, is announced; a Chief Digital Officer is appointed; and there are no less than 370,000 visits to Collections Online, while 155,000 read the blog. *New Zealand Birds Online*, launched in 2013, has its one-millionth visit.
- Karanga Aotearoa complete their largest repatriation with 114 human

remains, including toi moko from the American Museum of Natural History in New York.

- After the settlement of their claim to the Waitangi Tribunal, and a heads of agreement signed with the Crown, the Rongowhakaata iwi from Gisborne embark on the process of restoring their meeting house Te Hau ki Tūranga.
- As part of a research project tracing the histories of the LGBTI (Lesbian Gay Bisexual Transgender Intersex) community, a major collection is acquired from the late Carmen Rupe (1936–2011), a legendary transgender performer and activist. Working with the community, research is conducted on related people and places such as Chrissie Witoko and the Evergreen Coffee House managed by Carmen just off Cuba Street in Wellington. Meanwhile the art team buys a significant historical oil painting by English artist William Strutt from a private collection in London — *View of Mt Egmont, Taranaki, New Zealand, taken from New Plymouth, with Maoris driving off settlers' cattle* (1861).

2015/2016

- The Mahuki Innovation Hub launches.
- The website is upgraded, redesigned and streamlined, with more collections and exhibition content online.
- In September 2015, Te Papa hosts a major conference of the International Federation of Human Rights Museums in collaboration with Victoria University, including the inaugural Michael Volkerling Memorial Lecture presented by Professor Richard Sandell from the University of Leicester.
- A decades-long research project culminates in the publication by Te Papa Press of the encyclopedic, four-volume *The Fishes of New Zealand*.
- The Kaihautū Arapata Hakiwai and Māori staff continue the ongoing work, alongside other government agencies, of negotiating the settlement of Treaty claims with over twenty iwi, including cultural redress, access to taonga through digital databases, repatriation, and cultural centres.
- The ‘ahu ‘ula (cloak) and mahiole (headdress) gifted to Captain Cook by Hawaiian chief Kalani‘ōpu‘u in 1779 are transferred to the Bishop Museum in Honolulu on long-term ‘loan’.

2016/2017

- The annual report heralds Te Papa's most successful year to date with a record 1,578,292 visitors through the doors. Total visitor numbers reach 27,591,143 since opening.
- In October 2016 *Gallipoli* has its millionth visitor, making it the most successful exhibition in the museum's history. *Bug Lab: Te Aitanga a Pepeke*, an innovative display about insects, opens at Te Papa and then goes on tour. *Whales / Tohorā* clocks up 2.7 million visitors overseas. Meanwhile back home, sport is featured as Sir Peter Snell's Olympic medals go on display and an exhibition hotspot, *The Spirit of the Black Jersey*, opens to coincide with the Lions rugby tour.
- Hīnātore Learning Lab launches on level four, and at Tory Street a laboratory for DNA analysis opens, the first in a New Zealand museum, to support the science team's work of classifying plants and animals.
- Karanga Aotearoa host a major pōwhiri for a repatriation of 60 human remains from five German, Swedish and North American museums, including the Smithsonian in Washington DC.
- National Services Te Paerangi provides training and support for museums, galleries and iwi in the Far North, Waitangi, Waikato, Whanganui, Nelson, West Coast, Christchurch and Rēkohu (Chatham Islands).
- The Te Papa Foundation, a key part of the funds development strategy, is launched with much pizzazz and receives donations from high-profile figures in the arts and heritage sector.
- In June 2017 Te Papa's well-known midwinter Māori public programme is rebranded as *Matariki Rising*. The ever-popular kaumātua kapa haka livestreams to 900,000 viewers on Facebook. At Tory Street the 'Open House' event, in which the public visit collections, attracts 2756 people.
- A series of medals is put on temporary display: a suffragette medal given to a New Zealand-born activist in Scotland (1912), the Te Pahi medal presented to the Ngā Puhi chief in Sydney in 1806, and Peter Snell's Olympic gold medals from Rome (1960) and Tokyo (1964).

- Highlights of recent acquisitions demonstrate the diversity and range of the national collections: five works from Simon Denny's exhibition *Secret Power* from the 2015 Venice Biennale; a collection of ceramics (1972–86) by James Greig; a rare specimen and egg of the extinct laughing owl; a 1970s–80s battle shield from Papua New Guinea featuring 'The Phantom' comic book character; a terracotta sculpture, *Seven days*, by Māori potter Baye Riddell; and finally a homemade rimu skateboard from the 1950s and a cash register from the Wellington department store Kirkcaldie and Stains.
- In 2017 the Pacific team launch an ambitious co-collecting project with the Tongan community in South Auckland — Pikipikihama Kae Vaevae Manava/Joining our Vaka to Share our Life Stories.
- Geraint Martin starts work as the new CEO in May 2017.
- The Ngāti Toa iwi exhibition closes in March 2017, and the Rongowhakaata exhibition, *Ko Rongowakaata: The Story of Light and Shadow*, opens in September 2017, livestreamed on the website.

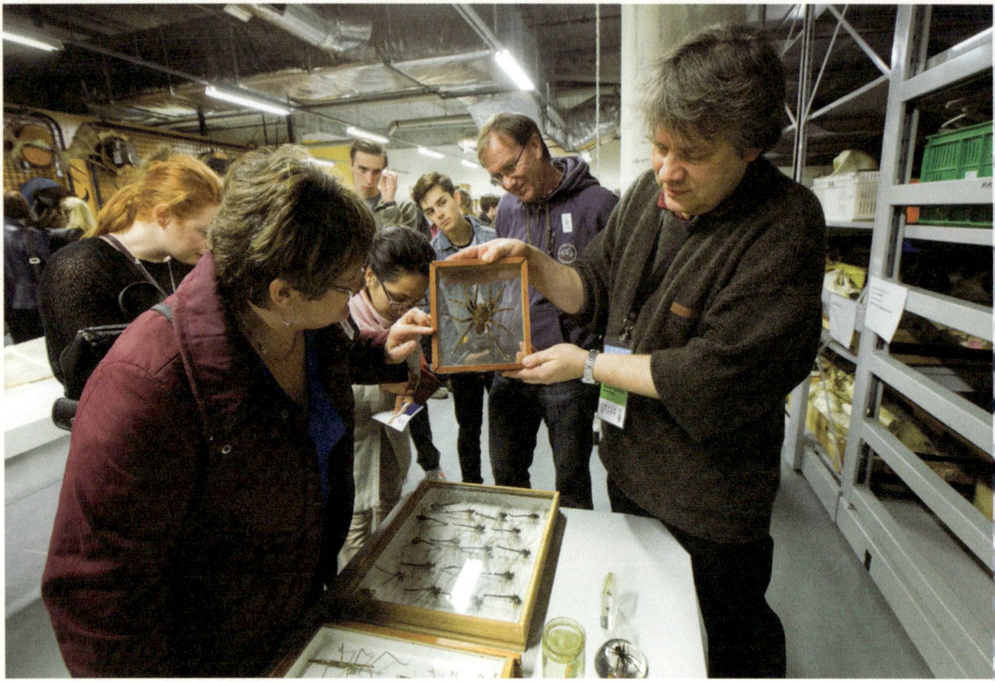

1.

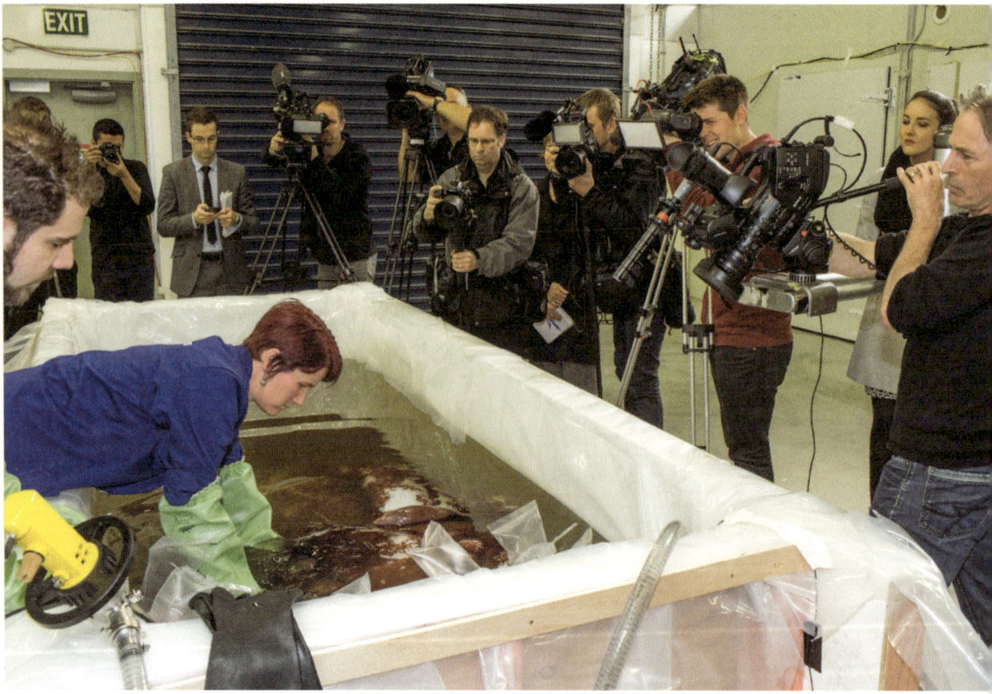

2.

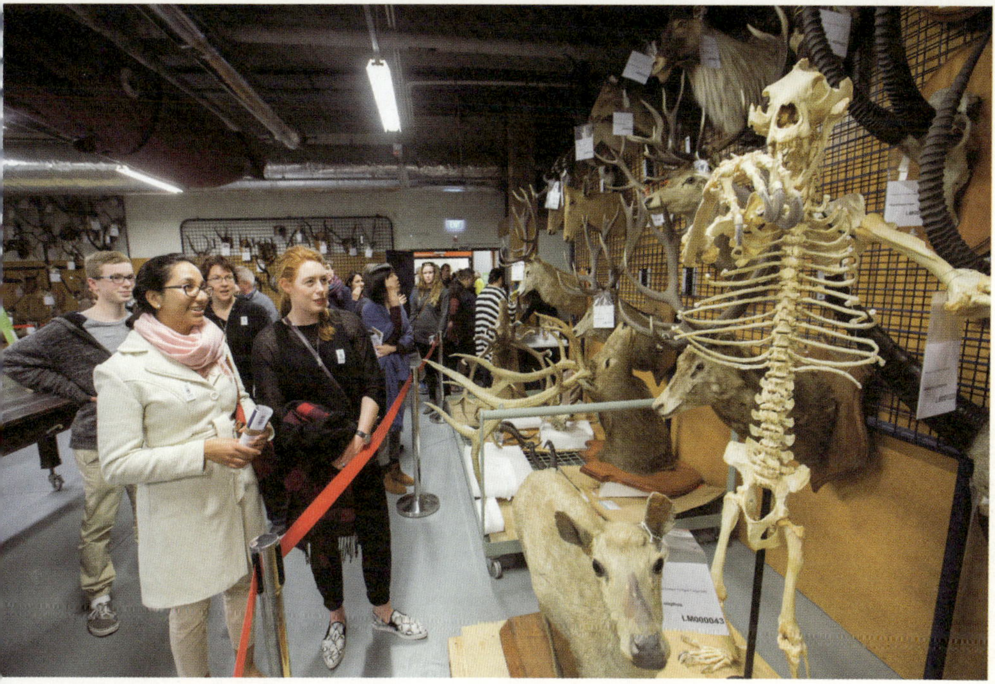

3.

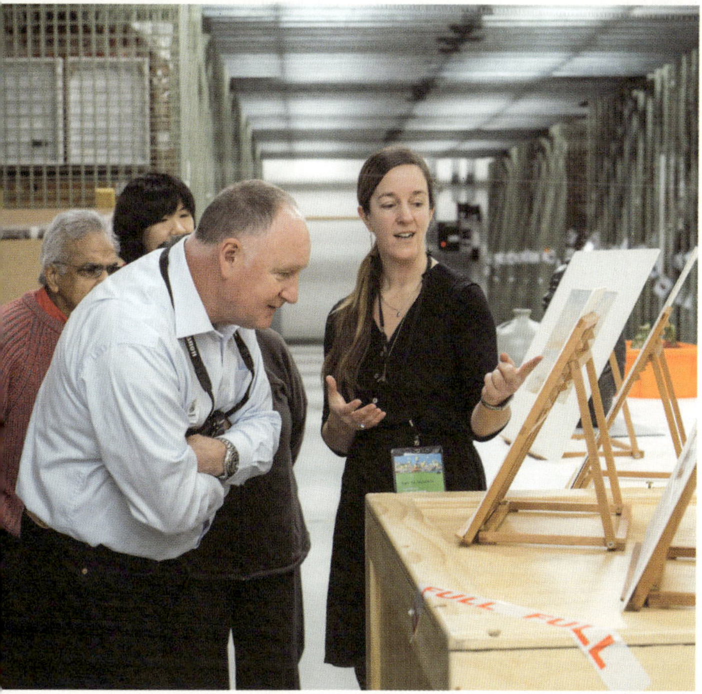

4.

1.

Te Papa entomologist Dr Phil Sirvid shows a spider from the collection to a curious visitor.

2.

The press view a specimen of a colossal squid in the natural environment collection at Tory Street.

3.

Visitors view the natural environment collections at Tory Street on an open day.

4.

Curator Rebecca Rice shows visitors a work from the art collection on an open day.

appendix B

current strategies and values

STRATEGIES[1]

Accessing all areas

Te Papa will share its collections, skills and knowledge with the diverse communities across Aotearoa New Zealand and overseas.

Being a forum for the future

As a cultural and intellectual leader, Te Papa will signpost pathways to the future by initiating, hosting and engaging in debates that explore a wide range of contemporary issues.

Housing the treasures

Taonga (treasures), within the guardianship of Te Papa will be at the heart of the Museum's activities.

Connecting with people

Te Papa will make learning an engaging and entertaining experience. Te Papa will set the highest possible standards for an integrated and welcoming experience.

Saving the planet

Te Papa will engage and excite by conducting leading-edge research and by communicating and modelling environmentally responsible practices that are smart, accessible and inspiring.

Mana taonga|Sharing authority

Te Papa will share decisionmaking with iwi (tribes), communities and individuals with respect to managing and understanding their taonga (treasures).

VALUES[2]

Mātauranga|Knowledge & learning

We actively seek and share knowledge, value intellectual rigour, learn from our experiences and mistakes, and promote questioning and debate among ourselves and our communities.

Whanaungatanga|Relationships

Caring for each other: we work collaboratively with colleagues, both internally and externally, respecting and honouring each other's mana (integrity), expertise and perspectives.

Kaitiakitanga|Guardianship

Caring for our collections: we care for and promote access to our collections, acknowledging that we hold them in trust for all New Zealanders and nourishing the whakapapa relationships between taonga and their communities.

Manaakitanga|Community responsibility

Caring for our communities: we welcome, include, inspire, respond to and collaborate with our communities, championing the importance of culture, heritage and natural history.

Hiranga|Excellence

We aspire to be first-class, professional, innovative, ground-breaking, relevant, engaging and commercially successful.

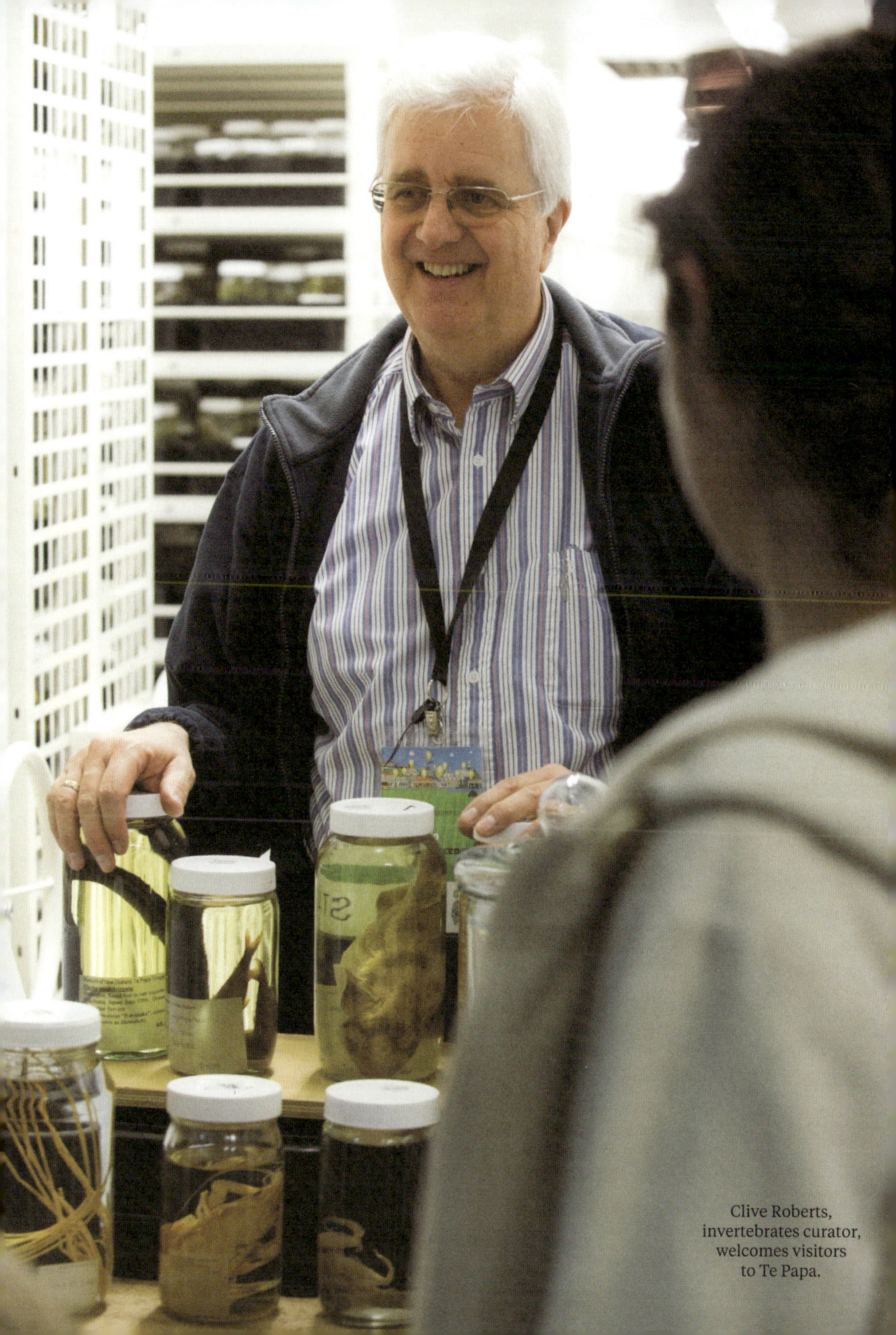

Clive Roberts, invertebrates curator, welcomes visitors to Te Papa.

appendix C
interviewees

All interviews were conducted by the author, unless noted below. Original cassette tapes, CDs and audio files, notes and transcripts of the interviews are housed in the Te Papa Archives, Wellington.

Dougal Austin — March and April 2009
Matiu Baker — May 2009
Seddon Bennington — March 2009
Lynne Carmichael — June 2017
Janet Davidson — August 2000
Migoto Eria — June 2017
Victoria Esson — July 2009
Ken Gorbey — March 2000, September 2008 and May 2009
Arapata Hakiwai — July 2000 and February 2009
Arapata Hakiwai interview by Philipp Schorch — June 2009
Te Herekiekie Herewini — April 2009
Michelle Hippolite — January 2009
Karl Johnstone — December 2008
Hirini Moko Mead — April 2006
Carolyn McGill — July 2017
Gerard O'Regan — June 2009
Ross O'Rourke — July 2000
Moana Parata — February 2009
Dion Peita — January 2009
Leon Perrie — June 2017
Betty Rewi — August 2001
Huhana Smith — January 2009 and November 2016
Mark Stocker — May 2017
Awhina Tamarapa — July 2000, February 2009 and April 2016
Megan Tamati-Quennell — April 2009
Rangimoana Taylor — May 2017
Rangi Te Kanawa — May 2009
Kukupa Tirakatene — May and June 2009
Lisa Ward — March 2009
Te Taru White — December 2008
Cliff Whiting — January 2000
Matariki Williams — November 2016
Miri Young — June 2017

glossary

This glossary is intended as an indicative guide only; it contains a very basic list of customary concepts related to caring for taonga, as well as Māori words in general use that are relevant to working in museums. Sources include the works listed in the endnote, to which readers are directed for further information.[1]

amo	upright support posts at the end of gables on the front of the house
aroha	love, respect, pity, compassion, show approval
atua	god, supernatural being, guardians or spiritual powers of the natural world
haka	posture dance
hapū	extended family group, subtribe or section of a large tribe, also word for 'pregnancy'
heke	rafter
hiki tapu	lift the tapu, ceremony for opening houses currently used for exhibitions
hoeroa	ceremonial staff made from whalebone
hongi	salute or greet by pressing noses together
hui	gathering, meeting, assembly, seminar, conference
huia	extinct bird, tail feathers used as chiefly adornment

iwi	tribe, nation, people, also word for 'bone(s)'
kai	food
kaiārahi	guide (literally 'one who leads')
kaihautū	Māori director
kaitaka	cloak made of fine flax with ornamental border
kaitiaki	guardian, caretaker, word designating Māori museum staff (literally 'one who cares')
kaitiakitanga	guardianship, stewardship of Māori taonga in museum collections
kākahu	cloak/s, garment, clothes
kapa haka	concert party, refers to group of performers and performing arts themselves
karakia	incantation, prayer
karanga	call of welcome to visitors in pōwhiri ceremony
kawa	cultural protocols (see tikanga)
kaumātua	elder or elders, old man (or woman)
kaupapa	plan, proposal, policy, reason
kaupapa Māori	modern term referring to Māori-driven projects, self-determination
kauri	native tree
kiwi	native species of bird
kōiwi	human remains
kōiwi tangata	human bone(s) or skeletal remains
kōrero	say, speak, talk, conversation, story
kōruru	carved gable mask of a house
kuia	old woman, grandmother
maihi	carved gables on the front of a house

mana	power, authority, prestige, respect; closely related to tapu ('potential power'), mana is the 'actual power or power itself', the 'actualisation' or 'realisation' of tapu
manaakitanga	the hosting of visitors
mana taonga	the power, authority and responsibility associated with the possession of taonga
mana whenua	the power, authority and responsibility arising from the possession of lands
manuhiri	visitors
Māori	person of Māori descent, indigenous to Aotearoa New Zealand; also ordinary, normal, natural
Māoritanga	explanation or meaning; in modern times denotes Māoriness, Māori culture
marae	space in front of a meeting house; can also refer generally to all the community facilities around the house
marae ātea	space in front of a meeting house where welcome ceremonies take place
māramatanga	enlightenment
mātauranga	knowledge
mātauranga Māori	modern term referring to the Māori system of knowledge or world view, as well as the body of knowledge to which it refers
mauri	spark of life, life essence
mere	short flat club or cleaver often made of greenstone
mihi	greet, acknowledge
moa	extinct species of native bird
mōhiotanga	understanding

moko	incised body adornment, tattoo
Moriori	the indigenous people of the Chatham Islands 800 kilometres east of New Zealand, descended from the same Polynesian settlers as Māori
muka	processed flax prepared for weaving
muri	future
noa	ordinary, normal, safe; sometimes referred to as the opposite/complementary value to tapu
pā	fortified village, former name for marae complex
paepae	threshold of house, line of kaumātua at welcome ceremony
Pākehā	person of European descent, as opposed to Māori
Papa, Papatūānuku	mother earth
papahou	form of Māori treasure box from northern New Zealand
pātaka	storehouse
patu	short club
pāua	brightly coloured seashell native to New Zealand
pepeha	proverb, saying (see also whakataukī)
pou	post, pole
pounamu	greenstone, jade (New Zealand nephrite)
poupou	carved side wall post or slab of a house
poutokomanawa	central free-standing post inside a house supporting the ridgepole
pōwhiri	welcoming ceremony
rangatira	chief
rangatiratanga	chieftainship, chiefly authority, power or sovereignty

rauawa	strakes of a canoe
taiaha	two-handled fighting or ceremonial staff
tā moko	tattoo
tangata	adult person (sing.)
tāngata	people (pl.)
tangata whenua	people of the land, indigenous people (Māori), specifically the local tribe who claim mana whenua, power or authority, over specific territory
tangi, tangihanga	funeral ceremony
taonga	property, treasure, anything highly prized
taonga puoro	traditional Māori wind instruments such as kōauau
tapu	sacred, special, state of being set apart
tauihu	carved prow of a war canoe
taurapa	carved sternpost of a war canoe
tekoteko	free-standing carved figure, usually at the front apex of a house
te reo Māori	the Māori language
tewhatewha	long-handled club
tikanga	customary rules or habits, set of beliefs associated with Māori cultural practices and procedures
tikanga taonga	customary Māori cultural practices employed in caring for taonga in museum collections, Māori collection care
tino rangatiratanga	phrase in the Māori text of the Treaty of Waitangi meaning absolute chieftainship or authority; today generally refers to aspiration for self-determination
tiriti	treaty
toi moko	respectful modern term for a decorated, tattooed preserved human head

tongarewa, tongarerewa	variety of greenstone, ear ornament, something precious (adjective)
tōtara	native timber favoured for carving
tukutuku	stitched latticework panels between posts in a house interior
tūpāpaku	corpse
tupuna	ancestor (pl. tūpuna)
waharoa	gateway
wāhi tapu	special places, sacred spots; also special repositories in museums for human remains
waiata	song
wairua	soul, spirit, spirituality
waka	canoe, vessel or container
waka huia	carved feather box, treasure box
waka taua	war canoe
wānanga	workshop, seminar, course of learning
whaikōrero	oration, formal speech
whakairo	to ornament with a pattern; in modern usage refers to wood carving
whakanoa	tapu-reducing ritual
whakapapa	genealogy
whakataukī, whakatauākī	proverb, saying
whānau	family, to give birth
whare	house
whare wānanga	school of learning
whare whakairo	carved house
whenua	land, afterbirth

notes

Introduction: Day one

1 Jenny Shipley quoted in Andrea O'Neil, '150 Years of News — Te Papa opens amid logo and name criticism', *The Dominion Post*, May 15, 2015, http://www.stuff.co.nz/dominion-post/68932713/150-years-of-news-Te-Papa-opens-amid-logo-and-name-criticism.

2 For visitor numbers and breakdown of audience see the Te Papa Annual Report 1998/1999, 5–6, 8–9, 33. Although 2 million visited (from February 1998 to February 1999), the official first year total is 1.68 million, taken from 30 June 1998 to 30 June 1999. A UMR survey conducted in December 1998 found that a quarter of New Zealanders and over 60 per cent of Wellingtonians had already been to Te Papa. See: 'Museum of New Zealand Te Papa Tongarewa: A summary report', Wellington, Te Papa Visitor and Market Research and UMR Insight Ltd, 1998, 3. Hereafter all annual reports are available from 'Annual Reports and Key Documents', Te Papa, accessed July 30, 2017, https://www.tepapa.govt.nz/about/what-we-do/annual-reports-and-key-documents.

3 For more information, see the visitor data in Chapter 3 and Appendix A.

4 See for example: Rosmarie Beier-de-Haan, 'Restaging Histories and Identities', in *A Companion to Museum Studies*, ed. Sharon Macdonald (Oxford and Malden: Blackwell, 2006), 186–97; Robert Janes, 'Museums, Corporatism and the Civil Society', in *Museum Studies: An Anthology of Contexts*, 2nd edn, ed. Bettina Messias Carbonell (Oxford and Malden: Wiley-Blackwell, 2012), 554.

5 See the Foreword to this volume. For Knell's work, see: Simon J. Knell, 'National Museums and the National Imagination', in *National Museums: New Studies from Around the World*, eds. Simon J. Knell, Peter Aronsson, Arne Bugge Amundsen, Amy Jane Barnes, Stuart Burch, Jennifer Carter, Viviane Gosselin, Sara A. Hughes and Alan Kirwan (London and New York: Routledge, 2010), 3–28; Simon J. Knell, *National Galleries: The Art of Making Nations* (London and New York: Routledge, 2016).

6 Barbara Kirshenblatt-Gimblett, 'Destination Culture', my notes from a lecture presented at Auckland Art Gallery, August 21, 1998. See also: Barbara Kirshenblatt-Gimblett, *Destination Culture: Tourism, Museums, and Heritage* (Berkeley: University of California Press, 1998).

7 Elaine Heumann Gurian, 'A Ray of Hope?' *Architecture/New Zealand* (February 1998): 78.

8 For an analysis of Te Papa in its national and international context, see: Conal McCarthy, 'Museums', *Te Ara — the Encyclopedia of New Zealand*, accessed July 1, 2017, https://teara.govt.nz/en/museums; Conal McCarthy, 'Museum of New Zealand Te Papa Tongarewa', in *The Encyclopedia of Global Archaeology*, ed. Claire Smith (Springer, 2014), 5114–16, accessed July 1, 2017, https://link.springer.com/referenceworkentry/10.1007/978-1-4419-0465-2_2294.

9 Ken Gorbey, 'Provocation: A New Te Papa L4 Cultural Exhibition Concept', paper presented to staff at Te Papa (January 25, 2017).

10 Ken Gorbey, 'Disneyland! Or the Te Papa-fication of New Zealand Museums', paper presented to the Stout Research Centre Conference *Antipodes: New Directions in New*

Zealand Culture and History, Victoria University of Wellington (September 4, 2009).

11 Kylie Message, *New Museums and the Making of Culture* (Oxford and New York: Berg, 2006).

12 Charlotte Macdonald, 'Race and Empire at Our Place: New Zealand's New National Museum', *Radical History Review* 75 (1999): 80–91.

13 See: Sarah Catherall, 'Te Papa Roasted for Poor Art Display,' *Sunday Star Times*, May 2, 1999; Jenny Harper, 'For the Sake of Your Art,' *Dominion*, June 2, 1999. For more commentary on art at Te Papa see Chapter 3.

14 Theodore Dalrymple, 'An Amusement Arcade Masquerading as a Museum', *New Statesman*, February 1, 1999; Rodney Wilson quoted in Jenny Chamberlain, 'Museum Wars', *North & South*, April 2000, 169.

15 'Te Papa Treats Art Like an Old Fridge — PM', *Evening Post*, January 25, 2000, 3.

16 Michael Goldsmith, 'Te Papa/Our Place and the Grammar of New Zealand Museumhood', paper presented to the annual conference of Social Anthropologists of Aotearoa New Zealand, Palmerston North (November 24–25, 2001).

17 See: Ryan Brown-Haysom, 'Book review essay: Crispin Paine, *Religious Objects in Museums: Private Lives and Public Duties*', *Museum Worlds: Advances in Research* 2 (2014): 235–40.

1: Getting to day one

1 For the history of these national institutions, and the history of museums in New Zealand generally, see: Richard Dell, 'Museums', in *An Encyclopedia of New Zealand*, ed. A.H. McLintock (Wellington: Government Printer, 1966), 602–05; Robert Falla, 'Museums', in *Oxford New Zealand Encyclopedia: Companion Volume to the Oxford Junior Encyclopedia*, eds. Laura Salt and John Pascoe (London: Oxford University Press, 1965), 255–57; Keith W. Thomson, *Art Galleries and Museums of New Zealand* (Wellington: Reed, 1981); Conal McCarthy, 'Museums', *Te Ara — the Encyclopedia of New Zealand*, accessed June 1, 2017, https://teara.govt.nz/en/museums.

2 For the history of the National Art Gallery, and related institutions such as the Academy of Fine Arts (now on Customhouse Quay), see: Tony Eden and Robin Kay, *Portrait of a Century: The History of the New Zealand Academy of Fine Arts 1882–1982* (Wellington: Millwood Press, 1983).

3 John M. MacKenzie, *Museums and Empire: Natural History, Human Cultures and Colonial Identities* (Manchester: Manchester University Press, 2009). That Victorian museums housed artworks integrated with other collections, before the emergence of academic disciplines demanded they be separated out, is a point not lost on those observers of late twentieth century museology. See: Christopher Whitehead, *Museums and the Construction of Disciplines: Art and Archaeology in Nineteenth-Century Britain* (London: Duckworth, 2009).

4 Roger Blackley, 'Art Galleries and Collections', *Te Ara — the Encyclopedia of New Zealand*, accessed June 13, 2017, http://www.TeAra.govt.nz/en/art-galleries-and-collections; Rebecca Rice, 'The State Collections of Colonial New Zealand Art: Intertwined Histories of Collecting and Display' (PhD thesis, Art History, Victoria University of Wellington, 2010).

5 Dell, 'Museums', 602.

6 Conal McCarthy, 'Displaying Natural History: Colonial Museum', in *The Amazing World of James Hector*, eds. Simon Nathan and Mary Varnham (Wellington: Awa Press, 2008), 49–61; Simon Nathan, *James Hector: Explorer, Scientist, Leader* (Wellington: Geoscience Society of New Zealand, 2015).

7 Amiria Henare, *Museums, Anthropology and Imperial Exchange* (Cambridge: Cambridge University Press, 2005).

8 Māori academic Hirini Moko Mead has argued that Pacific peoples had their own heritage institutions that preceded and paralleled some of the museum functions of preservation and display; for example, Māori had the marae, a complex of buildings for ceremonial and meeting purposes, which was an indigenous model for a museum. See: Sidney M. Mead, 'Indigenous Models of Museums in Oceania', *Museum* 35, no. 139 (1983): 98–101. For Māori involvement in and response to museums, see: Conal McCarthy, 'Carving Out a Place in the Better Britain of the South Pacific: Māori in New Zealand Museums and Exhibitions', in *Curating Empire: Museums and the British Imperial Experience*, eds. Sarah Longair and John McAleer (Manchester: Manchester University Press, 2012), 56–81.

9 Witness the publishing undertaken by the *Journal of the Polynesian Society* and the Board of Maori Ethnological Research, the field work of ethnologist Elsdon Best at the Dominion Museum, and the museum's expeditions to tribal areas where films of customary activities were shot by James MacDonald. See: Conal McCarthy, '"Empirical Anthropologists Advocating Cultural Adjustments": The Anthropological Governance of Āpirana Ngata and the Native Affairs Department', *History and Anthropology* 25, no. 2 (March 2014): 280–95; Tony Bennett, Fiona Cameron, Ben Dibley, Nélia Dias, Rodney Harrison, Ira Jacknis and Conal McCarthy, *Collecting, Ordering, Governing: Anthropology, Museums and Liberal Government* (Durham: Duke University Press, 2017).

10 For Māori arts and crafts, see: Roger Neich, *Carved Histories: Rotorua Ngati Tarawhai Woodcarving* (Auckland: Auckland University Press, 2001); Conal McCarthy, 'To Foster and Encourage the Study and Practice of Maori Arts and Crafts: Indigenous Material Culture, Colonial Culture and Museums in New Zealand', in *Craft & Community: The Material Culture of Place & Politics, 19th–20th Century*, eds. Janice Helland, Beverly Lemire and Alena Buis (Aldershot: Ashgate, 2014), 59–82. For Māori involvement in museum display, see: Conal McCarthy, *Exhibiting Māori: A History of Colonial Cultures of Display* (Oxford and New York: Berg, 2007), Chapter 2.

11 See: Conal McCarthy, 'From Curio to Taonga: A Genealogy of Display at New Zealand's National Museum, 1865–2001' (PhD thesis, Museum and Heritage Studies, Victoria University of Wellington, 2004), Chapters 2 and 3.

12 For an account of the museum's activities from the 1940s to the 1960s, see: Richard Dell, *Dominion Museum, 1865–1965* (Wellington: Dominion Museum, 1965). See also the unpublished manuscript of the longer version of this book: Richard Dell, 'The First Hundred Years of the Dominion Museum', unpublished manuscript, Te Papa Archives, Dell Ms papers 5156.

13 Conal McCarthy and Joanna Cobley, 'Museums and Museum Studies in New Zealand: A Survey of Historical Developments', *History Compass* 7 (2009), accessed January 1, 2017, http://onlinelibrary.wiley.com/doi/10.1111/j.1478-0542.2008.00587.x/abstract.

14 Tom Brooking, *Milestones: Turning Points in New Zealand History*, 2nd edn (Palmerston North: Dunmore, 1999).

15 For the *Te Maori* exhibition, see: Sidney M. Mead, ed., *Te Maori: Maori Art from New Zealand Collections* (New York: Heinemann and American Federation of Arts, 1984). For its impact, see: McCarthy, *Exhibiting Māori*, Chapter 4; Conal McCarthy, *Museums and Māori: Heritage Professionals, Indigenous Collections, Current Practice* (Wellington: Te Papa Press, 2011), Chapters 1 to 3.

16 Hamish Keith, 'Keynote address, Conference of the Art Gallery and Museums Association New Zealand', *AGMANZ Journal* 17, no. 3 (Spring 1986): 31–32. See also: Ken Gorbey, 'Editorial: New Zealand Museums — Is there life after *Te Maori*'? *AGMANZ Journal* 15, no. 4 (December 1984), 2–3.

17 McCarthy, *Exhibiting Māori*, Chapter 4. The dramatic change in the early 1980s should not diminish the substantial progress made in the 1970s, when professionals advocated for better facilities, more staff, new practices, and recognition of the Treaty. See: David Butts, 'Māori and Museums: The Politics of Indigenous Recognition' (PhD thesis, Museum Studies, Massey University, 2003); Thomson, *Art Galleries and Museums of New Zealand*.

18 James Belich, *Paradise Reforged: A History of the New Zealanders from the 1880s to the Year 2000* (Auckland: Allen Lane and Penguin, 2001), 392, 425, 463–65.

19 Belich, *Paradise Reforged*; Michael King, *The Penguin History of New Zealand* (Auckland: Penguin Books, 2003).

20 Ken Gorbey, 'Provocation: A New Te Papa L4 Cultural Exhibition Concept', paper presented to staff at Te Papa (January 25, 2017).

21 Mason Durie, *Te Mana, Te Kawanatanga: The Politics of Maori Self-Determination* (Auckland: Oxford University Press, 1998), 6–10.

22 For a comprehensive analysis of the Treaty in New Zealand politics and government in the 1980s, see Richard S. Hill, *Maori and the State: Crown-Maori Relations in Aotearoa/New Zealand 1950–2000* (Wellington: Victoria University Press, 2009). On the Treaty, see: Claudia Orange, *The Treaty of Waitangi* (Wellington: Allen & Unwin and Port Nicholson Press, 1987); Hugh Kawharu, *Waitangi: Maori and Pakeha Perspectives of the Treaty of Waitangi* (Auckland: Oxford University Press, 1989). On the Treaty and museums, see: David Butts, 'Maori, Museums, and the Treaty of Waitangi: The Changing Politics of Representation and Control', in *Museum Revolutions: How Museums Change and Are Changed*, eds. Simon J. Knell, Sheila Watson and Suzanne MacLeod (London and New York: Routledge, 2007), 215–27.

23 Butts, 'Māori and Museums'.

24 In 1900 Māori comprised a tiny rural minority, but by 2000 the tangata whenua were numerous (600,000 or 15 per cent of the total population), urbanised (83 per cent living in cities), and politicised. Belich, *Paradise Reforged*, 471–74.

25 Ibid., 479–80.

26 This list includes: Dunedin Public Art Gallery, 1996; Museum of Wellington City and Sea, 1999; Pātaka Art + Museum in Porirua, 2001; Aratoi Wairarapa Museum of Art and History in Masterton, 2002; Christchurch Art Gallery, 2003; and Puke Ariki in New Plymouth, 2003. Conal McCarthy, 'Museums', *Te Ara — the Encyclopedia of New Zealand*, accessed June 13, 2017, https://teara.govt.nz/en/museums.

27 On this topic of convergence and integration in GLAMS, see: Shannon Wellington, 'Building GLAMour: Converging Practice between Gallery, Library, Archive and Museum Entities in New Zealand Memory Institutions' (PhD thesis, Museum and Heritage Studies, Victoria University of Wellington, 2013). Other observers argue that Te Papa did *not* have much direct influence on local museums, aside from the demand for something new. Still others say that Te Papa spurred a counter-reformation of traditional, object-rich displays that avowedly swam against the tide of the new museology.

28 Peter Vergo, ed., *The New Museology* (London: Reaktion Books, 1989).

29 Gail Anderson, ed., *Reinventing the Museum: Historical and Contemporary Perspectives on the Paradigm Shift* (Lanham: Altamira Press, 2004).

30 See: Stephen E. Weil, 'From Being About Something to Being For Somebody: The Ongoing Transformation of the American Museum', *Daedalus* 128, no. 3 (Summer 1999): 229–58. See also: Stephen Weil, 'When the Audience Takes Centre Stage', *Melbourne Art Journal* 3 (1998): 5–13.

31 Deirdre C. Stam, 'The Informed Muse: The Implications of "The New Museology" for Museum Practice', in *Heritage, Museums and Galleries: An Introductory Reader*, ed. Gerard Corsane (Oxford and New York: Routledge, 2005), 54–70.

32 See: McCarthy, *Exhibiting Māori*, Chapter 5. Jette Sandahl, who has worked at Te Papa as well as in museums in Europe, has argued that, despite their bold political stance on global issues, one common feature of these new national museums was a lacklustre approach to design that she found 'conventional, formulaic, stereotypic — which in no way supported or facilitated, released or expressed innovative curatorial methods or alternative world views'. Jette Sandahl, 'Curating Across the Colonial and Other Divides', in *Curatopia: Museums and the Future of Curatorship*, eds. Philipp Schorch and Conal McCarthy (London and New York: Manchester University Press, forthcoming 2018).

33 Lindsay Archibald, 'Comparing the Canadian Museum of Civilization and Te Papa: Reinventing National Museums in the Late 20th Century' (Master's diss., Museum and Heritage Studies, Victoria University of Wellington, 2007). For museums and indigenous people in Canada, see: Ruth B. Phillips, *Museum Pieces: Towards the Indigenization of Canadian Museums* (Montreal and Kingston: McGill-Queen's University Press, 2011).

34 Darryl McIntyre and Kirsten Wehner, eds., *Negotiating Histories: National Museums — Conference Proceedings* (Canberra: National Museum of Australia, 2001); Graeme Davison, 'What Should National Museums Do? Learning from the World', in *Memory, Monuments and Museums: The Past in the Present*, ed. Marilyn Lake (Melbourne: Melbourne University Press, 2006), 91–109.

35 Richard West, et al., *The Changing Presentation of the American Indian: Museums*

and Native Cultures (Washington DC: Smithsonian Institution and University of Washington Press, 2006). For critical discussion of the NMAI, see: Amy Lonetree and Amanda J. Cobb, eds., *The National Museum of the American Indian: Critical Conversations* (Lincoln: University of Nebraska Press, 2008).

36 Ivan Karp and Steven D. Lavine, eds., *Exhibiting Cultures: The Poetics and Politics of Museum Display* (Washington: Smithsonian Institution Press, 1991); Joy Hendry, *Reclaiming Indigenous Culture: Indigenous People and Self-Representation* (New York: Palgrave MacMillan, 2005); Laura Peers and Alison K. Brown, eds., *Museums and Source Communities: A Routledge Reader* (London: Routledge, 2003).

37 See for example: McIntyre and Wehner, *Negotiating Histories*; Richard Gillespie, 'Making an Exhibition: One Gallery, One Thousand Objects, One Million Critics', *Meanjin* 60, no. 4 (2001): 118–19.

38 Sandahl, 'Curating Across the Colonial and Other Divides'. For the new museums' influence on European museology, see: Jette Sandahl, 'Living Entities', in *The Native Universe and Museums in the Twenty-First Century*, ed. Charlotte Heth (Washington: National Museum of the American Indian, 2005), 27–38.

39 'Te hokinga mai o nga taonga whakairo/The return of the art treasures', Hui wananga, National Museum, Saturday October 18, 1986. Report from Hirini Mead, Turoa Royal, Whata Winiata and Kuru Waaka on the seminar, as submission to *Nga Taonga o te Motu*, October 21, 1986. 'Te Maori general file', Te Papa Archives MU 487/1 box 2. See also: McCarthy, *Exhibiting Māori*, 155.

40 *Nga Taonga o Te Motu: Treasures of the Nation* (Wellington: Project Development Team for the National Museum of New Zealand and Department of Internal Affairs, 1985).

41 *A Concept for the Museum of New Zealand Te Papa Tongarewa* (Wellington: Museum of New Zealand Project Development Board, 1989); see also: Annual Report of the National Museum, 1989, 24.

42 This section draws on notes from two interviews with Ken Gorbey in September 2008 and May 2009. See Appendix C for the complete list of interviews.

43 Ken Gorbey, 'Driving Stakes into the Ground: Michael Blumenthal's Vision for a New Museum of German Jewish History', in *Die Ersten Achtzig Jahre The First Eighty Years: W. Michael Blumenthal zum Geburtstag* (Berlin: Society of Friends of the Jewish Museum, 2006), 155–63.

44 See: Andrea O'Neil, '150 Years of News: Te Papa opens amid logo and name criticism', *The Dominion Post*, May 15, 2015, http://www.stuff.co.nz/dominion-post/68932713/150-years-of-news-Te-Papa-opens-amid-logo-and-name-criticism.

45 See: Keith Stewart, 'Behind the Scenes at the Museum', *Quote Unquote* 35 (May 1996): 12–14; Diana Dekker, 'In the Brave New World of MONZ', *Evening Post*, August 3, 1996, 13; Nicola Legat, 'Cheryll Sotheran: New Zealander of the Year', *North & South*, January 1999, 48–53. For comments from a more recent interview with Sotheran, see: Wellington, 'Building GLAMour', Chapter 5.

46 Museum academic, professional and consultant David Butts points out that the appointment of people like Sotheran, Gorbey and others 'acknowledges the innovative examples of facility development, awareness of international standards

in professional practice and programming, and engagement with iwi emerging at that time in a number of regional institutions'. David Butts, pers. comm., July 2017.

47 On this under-researched topic, see: Ted Silberberg and Gail Dexter Lord, 'Balancing Mission and Money: Issues in Museum Economics', in *Museum Practice: The International Handbooks of Museum Studies*, vol. 2, ed. Conal McCarthy (Oxford and Malden: Wiley Blackwell, 2015), 151–78.

48 Cheryll Sotheran and Cliff Whiting, 'The Positioning of the Museum of New Zealand Te Papa Tongarewa', presented at *Repositioning the Museum: A forum for museums, stakeholder representatives and marketing support agencies*, Wellington, Museum Directors Federation (November 1–3, 1995).

49 Michael Volkerling, 'The Organisational Development of the Museum of New Zealand Te Papa Tongarewa', unpublished briefing paper, Wellington, Museum of New Zealand, 1992.

50 Gorbey, 'Provocation'.

51 Apirana T. Mahuika, 'Maori Culture and the New Museum', *Museum Anthropology* 15, no. 4 (1991): 9–10.

52 See: Ken Gorbey, 'The Challenge of Creating a Bicultural Museum', *Museum Anthropology* 15, no. 4 (1991): 7–8. For Māori community involvement, see: 'Museum Consult Iwi on New Facility Plans', *Kia Hiwa Ra*, March/April 1993, 27.

53 'Michael Volkerling Executive Director of the Board of Trustees, National Art Gallery Museum and War Memorial: Interviewed by Geri Thomas', *AGMANZ Journal* 19, no. 4 (1988): 14–17. See also: Michael Volkerling, 'Managing Change: Towards the Museum of New Zealand', paper presented to the AGMANZ conference, Wanganui (April 19, 1989).

54 For the Act, see: 'Annual Reports and Key Documents', Te Papa, accessed July 30, 2017, https://www.tepapa.govt.nz/sites/default/files/museum_of_new_zealand_te_papa_tongarewa_act_1992.pdf.

55 One wag in a local newspaper dubbed Cheryll Sotheran 'Te Mama o Te Papa': *Dominion*, February 14, 1998, 20.

56 For a full account of the name and other aspects of Te Papa's history, see: 'Our History', Te Papa, accessed June 30, 2017, https://www.tepapa.govt.nz/about/what-we-do/our-history. For the word 'papa' and its dialectal variations, see: Henry Williams, *A Dictionary of the Maori Language*, 7th edn (Wellington: GP Books, 1971), 436.

57 Ken Gorbey, letter to Sir Timoti Karetu, June 12, 2017. Another contributor to the name may have been Joe Malcolm of Te Arawa, who then worked in the project office. Variants of the phrase 'papa tongarewa' can be found in Te Arawa waiata, on which Malcolm was an expert.

58 For further visitors' comments, see: Conal McCarthy, 'A Theoretical Tour of the Museum', *Sites* 25 (Summer 1992): 81–117, appendix.

59 For a sample of some of the bizarre contemporary criticism of the brand, the building and the bicultural mission (and just about everything else to do with the museum), see the comments in: O'Neil, 'Te Papa opens amid logo and name criticism'.

60 Jock Phillips, draft memoirs, 2017, Chapter 8.
61 McCarthy, 'From Curio to Taonga', 345.
62 Gorbey, 'Provocation'.
63 Michaela Giebelhausen, ed., *The Architecture of the Museum: Symbolic Structures, Urban Contexts* (Manchester and New York: Manchester University Press, 2003).
64 See the documentary *Concert of Wills: Making the Getty Centre* (directed by Bob Essenhardt, Susan Froemke and Albert Maysles, 1997) to gauge the consequences of Richard Meier's design for the staff of the Getty in Los Angeles who had to work in the building. For a discussion of a more equitable balance between architects, designers and museum professionals, see: Suzanne MacLeod, *Reshaping Museum Space: Architecture, Design, Exhibitions* (Oxford and New York: Routledge, 2005).
65 This reading of Te Papa's architecture is based on notes taken during a discussion with architect Ivan Mercep, November 6, 1997. See also: Pete Bossley, *Te Papa: An Architectural Adventure* (Wellington: Te Papa Press, 1998).
66 For one of many critical views of the architecture, see: Anna Neill, 'National Culture and the New Museology', in *On Display: New Essays in Cultural Studies*, eds. Anna Smith and Lydia Wevers (Wellington: Victoria University Press, 2004), 180–96. For a more temperate assessment, see Peter Shaw, *A History of New Zealand Architecture* (Auckland: Hodder Moa Beckett, 2003).
67 'Day 1 Exhibitions conceptual plan', Museum of New Zealand Te Papa Tongarewa, Wellington, March 1994, 5. Te Papa Archives, MU 361 box 2.
68 William Tramposch, 'Exact Imaginings: The Museum as a Journey', in *New Trends in Museum Practice: Perspectives Nouvelles En Museologie*, eds. Michel Cote and Lisette Ferera (Quebec: ICOM Canada, 1997), 43–76. See also: William Tramposch, 'Te Papa: Reinventing the Museum', *Museum Management and Curatorship* 17, no. 4 (1998): 339–50.
69 Gaylene Preston and Anna Cotterill, *Getting to Our Place*, Gaylene Preston Productions, Wellington, 1999, accessed June 1, 2017, https://www.nzonscreen.com/title/getting-to-our-place-1999.
70 Te Papa was the first of many local heritage institutions to have a Māori name, followed by a host of others: Puke Ariki, Pātaka, Aratoi, Te Puia, Te Tuhi, Toitū, etc. It is the first and only national museum in the world to have an indigenous language name. Ironically, the only people who refused to use the Māori name, adopted universally by New Zealanders in preference to the longer form, were a handful of critics such as the editor of the *Dominion* who called it, illogically, 'Te Papa museum'.
71 On the long and circuitous process of coming up with this design, see *Getting to Our Place*.

2: A guided tour of the museum

1 This chapter is based on a number of sources, including the script of an introductory tour that I developed and delivered after the opening in 1998. The exhibits and other attractions are described as they were in February 1998, when I worked with them as a member of the education team.

2 Notes taken during a discussion with architect Ivan Mercep, November 6, 1997. See also: Pete Bossley, *Te Papa: An Architectural Adventure* (Wellington: Te Papa Press, 1998).
3 Conal McCarthy, '"Our Works of Ancient Times": History, Colonisation and Agency at the 1906–7 New Zealand International Exhibition', *Museum History Journal* 2, no. 2 (July 2009): 119–42. See also: Roger Neich, *Carved Histories: Rotorua Ngāti Tarawhai woodcarving* (Auckland: Auckland University Press, 2001).
4 In fact the exhibition *Blood Earth Fire* was not opened until 2006, but the original concept had always been to explore the interaction of people and land on level three. For the mixed success of the original aim to combine the exhibitions, see Chapter 3.
5 In May 2017 the Treaty was moved to a new exhibition, *He Tohu*, at the National Library in nearby Molesworth Street.
6 Until the paired artwork *Void* by Ralph Hōtere and Bill Culbert was installed in 2006.
7 For past exhibitions, see: 'Past Exhibitions 1998–2002', Te Papa, accessed March 30, 2017, https://www.tepapa.govt.nz/visit/whats-on/exhibitions/past-exhibitions/1998-2002-past-exhibitions.
8 Barbara Kirshenblatt-Gimblett, *Destination Culture: Tourism, Museums, and Heritage* (Berkeley: University of California Press, 1998), 175.
9 On the first plans, which I saw in 1992, this space was devoted to a cafeteria for staff. By the time Te Papa opened, it had become a restaurant, with fine dining under a celebrated chef, Adam Newell. Such is the metamorphosis of the contemporary museum.
10 From 2009, this space was dominated by a display of a colossal squid in its own custom-made case.
11 See the profile of Ngāti Toa kaumātua Te Waari Carkeek in Chapter 5.
12 See Chapter 4.
13 See Chapter 5 for later developments with this issue.
14 For more information on *Parade* 1998–2001, and images of the artworks, see: '*Parade*', accessed June 1, 2017, http://collections.tepapa.govt.nz/Topic/908.
15 In a scene from the documentary *Getting to Our Place* (Gaylene Preston Productions, Wellington, 1999) the chair of the board, Ron Trotter, is heard saying, in a debate about art being integrated with other media in exhibitions, that he likes his drinks straight 'and you're giving us cocktails'.

3: What the staff intended ... and what the critics thought

1 On this topic, see: Kathleen McLean, 'Museum Exhibitions and the Dynamics of Dialogue', in *Reinventing the Museum: Historical and Contemporary Perspectives on the Paradigm Shift*, ed. Gail Anderson (Walnut Creek: Altamira, 2004), 193–211.
2 For research on Te Papa exhibits and the complex interplay between intentions and reception, see: Lynne Carmichael Allan, 'Giving and Receiving: A Case Study of the Stowaways Exhibit in Blood Earth Fire Whāngai Whenua Ahi Kā' (Master's diss., Museum and Heritage Studies, Victoria University of Wellington, 2008). For

a complete set of exhibition development documents for day-one exhibitions, see: 'Exhibition Concept, Design and Development Documents 1992–1997', Te Papa Archives, series MU 361.

3 Kerry Jimson, 'Translating Museum Meanings: A Case for Interpretation', in *Museum Practice: International Handbooks of Museum Practice*, vol. 2, ed. Conal McCarthy (Oxford and Boston: Wiley Blackwell, 2015), 529–50.

4 Tim Walker, pers. comm., June 5, 2017.

5 These included: novelist Nigel Cox; children's author Johanna Mary; polymath Michael Keith; and playwright/scriptwriter, and later Senior Writer at Te Papa, Kerry Jimson. On his experiences at Te Papa and the Jewish Museum Berlin, where he worked with Ken Gorbey and Christine Fitzgerald, see: Nigel Cox, *Phone Home Berlin: Collected Non Fiction* (Wellington: Victoria University Press, 2007).

6 See the critical comments of art historian Mark Stocker, now a curator at Te Papa, along with Ian Wedde's response, in 'Te Papa: Not "Our Place" for Scholars', *City Voice*, December 16, 1999, 18.

7 Ken Gorbey, Letter to the editor, *Evening Post*, February 17, 1999.

8 All interviews are listed in Appendix C. Whiting was, of course, an art educator as well as an artist, and I remember he showed a keen interest in public programmes at Te Papa in which I was involved.

9 Warren Barton, 'Wonders of Our World Revealed', *Dominion*, February 10, 1998, 8.

10 'Ancient Lands: 90% Concept Design', Museum of New Zealand Te Papa Tongarewa, Wellington, 1996.

11 'Dinosaur Man Chuffed', *Contact*, November 11, 1999, 17.

12 Greg Motu, 'How Can the Natural History Components of Museums Become More Relevant to Iwi Interests?' *New Zealand Museums Journal* 26, no. 2 (Summer, 1997): 31–33. For another Māori natural history exhibition at Auckland Museum, *Te Ao Turoa*, developed by Mere Roberts, see: Chanel Clarke, 'Te Ao Turoa', *Te Ara: Journal of Museums Aotearoa* 27, no. 1 (2002): 23–26.

13 Kay Haughey, 'Mountains to Sea: Summative Evaluation Report', Wellington, Te Papa Visitor and Market Research, July 2001.

14 Jo Brehaut, 'Awesome Forces: Summative Evaluation', Wellington, Te Papa Visitor and Market Research, 2002, 4–5.

15 Ibid., 5.

16 Edward Poot, 'Finding Ourselves at Te Papa', *New Zealand Geographic*, 1998, accessed July 31, 2017, https://www.nzgeo.com/stories/finding-ourselves-at-te-papa.

17 See: 'Trip Advisor: Reviews Museum of New Zealand', accessed June 15, 2017, https://www.tripadvisor.ie/Attraction_Review-g255115-d257133-Reviews-Museum_of_New_Zealand_Te_Papa_Tongarewa-Wellington_Greater_Wellington_North_Island.html.

18 Barton, 'Wonders of Our World Revealed'.

19 Interview with Cliff Whiting, 'Ngā Wawata o Te Iwi Māori: A Māori Perspective', *Wanganui Chronicle*, February 16, 1998. Another controversy was speaking rights for women — see the argument between Cliff Whiting and Sir Ron Trotter captured in the documentary *Getting to Our Place*.

20 Brendan Cole, 'Our Place Shows the Way We Were, Are, and Will Be', *Taranaki Daily News*, February 14, 1998, 22. See also: C. Watson, 'Post-occupancy Evaluation for the Visitor Communications Group', Wellington, Te Papa Visitor and Market Research and Watson Consultancy Ltd, 1997. These comments are typical of those from Pākehā visitors heard on guided tours that I conducted while working at Te Papa from February 1998 to March 2000.

21 James Belich quoted in Simon Robinson, 'The Arts/Museums: Where the Heart is', *Time International*, February 16, 1998, accessed July 26, 2000, Electronic Library Australasia, http://www.e library.com.

22 Arapata Hakiwai interview, February 15, 2009, Te Papa Archives (Appendix C). See also the section on iwi relationships and the marae, Chapter 5.

23 For more detail on the way this played out, see Conal McCarthy, *Exhibiting Māori: A History of Colonial Cultures of Display* (Oxford and New York: Berg, 2007).

24 Arapata Hakiwai, 'Mana Whenua', *Open Eyes*, June 1998, 1.

25 Ibid.

26 Conal McCarthy, 'Mana Whenua: Summative Evaluation Report', Te Papa Visitor and Market Research and Victoria University of Wellington, 2001. See also McCarthy, *Exhibiting Māori*, Chapter 5.

27 Awhina Tamarapa, pers. comm., March 2017.

28 Ngāti Hinewaka's ongoing relationship with Te Papa has involved building collections, producing a video, the staging of their own exhibition in Masterton, and a tourism project. On Mākōtukutuku, see: Lindsay Archibald, 'Comparing the Canadian Museum of Civilisation and Te Papa: Reinventing National Museums in the Late 20th Century' (Master's diss., Museum and Heritage Studies, Victoria University of Wellington, 2007).

29 'Mana Whenua: 90% Concept Development', Museum of New Zealand Te Papa Tongarewa, Wellington, 1994, 19.

30 On this point, see: Nicholas Thomas, 'A Second Reflection: Presence and Opposition in Contemporary Maori Art', *Journal of the Royal Anthropological Institute* 1 (1995): 23–46.

31 See the comments from staff during interviews in McCarthy, 'From Curio to Taonga: A Genealogy of Display at New Zealand's National Museum, 1865–2001' (PhD thesis, Museum and Heritage Studies, Victoria University of Wellington, 2004), 370. This chapter also contains a range of external reviews.

32 McCarthy, 'Mana Whenua'. Despite this success, it should be acknowledged that any Māori exhibition is likely to be popular with international visitors, who make up a large part of a museum audience.

33 Ibid., 26.

34 Ibid., 63. For more comments, see this report, and McCarthy, *Exhibiting Māori*, Chapter 5.

35 See McCarthy, *Exhibiting Māori*, Chapter 5. Since the 2000s staff have been keen to update the exhibition, which has seen several 'refreshments'. It underwent redesign in late 2001 during the installation of the Tūhoe iwi exhibition. Later Māori curators wanted to completely replace the exhibition, but plans have been delayed.

36 Jenny Harper, 'The Bicultural Buffer Zone: Art, Maori Art, Museums and Their Markets', paper presented to the Art Association of Australia Conference, Canberra (October 5, 1997). Maria Brown, 'Representing the Body of a Nation: The Art Exhibitions of New Zealand's National Museum', *Third Text* 16, no. 3 (2002): 285–94.

37 Margaret Jolly, 'On the Edge? Deserts, Oceans, Islands', *The Contemporary Pacific* 13, no. 2 (Fall 2001): 445–46. In contrast, see: Lorenzo Veracini and Adrian Muckle, 'Reflections of Indigenous History Inside the National Museums of Australia and Aotearoa New Zealand and Outside of New Caledonia's Centre Culturel Jean-Marie Tjibaou', *Electronic Journal of Australian and New Zealand History*, accessed February 17, 2003, www.jcu.edu.au/aff/history/articles.

38 See comments from visitors in the 'soft opening' (trial run), Watson, 'Post-occupancy Evaluation'.

39 Peter Munz, 'Te Papa and the Problem of Historical Truth', *History Now/Te Pae Tawhito o te Wā* 6, no. 1 (2000): 13–16. See also: Nick Barnett, 'The Invasion Evasion', *Dominion*, November 1, 1999, 11. For a discussion of controversies in Australia over the museum representation of dark history, see: Mathew Trinca, 'Museums and the History Wars', *History Australia: Journal of the Australian Historical Association* 1, no. 1 (December 2003): 85–97.

40 Hakiwai interview, 2000. See McCarthy, 'From Curio to Taonga', Chapter 5.

41 See Sean Mallon, 'Afterword: Pacific Voices in the Bicultural Museum', in Conal McCarthy, *Museums and Māori: Heritage Professionals, Indigenous Collections, Current Practice* (Wellington: Te Papa Press, 2011), 248–54.

42 Janet Davidson, 'Mana Pasifika', *Open Eyes* 29, August 1998, 1. As well as the seven Pacific Island groups from the South Pacific, there were also objects from New Caledonia and Vanuatu.

43 'Focus on Pacific People', *Dominion*, February 12, 1998, 4.

44 Ibid.

45 Sean Mallon, 'Against Tradition', *The Contemporary Pacific* 22, no. 2 (2010): 362–81. For an example of how curators developed these ideas in the later exhibition, see: Sean Mallon, Kolokesa Mahina-Tuai and Damon Salesa, eds., *Tangata O Le Moana: New Zealand and the People of the Pacific* (Wellington: Te Papa Press, 2012).

46 See the exhibition planning documents ('Concept Design', 'Developed Design') in the Te Papa Archives. According to architect Pete Bossley, *Signs of a Nation* was the 'hinge' of the space. See: McCarthy, *Exhibiting Māori*, 170.

47 Gaylene Preston and Anna Cotterill, *Getting to Our Place*, Gaylene Preston Productions, Wellington, 1999, accessed June 1, 2017, https://www.nzonscreen.com/title/getting-to-our-place-1999.

48 Christine Fitzgerald and Paul MacLennan, 'Treaty of Waitangi: Front End Evaluation', Te Papa Visitor and Market Research, Wellington, 1995; Christine Fitzgerald and Paul MacLennan, 'Treaty of Waitangi: Front End Evaluation', Wellington, Te Papa Visitor and Market Research, January 1996.

49 As Jock Phillips remembers it, the empty, contemplative space was a deliberate contrast to all the other exhibitions, which 'were content and object heavy'. The idea was to focus on words but, he says, 'I think many of the critics take the exhibition

out of its physical context which is the key to understanding it.' Jock Phillips, pers. comm., July 2017.

50 Paul Thompson interview by Julia Waite, 2008, Te Papa Archives. See also: Julia Waite, 'Under Construction: National Identity and the Display of Colonial History at the National Museum of Singapore and the Museum of New Zealand Te Papa Tongarewa' (Master's diss., Museum and Heritage Studies, Victoria University of Wellington, 2009). Upstairs, there was more information, a timeline of the Treaty in New Zealand history, and an intriguing computer interactive that forced visitors to make difficult decisions about Tribunal claims.

51 'The Treaty of Waitangi: Concept Development', Museum of New Zealand Te Papa Tongarewa, Wellington, May 1996, 2.

52 Paul Hudson, 'Hype and Glory: A British Perspective on the Museum of New Zealand/Te Papa Tongarewa', *People's History: Newsletter of the Historical Branch* 27 (March 1998): 1.

53 Kylie Message, *New Museums and the Making of Culture* (Oxford and New York: Berg, 2006), 186–88. In other critical accounts, Paul Williams wrote about a reformed nationhood exhibited through an idealised biculturalism. Paul Williams, 'Reforming Nationhood: The Intersection of Free Market and Biculturalism at the Museum of New Zealand Te Papa Tongarewa', in *South Pacific Museums: Experiments in Culture*, eds. Chris Healy and Andrea Witcomb (Melbourne: Monash E-Press, 2006), 2.1–2.16. See also: James Gore, 'Representations of History and Nation in Museums in Australia and Aotearoa New Zealand: The National Museum of Australia and the Museum of New Zealand Te Papa Tongarewa' (PhD thesis, History, University of Melbourne, 2002). Probably the most comprehensive analysis of the exhibition, which looked at its development as well as the political context, is: Bain Attwood, 'Difficult Histories: The Museum of New Zealand Te Papa Tongarewa and the Treaty of Waitangi Exhibit', *The Public Historian* 35, no. 3 (2013): 46–71.

54 Jock Phillips, pers. comm., July 31, 2017.

55 These comments are taken from Jock Phillips' draft memoir (2017). Later Phillips went on to lead the development of the electronic encyclopedia of New Zealand, *Te Ara*.

56 'Displays Define Kiwi Identity', *Evening Post*, February 10, 1998, 6. Despite this explicit intention to foreground the constructedness of cultural identity, the way in which this article is titled suggests the point was lost on the journalist.

57 Jock Phillips, 'Our History, Our Selves: The Historian and National Identity', *New Zealand Journal of History* 30, no. 2 (1996): 116.

58 Amiria Henare, *Museums, Anthropology and Imperial Exchange* (Cambridge: Cambridge University Press, 2005), 277–78. Barbara Kirshenblatt-Gimblett told me after visiting Te Papa that she thought this exhibit was the DNA of the museum because it traced its exhibitionary roots in the world's fairs, international exhibitions and tourism.

59 Jock Phillips, pers. comm., July 31, 2017.

60 Phillips, 'Our History, Our Selves', 111.

61 Phillips, in Waite, 'Under Construction', 54.

62 'Displays Define Kiwi Identity'.

63 Ibid.

64 Val Aldridge, 'A Passport to the Past', *Dominion*, February 17, 1998.

65 Ann Bailey, *Inform* 4, no. 1 (June 1998). See also: Jock Phillips, 'History of Immigration', *Te Ara — the Encyclopedia of New Zealand*, accessed July 15, 2017, https://teara.govt.nz/en/history-of-immigration.

66 On the community gallery, see: Stephanie Gibson, 'Te Papa and New Zealand's Indian Communities: A Case Study about Exhibition Development', *Tuhinga* 14 (2003): 41–60. Christy Ballard, 'The Negotiation of Narratives: A Case-Study of the Indian Community Exhibition "Aainaa: Reflections through Indian Weddings" at Te Papa' (Master's diss., Museum and Heritage Studies, Victoria University of Wellington, 2005). Michael Fitzgerald, 'Te Papa's Community Gallery: Presenting Migrant Stories at Our Place', *New Zealand Journal of History* 43, no. 2 (October 2009): 198–207.

67 Michael Fitzgerald, 'Migrant Stories at Our Place', *LINKZ* 39 (2008): 11.

68 I recall one incident during the development of the exhibition in the project office, when interpreter Jane Martin had to mediate between the views of different factions of the Chinese community. The Advisory Group, nervous about the racist backlash in response to recent Chinese migrants, wanted to change a label about a teenage boy from Malaysia, who when asked what he wanted to do when he grew up, replied that he wanted to go and make lots of money.

69 Steven Young, 'An Asian at My Museum', *City Voice*, February 28, 1998.

70 Vera Mey, 'Commonplace: Towards a Post-ethnic Understanding of Identity and Representation of Asian New Zealanders for Museum Practice' (Master's diss., Museum and Heritage Studies, Victoria University of Wellington, 2010).

71 Bailey, *Inform* 4, no. 1.

72 Hudson, 'Hype and Glory', 1998, 2.

73 'Passports: Visitor analysis', Wellington, Te Papa Visitor and Market Research, E Docs 403260, September 2002.

74 See Appendix A for other history exhibitions, including *A Slice of Heaven* (2010–17). For curators' blogs on aspects of New Zealand history in relation to this show, see: 'Te Papa blog: Exhibitions', accessed July 15, 2017, http://blog.tepapa.govt.nz/category/exhibitions/slice-of-heaven-20th-century-aotearoa. See also: Kirstie Ross, 'Materialising Social History in Museums', *Te Ara: Journal of Museums Aotearoa* 32, no. 1–2 (December 2007), accessed July 15, 2017, http://www.museumsaotearoa.org.nz/materialising-social-history-museums.

75 In his memoirs Phillips writes: 'Those years at Te Papa were among the most exciting (along with the most frustrating!) of my life; and through the friends I made there and the lessons I learnt, they changed my life and my approach to history.'; Jock Phillips, draft memoirs, 2017.

76 After leaving Te Papa in 2001, Labrum was a lecturer in history at Waikato University, and visual and material culture at Massey University, before returning as Head of New Zealand and Pacific Cultures. See: Bronwyn Labrum, 'Material Histories in Australia and New Zealand: Interweaving Distinct Material and Social

Domains', *History Compass* 8, no. 8 (2010): 805–16; Bronwyn Labrum, 'Historicizing the Museum's Recent Past: History Exhibitions at the Museum of New Zealand Te Papa Tongarewa, 1998–2008', *Museum History Journal* 5, no. 1 (2011): 29–52.

77 Ken Gorbey interview with Conal McCarthy, May 2009, Te Papa Archives (Appendix C).

78 See the scene from *Getting to Our Place* where Jenny Gibbs and other board members complain about art. See also: Paul Fisher, 'Mighty MONZ: Artless at Heart', *North & South*, October 1994, 70–80.

79 See: Mark Amery, 'Visual Arts: Interpreting Our Dreams at Te Papa', *Evening Post*, 1998, undated press clipping in Te Papa library; Damian Skinner, 'Review: Dream Not Fully Realised', *Dominion*, May 4, 1998.

80 Megan Tamati-Quennell, 'Facing IT', *Open Eyes*, October 30, 1998, 3.

81 Ian Wedde, pers. comm., June 6, 2017. It is important to acknowledge the numerous art commissions in this context. Lisa Reihana, Jacqueline Fraser, and City Group with Greg Semu, produced artworks that referenced Te Papa's collections.

82 Ian Wedde quoted in Mike Houlihan, 'Te Papa: A Treat in Store for Art Lovers', *Evening Post*, August 25, 1998, 5.

83 Ken Gorbey, 'Provocation: A New Te Papa L4 Cultural Exhibition Concept', paper presented to staff at Te Papa (January 25, 2017), 3.

84 Pierre Bourdieu and Alain Darbel, *The Love of Art: European Art Museums and Their Public*, trans. Caroline Beattie and Nick Merriman (Oxford and Cambridge: Polity Press in association with Blackwell, 1991); Tony Bennett, Michael Emmison and John Frow, *Accounting for Tastes: Australian Everyday Cultures* (New York: Cambridge University Press, 1999); Michael Grenfell and Cheryl Hardy, *Art Rules: Pierre Bourdieu and the Visual Arts* (Oxford and New York: Berg, 2007); David D.M. Mason and Conal McCarthy, '"The Feeling of Exclusion": Young People's Perceptions of Art Galleries', *Museum Management and Curatorship* 21 (2006): 20–31; McCarthy, *Exhibiting Māori*, 154–55; Conal McCarthy, 'The Rules of (Māori) Art: Bourdieu's Cultural Sociology and Māori Visitors in New Zealand Museums', *Journal of Sociology* 49, no. 2–3 (June 2013): 108–30; Claire Adele Baker, 'Good Intentions: A case study of social inclusion and its evaluation in local public art galleries' (Master's diss., Museum and Heritage Studies, Victoria University of Wellington, 2014).

85 Tim Walker, pers. comm., June 2017. Wedde remembers that focus groups early in the process were useful in focusing the team on broad 'social values'. Ian Wedde, pers. comm., June 2017.

86 Tim Walker, pers. comm., June 2017.

87 Philip Wright, 'The Quality of Visitors' Experiences in Art Museums', in *The New Museology*, ed. Peter Vergo (London: Reaktion Books, 1989), 119–48. For a recent survey of these now well-established ideas, see: Christopher Whitehead, *Interpreting Art in Museums and Galleries* (London and New York: Routledge, 2012). For local examples, see: Nicola Caldwell (Master's diss., Museum and Heritage Studies, Victoria University of Wellington, forthcoming 2018).

88 See: Marcia Pointon, ed., *Art Apart: Art Institutions and Ideology Across England*

and North America (Manchester and New York: Manchester University Press, 1994). For the 'new' art history, see: A.L. Rees and Frances Borzello, eds., *The New Art History* (London: Camden Press, 1986); Sharon Macdonald and Gordon Fyfe, eds., *Theorizing Museums: Representing Identity and Diversity in a Changing World*, Sociological Review Monograph (Cambridge: Blackwell, 1996). I remember the last title being advertised on the noticeboard in the project office in 1996.

89 Tim Walker, pers. comm., June 2017.

90 Tim Walker quoted in Katy Corner, 'Bombarding with Art', *City Voice*, February 12, 1998.

91 Anthony Hubbard, 'Modern History', *Sunday Star-Times*, January 25, 1998.

92 Ibid.

93 Ibid.

94 Ian Wedde, 'Our Place in the World', *Listener*, February 14, 1998, 162.

95 Ian Wedde, pers. comm., June 6, 2017. On this point, see Paul Rayner's comment that the public were not at all fazed by the juxtaposition: Rayner in Zoe Alderton, *The Spirit of Colin McCahon* (Newcastle: Cambridge Scholars Press, 2015), 327. See also: Mark Amery, 'Back, Beyond and Here', *The Big Idea*, November 25, 2010.

96 Mark Amery, 'Boundaries of Art Blurred', *Sunday Star-Times*, February 8, 1998, 5.

97 'Te Papa Treats Art Like an Old Fridge — PM', *Evening Post*, January 25, 2000, 3.

98 See, for example: Rachel Kent, 'Museum of New Zealand Te Papa Tongarewa', *Art Asia Pacific* 20 (1998): 84–85; Robert Leonard, 'Papa's Bag', *Artforum* 36, no. 5 (January 1998); Josie McNaught, 'State of the Art', *Dominion*, May 15, 1999; William McAloon, 'Hang Ups', *Listener*, November 10, 2001, 50–51.

99 See: Gabrielle West, 'Why Keep It If You Can't See It! An Investigation into Public and Professional Attitudes Towards Collection Care, Access and Utilisation in New Zealand Museums' (Master's diss., Museum and Heritage Studies, Victoria University of Wellington, 2011).

100 Hamish Keith, 'Let's Have More Museum and Less McDonald's', *New Zealand Herald*, January 31, 2000, A19.

101 In Bourdieu's work, aesthetic tastes are not innate but the product of cultural capital, and activities such as visiting art galleries are determined by social positioning. See: Pierre Bourdieu, *Distinction: A Social Critique of the Judgement of Taste*, trans. Richard Nice (London: Routledge and Kegan Paul, 1984). Originally published as *La Distinction* (Paris: Minuit, 1979).

102 Tim Walker, pers. comm., 2017. See also: Tim Walker, 'Book review: *Museums and the Public Sphere*, by Jennifer Barrett', *Visitor Studies Journal* 15, no. 1 (January 2012): 118–20.

103 Kay Haughey, 'Parade: Summative Evaluation', Wellington, Te Papa Visitor and Market Research, April 2001. Complaints about the display of art barely registered in a huge visitor research sample numbering over 30,000. See: Lee Davidson and Pamela Sibley, 'Audiences at the New Museum: A Profile of Visitors to the Museum of New Zealand Te Papa Tongarewa', *Visitor Studies* 14, no. 2 (2011): 176–94.

104 Virginia Fraser, 'Te Papa Tongarewa', *Art Monthly Australia* 110 (June 1998): 13–16.

105 Ibid., 15.

106 Ibid., 16.
107 *Evening Post*, October 5, 1998, 4.
108 Hudson, 'Hype and Glory', 1.
109 Ibid., 2.
110 Jenny Chamberlain, 'Museum Wars', *North & South*, April 2000, 52.
111 Joe Bennett, 'Kids Delight in Te Papa's Energetic Chaos', *Evening Post*, July 8, 1998, 4.
112 Brendan Cole, 'Our Place Shows the Way We Were, Are, and Will Be', *Taranaki Daily News*, February 14, 1998, 20–23.
113 Neil Cossons quoted in Poot, 'Finding Ourselves at Te Papa'.
114 Peter Franks, 'Te Papa: A National Treasure House', *Taranaki Daily News*, June 12, 1998; Denis Dutton, 'State Treasure or Dog's Breakfast?', *Evening Post*, May 24, 1998.
115 Kerry Prendergast, Letter to the editor, *Evening Post*, January 27, 2000.
116 Henare Blackman and Sandra Potiki, Letter to the editor, *Listener*, February 26, 2000.
117 'Editorial: Te Papa: The People's Verdict', *Evening Post*, October 5, 1998, 4.
118 For her response to the critics, see: Cheryll Sotheran, 'Crowds Testament to Te Papa's Success', *Evening Post*, September 2, 1998, 20.
119 Peter Hall, 'Pulling Them In: Where Exhibits and Entertainment Meet', *New York Times*, May 2, 2001.
120 See: Rosie Millard, *The Tastemakers: UK Art Now* (London: Thames & Hudson, 2001).
121 Neil Harris, in Philip Nowlen, 'A View From the Top: Reaching Out to an Increasingly Diverse Range of People is a Major Challenge to US Museums', *Museums Journal* (June 1995): 29. See also: Tony Bennett, *The Birth of the Museum: History, Theory, Politics* (London: Routledge, 1995), 164.
122 On this ahistorical analysis of new museums, see: Andrea Witcomb, *Re-Imagining the Museum: Beyond the Mausoleum* (London and New York: Routledge, 2003).
123 Nick Prior, 'Having One's Tate and Eating It: Transformations of the Museum in the Hypermodern Era', in *Art and Its Publics: Museum Studies at the End of the Millennium*, ed. Andrew McClellan (Oxford and Malden: Blackwell, 2003), 51–74.
124 See the summary of annual visitation from 2002–11 in the Te Papa Annual Report 2010–2011, 8.
125 For visitor figures see the annual reports on the Te Papa website, 'Annual Reports and Key Documents', accessed June 1, 2017, https://www.tepapa.govt.nz/about/what-we-do/annual-reports-and-key-documents/annual-reports-and-key-documents-archive. (See also Appendix A for visitor numbers between 1998 and 2017.)
126 According to the annual reports, the National Museum recorded fluctuating annual attendance of roughly 250,000 p.a. in the 1980s, rising to over 400,000 in 1986/87 during the *Te Maori* exhibition. A current research project, The Long View, led by Dr Lee Davidson of Victoria University's Museum and Heritage Studies programme, aims to compile and analyse long-term visitation patterns in Australian and New Zealand galleries and museums.
127 Te Papa Annual Report 1998–1999, 2–3.
128 Although the linkage of social class and museum visiting was still present, the

dominance of highly educated professionals was dramatically reduced. See also: 'Te Papa's Audience', Te Papa Annual Report 1998–1999, 6–7; McCarthy, 'From Curio to Taonga', 347–49.

129 Megan Lane, 'Pulling in the Crowds', *Evening Post*, February 13, 1999. Another notable statistic was the reported length of stay at Te Papa (141 minutes — 2 hours 20), well above the international average (Te Papa Annual Report 1998–1999, 6).

130 'Te Papa Ministerial Briefing', 2008, 23. Generally these respondents were happy with their visit, and the visitor satisfaction rating was very high. From 1998–2001, 95 per cent of Te Papa's visitors rated their experience as being from 'good to excellent'. The average individual rating was 8.3/10, with 27 per cent of visitors rating Te Papa a full 10/10. In addition, 99 per cent of Te Papa's visitors reported that they would recommend it to others. See Te Papa annual reports 1998–2001.

131 See graph, Te Papa Annual Report 2010–2011, 8.

132 For a revealing insight into thinking at Te Papa at the time, see: Alan Smith, 'The Museum as a Forum for the Nation: The Web's Impact', paper presented to the 'Museums and the web' conference (1998), accessed May 1, 2017, http://www.museumsandtheweb.com/mw98/papers/smith_a/smith_a_paper.html. For museums and the digital, see: Ross Parry, ed., *Museums in a Digital Age*, Leicester Readers in Museum Studies (London and New York: Routledge, 2010).

133 C. Watson, 'Post-occupancy Evaluation for the Visitor Communications Group', Wellington, Te Papa Visitor and Market Research and Watson Consultancy Ltd, 1998, 118–20.

134 *Evening Post*, October 5, 1998, 4.

135 Conal McCarthy, 'Before *Te Maori*: A Revolution Deconstructed', in *Museum Revolutions: How Museums Change and Are Changed*, eds. Simon J. Knell, Sheila Watson and Suzanne MacLeod (London and New York: Routledge, 2007), 117–33.

136 For further discussion of Māori visitation, see: Gerard O'Regan, *Bicultural Developments in Museums of Aotearoa: What is the Current Status? Ki te Whakamana i te Kaupapa Tikanga-a-Rua ki Roto i nga Whare Taonga o te Motu: Kei hea e tu ana?* (Wellington: Te Papa National Services and Museums Association of Aotearoa, 1997); Conal McCarthy, 'Hailing the Subject: Maori Visitors, Museum Display and the Sociology of Cultural Reception', *New Zealand Sociology* 21, no. 1 (June 2006), 108–30; McCarthy, 'The Rules of (Māori) Art'.

137 See Te Papa Annual Report 2002–2003, 3. See also: McCarthy, *Exhibiting Māori*, Chapter 5; McCarthy, *Museums and Māori*, 191–93.

138 See McCarthy, *Museums and Māori*, 191, box 29.

139 For thoughts on why this may be happening, see: McCarthy, 'The Rules of (Māori) Art'.

4: Biculturalism and beyond

1 Documents and resources used in this chapter include: the Te Papa website, www.tepapa.govt.nz; 'Kete Intranet Resources', 2005; National Services Te Paerangi resource guides; and interviews conducted in 2000, 2008–09 and 2016–17 (now stored in the Te Papa Archives).

2 See: Conal McCarthy, *Museums and Māori: Heritage Professionals, Indigenous Collections, Current Practice* (Wellington: Te Papa Press, 2011).

3 For Māori words and phrases in this chapter, see the Glossary. For a comprehensive glossary of Māori words and concepts compiled from Māori sources, see: McCarthy, *Museums and Māori*, 263–70.

4 Te Papa Annual Report 2005–2006, 12–13.

5 Te Papa Annual Report 2008–09, 18.

6 Cath Nesus, 'Making the Connection: Biculturalism at Work', *Te Ara: Journal of Museums Aotearoa* 29, no. 1 (May 2004): 12–15.

7 Hereafter all quotes are taken from the alphabetical list of interviewees (Appendix C).

8 Hirini Moko Mead, 'The Nature of Taonga', in Mark Lindsay, ed., *Taonga Maori Conference* (Wellington: National Museum and Department of Internal Affairs, 1990), 64–69; Paul Tapsell, 'The Flight of Pareraututu: An Investigation of Taonga from a Tribal Perspective', *Journal of the Polynesian Society* 106, no. 4 (1997): 323–74.

9 Arapata Hakiwai and Philipp Schorch, 'Mana Taonga and the Public Sphere: A Dialogue between Indigenous Practice and Western Theory', *International Journal of Cultural Studies* 17, no. 2 (2014): 197–98.

10 'Iwi Relationships', Te Papa Annual Report 2005–2006, 26. See also Te Papa Annual Report 1995, 16.

11 Nesus, 'Making the Connection', 14.

12 See: Paul Tapsell, 'Taonga, Marae, Whenua — Negotiating Custodianship: A Maori Tribal Response to Te Papa: The Museum of New Zealand', in *Rethinking Settler Colonialism: History and Memory in Australia, Canada, Aotearoa New Zealand and South Africa*, ed. Annie Coombes (Manchester: Manchester University Press, 2006), 86–99. See also: Conal McCarthy, *Exhibiting Māori: A History of Colonial Cultures of Display* (Oxford and New York: Berg, 2007), 168.

13 Notes from a speech by Te Taru White, Museums Aotearoa Conference, Pātaka, Porirua, 2005.

14 Hakiwai and Schorch, 'Mana Taonga and the Public Sphere', 197–98.

15 Conal McCarthy, Eric Dorfman, Arapata Hakiwai and Āwhina Twomey, 'Mana Taonga: Connecting Communities with New Zealand Museums through Ancestral Māori Culture', *Museum International* 257–60 (2015): 5–15; Arapata Hakiwai, Conal McCarthy and Philipp Schorch, 'The Figure of the Kaitiaki: Learning from Māori Curatorship Past and Present', in *Curatopia: Museums and the Future of Curatorship*, ed. Philipp Schorch and Conal McCarthy (London and New York: Manchester University Press, forthcoming 2018).

16 'Karanga Aotearoa Repatriation Programme', Te Papa, accessed July 30, 2017, https://www.tepapa.govt.nz/about/repatriation.

17 Arapata Hakiwai, 'Virtual Repatriation: A Database of Māori Taonga in Overseas Museums', Ngā Pae o te Māramatanga, University of Auckland, accessed July 1, 2017, http://www.maramatanga.co.nz/project/virtual-repatriation-database-m-ori-taonga-overseas-museums. See also: Arapata Hakiwai, 'Digitisation & Research. Part One: Video Presentation', May 2012, accessed July 1, 2017, http://mediacentre.maramatanga.ac.nz/content/digitisation-research-part-one-arapata-hakiwai.

18 'Mātauranga Māori Strategy: He Ara Whainga', Museum of New Zealand Te Papa Tongarewa, Wellington, 2004.

19 See: Karl Johnstone, 'Mātauranga Māori and Museum Practice', *He Rauemi: Resource Guides*, Issue No. 31 (Wellington: National Services Te Paerangi, Museum of New Zealand Te Papa Tongarewa, 2006), accessed June 1, 2017, https://www.tepapa.govt.nz/sites/default/files/31-matauranga-maori-and-museum-practice_0.pdf; Te Ahukaramū Charles Royal, 'Mātauranga Māori and Museum Practice: A Discussion', National Services Te Paerangi, Museum of New Zealand Te Papa Tongarewa, Wellington, 2007.

20 This description is drawn from an earlier research report for the above discussion document: Te Ahukaramū Charles Royal, 'Mātauranga Māori and Museum Practice: A Discussion — Report Prepared by Te Ahukaramū Charles Royal for National Services Te Paerangi', National Services Te Paerangi, Wellington, 2004.

21 Royal, 'Mātauranga Māori and Museum Practice' (2004), n.p.

22 Royal, 'Mātauranga Māori and Museum Practice' (2007), 1.

23 Te Papa Annual Report 2005–2006, 7.

24 See Paul Tapsell, 'Taonga: A Tribal Response to Museums' (PhD thesis, Anthropology, University of Oxford, 1998), 28.

25 Te Papa Annual Report 2005–2006, 31.

26 For an in-depth study of how biculturalism works out internally in policy and practice, see Tanja Schubert-McArthur, '"Walking the Talk"? An Ethnography of Biculturalism at Te Papa' (PhD thesis, Anthropology, Victoria University of Wellington, 2014).

27 'Board News and Notes: New Māori Leadership Model', Museum of New Zealand Te Papa Tongarewa, Wellington, August 1995.

28 Cliff Whiting quoted in Anne French, 'Setting Standards', *Architecture/New Zealand* (1998): 72.

29 Seddon Bennington interview with Conal McCarthy, March 2009, Te Papa Archives.

30 *Tātai Kōrero* 32 (October 2004): 7.

31 Te Taru White interview with Conal McCarthy, December 2008, Te Papa Archives.

32 Schubert-McArthur, '"Walking the Talk"?'.

33 'Interview with Dr Michael Volkerling', *Rotorua Daily Post*, February 19, 1990. For later iterations of the new Māori department, see McCarthy, *Exhibiting Māori*, 2007.

34 Dr Ngata, who is also chair of the Māori Language Commission Te Taura Whiri i Te Reo Māori, is of Te Aitanga-a-Hauiti, Ngāti Ira and Ngāti Porou descent. His research interests include the revitalisation of indigenous language and knowledge, digital technology and museums. See for example: Billie Lythberg, Wayne Ngata and Amiria Salmond, 'Curating the Uncommons: Taking Care of Difference in Museums', in *Curatopia*.

35 See Schubert-McArthur, '"Walking the Talk"?'.

36 'Kete: Intranet Resources', Resource 6: Biculturalism, Te Papa, 2005.

37 Moana Davey interview.

38 For more detail on these matters, see: McCarthy, *Museums and Māori*, Chapter 5; see also McCarthy, Dorfman, Hakiwai and Twomey, 'Mana Taonga'.

39 Awhina Tamarapa, 'Museum Kaitiaki: Māori Perspectives on the Presentation and Management of Māori Treasures and Relationships with Museums', in *Curatorship: Indigenous Perspectives in Postcolonial Societies — Proceedings of Conference, May 1994*, eds. Michael Ames and Mina McKenzie (Ottawa: Canadian Museum of Civilization, 1996), 160–69.

40 Ibid.

41 Sidney M. Mead, ed., *Te Maori: Maori Art from New Zealand Collections* (New York: Heinemann American Federation of Arts, 1984).

42 See Johnstone, 'Mātauranga Māori and Museum Practice'.

43 On this point, see: Rose Evans, 'Tribal Involvement in Exhibition Planning and Conservation Treatment: A New Institutional Approach', *ICOM Ethnographic Conservation Newsletter* 19 (1999): 13–16; Rose Evans, 'Conservation in a Changing Museum Context: A Case Study at the Museum of New Zealand Te Papa Tongarewa', *New Zealand Museums Journal* 26, no. 1 (1996): 39–41.

44 On this point, see: Paul Tapsell, *Ko Tawa: Māori Treasures of New Zealand* (Auckland: David Bateman and Auckland Museum, 2006).

45 Māori terms are also listed in the Glossary. See also: Anne Salmond, 'Nga Huarahi O Te Ao Maori/Pathways in the Maori World', in *Te Maori*, ed. Sidney M. Mead, 118; Mead, 'The Nature of Taonga'; Amiria Henare, 'Taonga Maori: Encompassing Rights and Property in New Zealand', in *Thinking Through Things: Theorising Artefacts in Ethnographic Perspective*, eds. Amiria Henare, Martin Holbraad and Sari Wastell (London and New York: Routledge, 2007), 47–67.

46 See also: Huhana Smith, 'Mana Taonga and the Micro World of Intricate Research and Findings Around Taonga Maori at the Museum of New Zealand Te Papa Tongarewa', *SITES: A Journal of Social Anthropology and Cultural Studies. Special Issue: Matter in Place* 6, no. 2 (2009): 7–31.

47 See 'Taiaha kura, Kimihia', Te Papa Collections Online, accessed July 1, 2017, http://collections.tepapa.govt.nz/object/160286.

48 See: 'Iwi and Te Papa', Te Papa, accessed July 1, 2017, https://www.tepapa.govt.nz/about/what-we-do/iwi-tribes-and-te-papa. See also: '1998–2002 Past Exhibitions', Te Papa, accessed July 1, 2017, https://www.tepapa.govt.nz/visit/whats-on/exhibitions/past-exhibitions/1998-2002-past-exhibitions.

49 'Message from Te Taru White', *Tātai Kōrero* (2004): 5.

50 Ana Sciascia, 'Iwi Exhibitions at Te Papa: A Ngāi Tahu Perspective' (Master's diss., Museum and Heritage Studies, Victoria University of Wellington, 2012).

51 Arapata Hakiwai, 'He Mana Taonga, He Mana Tangata: Māori Taonga and the Politics of Māori Tribal Identity and Development' (PhD thesis, Museum and Heritage Studies, Victoria University of Wellington, 2014).

52 See 'Whiti Te Rā! The Story of Ngāti Toa Rangatira', Te Papa, accessed July 1, 2017, https://www.tepapa.govt.nz/about/past-exhibitions/2017-past-exhibitions/whiti-te-ra-story-ngati-toa-rangatira.

53 Hakiwai, quoted in Conal McCarthy, 'The Practice of Repatriation: A Case Study from New Zealand', in *Museums and Restitution: New Practices, New Approaches*, eds. Louise Tythacott and Kostos Arvanitis (Aldershot: Ashgate, 2014), 71–84.

54 Te Papa Annual Report 2015–2016, 11. This vision is underpinned by Hakiwai's own research: see Hakiwai, 'He Mana Taonga'.

55 See 'Repatriation: Karanga Aotearoa', Te Papa accessed May 1, 2017, http://www.tepapa.govt.nz/aboutus/repatriation/Pages/overview.aspx.

56 For an excellent account of their work in the wider context of repatriation, see: Coralie O'Hara, 'Repatriation in Practice: A Critical Analysis of the Repatriation of Human Remains in New Zealand'(Master's diss., Museum and Heritage Studies, Victoria University of Wellington, 2012).

57 McCarthy, Schorch and Hakiwai, 'The Figure of the Kaitiaki'.

58 For an analysis of contemporary collecting at Te Papa, see: Matariki Williams, 'Ka Hao te Rangatahi: How Contemporary Māori Society is Collected at Te Papa Tongarewa' (Master's diss., Museum and Heritage Studies, Victoria University of Wellington, 2014).

59 For more on this topic, see: Matariki Williams, Te Papa blog, 'Curating to Heal: Ways of Creating Sovereign Spaces in Museums', April 2017, accessed July 31, 2017, http://blog.tepapa.govt.nz/2017/04/20/curating-to-heal-ways-of-creating-sovereign-spaces-in-museums. An example of this kind of collecting is the current proposal to acquire the artwork that Māori curatorial collective Mata Aho showed in mid 2017 at the major art fair *documenta14* at Kassel, Germany, which includes the work, plus the Instagram account and a related website (the first time that Te Papa will have 'harvested' digital heritage).

60 Puawai Cairns, pers. comm., June 2017. In applying these ideas, Cairns is acquiring a range of material from artist James Webster, who has been spearheading a revival of the creation and performance of karetao (puppets), as well as developing his own unique hybrid form that combines the karetao with taonga puoro (wind instruments). The collection includes a digital record of a performance with three karetao at Te Papa during Te Wiki o te Reo Māori.

61 On this topic, see: Conal McCarthy, *Indigenous Museology: Insights from Australia and Aotearoa New Zealand* (London and New York: Routledge, forthcoming 2018).

62 Arapata Hakiwai interviewed by Phillipp Schorch, June 2009.

63 Brigitte Bönisch-Brednich and Richard Hill, 'Fitting Aotearoa into New Zealand: Politico-Cultural Change in a Modern Bicultural Nation', in *Historical Justice in International Perspective: How Societies Are Trying to Right the Wrongs of the Past*, ed. Manfred Berg and Bernd Schaeffer (Washington DC and Cambridge: German Historical Institute and Cambridge University Press, 2009), 239–63, 254.

64 Arapata Hakiwai seminar MHST515, Museum and Heritage Studies class, Victoria University of Wellington, September 2008. See also: James Ritchie, *Becoming Bicultural* (Wellington: Huia/Daphne Brasell Associates, 1992).

65 For a sample of the voluminous critical literature on Te Papa and biculturalism, see the bibliography in McCarthy, *Museums and Māori*.

66 Dominic O'Sullivan, *Beyond Biculturalism: The Politics of an Indigenous Minority* (Wellington: Huia, 2007), 207–08. Tino rangatiratanga has been translated as absolute chieftainship or sovereignty, as guaranteed in article two of the Māori version of the Treaty of Waitangi.

67 Paul Meredith, 'Hybridity in the Third Space: Rethinking Bi-Cultural Politics in Aotearoa/New Zealand', paper presented at Te Oru Rangahau Māori Research and Development Conference, Massey University, Palmerston North (1998), 21.
68 For the most comprehensive analysis of biculturalism in practice at Te Papa, see Schubert-McArthur, '"Walking the Talk"?'.
69 For a full discussion of these issues, see McCarthy, *Museums and Māori*, Chapter 8.
70 David Butts, 'Maori and Museums: The Politics of Indigenous Recognition' (PhD thesis, Museum Studies, Massey University, 2003).
71 For binationalism, see: Roger Maaka and Augie Fleras, *The Politics of Indigeneity: Challenging the State in Canada and Aotearoa New Zealand* (Dunedin: University of Otago Press, 2005). In his role as Director Ngā Manu Atarau, Charles Royal is exploring how new ideas such as interculturalism might be expressed, which may very well result in radical changes to Māori policy and practice at Te Papa, including the marae, relationships with iwi, etc.

5: The museum at work in 2017

1 Gabrielle West, 'Why Keep It If You Can't See It! An Investigation into Public and Professional Attitudes Towards Collection Care, Access and Utilisation in New Zealand Museums' (Master's diss., Museum and Heritage Studies, Victoria University of Wellington, 2011).
2 Conal McCarthy, 'Grounding Museum Studies: Introducing Practice', in *Museum Practice: The International Handbooks of Museum Studies*, vol. 2, ed. Conal McCarthy (Oxford and Malden: Wiley Blackwell, 2015), xxxv–lii.
3 Space restrictions obviously limit the number of staff whose roles are able to be discussed here, however a good idea of the wide variety of work and the many people who undertake it can be gained from browsing the museum's website and annual reports.
4 McCarthy, *Museums and Māori: Heritage Professionals, Indigenous Collections, Current Practice* (Wellington: Te Papa Press, 2011), Chapter 4.
5 Michele Fontana, 'Science Museum in a Pizza Box: Performance, Museum Tour Guiding, and Science Communication' (PhD thesis, Theatre Studies, Victoria University of Wellington, 2015).
6 Philipp Schorch, 'Te Papa: A Forum for the World? A Narrative Exploration of a Global Public Sphere' (PhD thesis, Museum and Heritage Studies, Victoria University of Wellington, 2010).
7 John Simmons, 'Collection Care and Management: History, Theory and Practice', in *Museum Practice*, vol. 2, ed. Conal McCarthy, 221–47; Patrick J. Boylan, 'The Museum Profession', in *A Companion to Museum Studies*, ed. Sharon Macdonald (Malden: Blackwell, 2006), 415–30.
8 Carolyn McGill, collection manager, Te Papa, comments in MHST512 Practicum class, May 2015.
9 On this topic, see: Rebecca Loud, 'Never Let Me Go? A Case Study of Deaccessioning and Disposal Undertaken at Museum of Wellington City and Sea' (Master's diss., Museum and Heritage Studies, Victoria University of Wellington, 2013); Amy

Hackett, 'Trash or Treasure? Te Papa and the Collecting of Everyday Material Culture' (Master's diss., Museum and Heritage Studies, Victoria University of Wellington, 2017).

10 The whole history collection, comprising other objects such as textiles, numbers some 40,000 objects in total. See History section, in *Icons: Ngā Taonga: From the Museum of New Zealand Te Papa Tongarewa* (Wellington: Te Papa Press, 2004).

11 Te Papa Annual Report 2016–2017. See Appendix A in this volume.

12 West, 'Why Keep It If You Can't See It!'.

13 See 'Our Curators', Te Papa, accessed June 1, 2017, https://www.tepapa.govt.nz/our-curators.

14 Conal McCarthy, Commentary, in *The Future of Natural History Museums*, ed. Eric Dorfman (London and New York: Routledge, 2017), 217–28.

15 Dan Hikuroa, pers. comm., July 31, 2017.

16 'Past Exhibitions', Te Papa, accessed June 1, 2017, https://www.tepapa.govt.nz/about/past-exhibitions/2017-past-exhibitions/european-splendour-1500-1800.

17 See: 'Te Pahi Medal on Display', Te Papa, accessed June 1, 2017, https://www.tepapa.govt.nz/about/press-and-media/press-releases/2017-news-and-media-releases/te-pahi-medal-on-display-te-papa.

18 Conal McCarthy and Mark Stocker, eds., *Colonial Gothic to Māori Renaissance: Essays in Memory of Jonathan Mane-Wheoki* (Wellington: Victoria University Press, 2017).

19 The directors of each of these make up the executive team with the CEO and Kaihautū. For an organisational chart, see: https://www.tepapa.govt.nz/about/what-we-do/organisation-structure.

20 'Te Papa Learning Philosophy: Draft for Consideration', Te Papa Learning Innovation, Wellington, 2016.

21 Ati Teepa, 'Bug Lab Public Programme: Wrap Report', Te Papa Learning Innovation, Wellington, 2017.

22 'Hīnātore | Learning Lab', Te Papa, accessed July 30, 2017, https://www.tepapa.govt.nz/learn/hinatore-learning-lab.

23 Sarah Powell, 'Towards a Collected Commons: Two Case Studies Examining New Zealand Collecting Domains Establishing Open GLAM Practices for Digital Collections' (Master's diss., Museum and Heritage Studies, Victoria University of Wellington, 2016).

24 'Mahuki', Te Papa, accessed June 1, 2017, http://www.mahuki.org.

25 'National Services Te Paerangi', Te Papa, accessed June 1, 2017, https://www.tepapa.govt.nz/learn/for-museums-and-galleries/national-services-te-paerangi.

26 McCarthy, *Museums and Māori*, 16–17, 100–101, 141, 211–15.

27 Outcome 6, *Statement of Intent* 2009–2012, 18. For the Kaihautū's report on these activities see the Te Papa Annual Report 2005–2006, 16–18, 26.

28 For the incorporation of Māori values within the organisational culture, see: 'Te Papa: Our Values', eDOCs813896, Kupenga, Museum of New Zealand Te Papa Tongarewa, Wellington, n.d. For an ethnographic analysis of how this worked in practice, see Tanja Schubert-McArthur, '"Walking the Talk"? An Ethnography

of Biculturalism at Te Papa' (PhD thesis, Anthropology, Victoria University of Wellington, 2014).

29 Cath Nesus, 'Making the Connection: Biculturalism at Work', *Te Ara: Journal of Museums Aotearoa* 29, no. 1 (May 2004): 13.

6: Learning from the first 20 years

1 'Te Papa Marks a Record Year for Gallipoli: The Scale of Our War', Te Papa press release, accessed July 1, 2017, https://www.tepapa.govt.nz/about/press-and-media/press-releases/2016-news-and-media-releases/te-papa-marks-record-year-for. At the time of writing, the exhibition had been seen by 1.5 million people.

2 For more on renewal, see: 'Renewal and Property', Te Papa, accessed June 1, 2017, https://www.tepapa.govt.nz/support-join/te-papa-foundation/renewal-and-property-te-papa-foundation.

3 David Fleming, pers. comm., March 2, 2017.

4 Conal McCarthy, 'The Rules of (Māori) Art: Bourdieu's Cultural Sociology and Māori Visitors in New Zealand Museums', *Journal of Sociology* 49, no. 2–3 (June 2013): 108–30. Much research remains to be done in analysing the very large Te Papa visitor profile. For an initial study, see: Lee Davidson and Pamela Sibley, 'Audiences at the New Museum: A Profile of Visitors to the Museum of New Zealand Te Papa Tongarewa', *Visitor Studies* 14, no. 2 (2011): 176–94.

5 Lee Davidson, 'Visitor Studies: Toward a Culture of Reflective Practice and Critical Museology for the Visitor Centred Museum', in *Museum Practice: International Handbooks of Museum Studies*, vol. 2, ed. Conal McCarthy (Oxford and Malden: Wiley Blackwell, 2015), 503–27.

6 See: Suzette Major and Tamarisk Sutherland, 'Strategic Partnerships Between Museums and Corporate Organisations: The "Marriage" of the Museum of New Zealand Te Papa Tongarewa and Tower', in *Museum Marketing: Competing in the Global Marketplace*, ed. Ruth Rentschler and Anne-Marie Hede (London and New York: Routledge, 2011).

7 Ken Gorbey, 'Disneyland! Or the Te Papa-fication of New Zealand Museums', paper presented to the Stout Research Centre Conference 'Antipodes: New Directions in New Zealand Culture and History', Victoria University of Wellington (September 4, 2009).

8 An INTERCOM conference on museums and tourism in Rotorua in 2008 finally turned around this ingrained attitude, and Te Papa was seen as a leader in this field.

9 Anna Abernathy, 'Innovative and Non-traditional Revenue Generation in New Zealand Museums' (MA thesis, Museum and Heritage Studies, Victoria University of Wellington, 2016).

10 For the digital directorate see 'Organisation Structure', Te Papa, accessed June 1, 2017, https://www.tepapa.govt.nz/about/what-we-do/organisation-structure.

11 See Chapter 5. For a recent review of these developments, see: the Kiwilooseinmuseums blog review, accessed June 1, 2017, https://kiwilooseinmuseums.wordpress.com/2017/03/13/te-papa-the-lean-canvas-model/?blogsub=confirming#blog_subscription-5.

12 Ross Parry, 'New Media Seminar: The Post Digital Museum', YouTube presentation, accessed June 1, 2017, https://www.youtube.com/watch?v=xx8IjvPGYZY. See also: Seb Chan, 'Tackling Ross Parry's Post-digital Normativity on a Daily Basis with Visitors', Fresh and newer blog post, December 13, 2013, http://www.freshandnew.org/2013/12/tackling-ross-parrys-post-digital-normativity-daily-basis.

13 See: Shannon Wellington and Gillian Oliver, 'Reviewing the Digital Heritage Landscape: The Intersection of Digital Media and Museum Practice', in *Museum Practice*, vol. 2, ed. Conal McCarthy, 577–98; David M. Mason and Conal McCarthy, 'Museums and the Culture of New Media: An Empirical Model of New Zealand Museum Websites', *Museum Management and Curatorship* 23, no. 1 (2008): 63–80.

14 Te Papa Annual Report 2010–2011, 13, 17.

15 Amy Hackett, 'Trash or Treasure? Te Papa and the Collecting of Everyday Material Culture' (Master's diss., Museum and Heritage Studies, Victoria University of Wellington, 2017).

16 Sara Selwood and Stuart Davies, 'Policies, Frameworks and Legislation: The Conditions under which English Museums Operate', in *Museum Practice*, vol. 2, ed. Conal McCarthy, 43–68.

17 For a complete list see 'Past Exhibitions', Te Papa, accessed June 1, 2017, https://www.tepapa.govt.nz/visit/whats-on/past-exhibitions.

18 Te Papa, Annual Report 2001, 4.

19 See for example in Appendix A the dire consequences of the 'failure' of touring shows at Te Papa for the overall budget in 2013/14. On the pitfalls of blockbusters, see: Alan Wallach, 'Norman Rockwell at the Guggenheim', in *Art and Its Publics: Museum Studies at the Millennium*, ed. Andrew McClellan (Oxford: Blackwell, 2003), 97–115.

20 In 2017 Wellington City Council announced that a Film Museum and Convention Centre in partnership with Peter Jackson would be built opposite Te Papa.

21 Jock Phillips, 'Review: Wellywood Goes to War,' *reCollections: Journal of the National Museum of Australia* 11, no. 1 (2016), accessed July 15, 2017, http://recollections.nma.gov.au/issues/volume_11_number_1/exhibition_reviews/gallipoli.

22 See '*Bug Lab*', Te Papa, accessed June 1, 2017, https://www.tepapa.govt.nz/about/past-exhibitions/2017-past-exhibitions/bug-lab.

23 On this exhibition, see: Anton Berndt, 'The State of Play: An Exploration of Games and Their Value in Museum Exhibitions' (MA thesis, Museum and Heritage Studies, Victoria University of Wellington, 2011).

24 Nicholas Thomas, *The Return of Curiosity: What Museums Are Good for in the 21st Century* (London: Reaktion Books, 2016). Thomas is the director of the Museum of Anthropology and Archaeology at Cambridge.

25 Ibid., 143.

26 Ibid., 145.

27 Lynette Townsend, 'Seen and Not Heard? Collecting the History of New Zealand Childhood' (MA thesis, Museum and Heritage Studies, Victoria University of Wellington, 2008); Chloe Searle, 'Collecting for New Zealand: Examining What the Museum of New Zealand Te Papa Tongarewa Should Collect' (Master's diss.,

Museum and Heritage Studies, Victoria University of Wellington, 2010).

28 See: Matariki Williams, 'Ka Hao te Rangatahi: How Contemporary Māori Society is Collected at Te Papa Tongarewa' (Master's diss., Museum and Heritage Studies, Victoria University of Wellington, 2014).

29 Bronwyn Labrum, *Real Modern: Living in New Zealand in the 1950s and 1960s* (Wellington: Te Papa Press, 2015).

30 See: Bronwyn Labrum, 'Collecting, Curating and Exhibiting Material Histories in a Post-Settler Society', in *Curatopia: Museums and the Future of Curatorship*, eds. Philipp Schorch and Conal McCarthy (London and New York: Manchester University Press, forthcoming 2018).

Appendix A: Selected highlights 1998–2017

1 Information sourced from: 'Annual Reports and Key Documents', Te Papa, accessed June 1, 2017, https://www.tepapa.govt.nz/about/what-we-do/annual-reports-and-key-documents/annual-reports-and-key-documents-archive. See also *Icons: Ngā Taonga: From the Museum of New Zealand Te Papa Tongarewa* (Wellington: Te Papa Press, 2004).

Appendix B: Current strategies and values

1 Te Papa Annual Report 2010–2011, 13.

2 Ibid., 17.

Glossary

1 See Hirini Moko Mead, *Tikanga Maori: Living by Maori Values* (Wellington: Huia, 2003); Roger Neich, *Carved Histories: Rotorua Ngati Tarawhai Woodcarving* (Auckland: Auckland University Press, 2001); Henry Williams, *A Dictionary of the Maori Language*, 7th edn (Wellington: GP Books, 1971).

image credits

All photography by Te Papa photographers Michael Hall, Norm Heke, Maarten Holl, Jan Nauta, Michael O'Neill, Jean-Claude Stahl, Kate Whitley, Herbert Webb and Warwick Wilson, except for page 23 (top): Alexander Turnbull Library, Wellington, permission courtesy Tom Scott; page 31 (bottom): Alexander Turnbull Library, Wellington, PAColl-5932-21; page 33 (bottom): Alexander Turnbull Library, Wellington, EP/1997/0787/28A-F; page 41 (top): author's collection; page 75 (top): Alexander Turnbull Library, Wellington, EP-1998-2243-8; page 111 (bottom): Amanda Rogers; page 154 (top): Tamara Koglar; page 155 (top): Jane Ussher; page 155 (bottom): Lara Shepherd.

acknowledgements

Writing an institutional history involves, as Raphael Samuel said of social history, the 'work of a thousand hands'.

If not thousands, there are many people to thank for their help with this book. First, thanks to the former staff of Te Papa who were there in the beginning, and gave advice, photographs and valuable information during the research: Ken Gorbey, Sean Sweeney, Ian Wedde, Jock Phillips, Tim Walker, Karen Mason, Hema Temara, Michelle Taylor, Neil Anderson, Alan Smith, Diana Minchall and Bronwyn Simes.

Second, thanks to current staff, who provided help and assistance with the project: Arapata Hakiwai, Puawai Cairns, Carolyn Roberts-Thompson, Raewyn Smith-Kapa, Bronwyn Labrum, Sean Mallon, Claire Regnault, Stephanie Gibson, Martin Lewis, Jennifer Twist, Anna Abernathy, Migoto Eria, Matariki Williams, Lucy Jackson and Lynne Carmichael, including those staff who were interviewed for the profiles in chapter 5: Rangimoana Taylor, Mark Stocker, Leon Perrie, Miri Young, Carolyn McGill and Te Waari Carkeek.

I am indebted to Simon Knell for his insights, as an acute observer who has visited literally hundreds of museums and galleries worldwide. Thanks also to Dr David Butts for reading the manuscript and providing helpful feedback and useful suggestions.

Lastly, heartfelt thanks to Nicola Legat and the team at Te Papa Press for their hard work in bringing this publication to life.

Index

Page numbers in **bold** refer to photographs and illustrations

First published in New Zealand in 2018 by
Te Papa Press, PO Box 467, Wellington, New Zealand
www.tepapapress.co.nz

TE PAPA
PRESS

TE PAPA® is the trademark of the Museum
of New Zealand Te Papa Tongarewa
Te Papa Press is an imprint of the Museum
of New Zealand Te Papa Tongarewa

A catalogue record is available from the
National Library of New Zealand

ISBN 978-0-9941362-6-8

Design by Kate Barraclough
Digital imaging by Jeremy Glyde
Printed in China by 1010 Printing International Ltd
Front cover image: The museum from Cable Street, Wellington